From one citizen to another.
This book I quite seriously believe all people should read. It is not very hard to read so I think you'll enjoy it.

You don't need to return it when your finished, I have another copy.

Lance DiBella

READ THIS BOOK!

FOUND by Ali Haimson & Corinna

at Boxcar Books, Bloomington, IN

# FOUND

THE BEST LOST, TOSSED, AND FORGOTTEN ITEMS
FROM AROUND THE WORLD

DAVY ROTHBART

A FIRESIDE BOOK
Published by Simon & Schuster
*New York London Toronto Sydney*

FIRESIDE
Rockefeller Center
1230 Avenue of the Americas
New York, NY 10020



For information regarding special discounts for bulk purchases,
please contact Simon & Schuster Special Sales at 1-800-456-6798
or business@simonandschuster.com

Manufactured in the United States of America

20 19 18 17 16

Library of Congress Cataloging-in-Publication Data is available.

ISBN-13: 978-0-7432-5114-3
ISBN-10: 0-7432-5114-8

*Found* is an uncommon tribute to and commentary on everyday life—a collage of disparate "found" items sent in by readers across the nation, ranging from love letters to doodles to shopping lists. Consistent with the entirely random way in which they have been found, no connection, relationship, or association between the individual items included in the book is intended or should be inferred from the manner in which they are displayed. Names and identifying characteristics of certain of the authors and creators of the "found" items and certain people featured in them have been changed.

AY, WHAT UP?!

welcome to

# FOUND

!!!!!!!!

POINT GUARD'S LETTER

Late one snowy night in Chicago I left my friend's apartment and went out to my car. On the windshield I found a note intended for someone else, a guy named Mario.

Since grade school I've been collecting notes, letters, photographs, and other stuff I found on the ground. It always amazed me how powerfully I could connect with a person I'd never met just by reading a half-page love letter left behind on a park bench or the city bus. When I discovered Amber's note to Mario, I was so moved by its blend of anger and longing that I knew I needed to find a way to share it with the world. A few days later, driving from one small Mississippi town to the next, I had an idea: Why not create a magazine and publish Amber's note, along with the rest of the incredible finds my friends and I had turned up over the years?

Mario,
I fucking hate you
you said you had to
work then whys
your car HERE
at HER place??
You're a fucking
LIAR. I hate you
I fucking hate you
Amber
PS Page me later

As I traveled around the country the next few months, I passed out flyers inviting folks to send in stuff they'd found. At first, I didn't hear anything. Then, suddenly, I did. Found notes came in from as far away as Alaska and Bangladesh. They were by turns beautiful, hilarious, and heartbreaking. Once I'd gathered a decent stack of material and combed through my own collection of found stuff, my friend Jason Bitner and I went to work for three nights cutting and pasting with scissors and tape and put together the first issue of *FOUND Magazine*.

The response completely stunned and overwhelmed me. New Found stuff began pouring in from all over the globe. I had no idea so many people shared my fascination with found stuff and other people's lives. Folks have written in who've been collecting these types of treasures since before my parents were born. And then a lot of people — particularly in small, rural towns — have said "All these years I've been picking up stuff off the street and everyone here thinks I'm a freak. But now I see that I am not alone!" I love that. It's exciting to sense an invisible community emerging from the shadows and finding each other.

But what I love most about this project is that everyone can play. People who've never been into finding things before have told me that they've begun to look at the world in a new way. We've gotten finds from dozens of countries and every state in the U.S. Finds arrived one week from both Iceland and Greenland, which I thought was kind of a coup. Kids as young as 6 years old have sent in their finds.

I ask folks to name their finds, just as they'd name a painting or a song or a story they'd written. Picking a note up from the ground — something that everyone else has walked past and seen as trash — seems to me an equally noble act of creation. We're always careful to give credit to the person who's found each item; they deserve recognition for rescuing their find from the gutter and giving it new life.

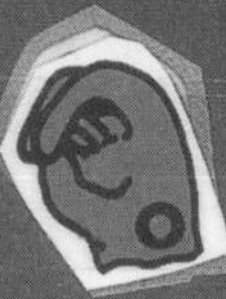

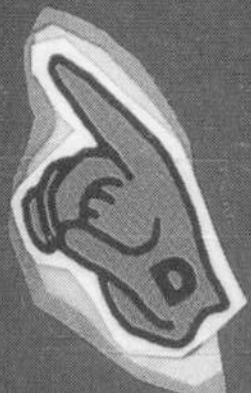


Found notes and letters open up the entire range of human experience; they offer a shortcut directly into people's minds and hearts. We often feel most alive when we're glimpsing someone at their most honest and raw. I think that's because when we read these notes, there's a powerful moment of recognition; we see another person – maybe someone very different from us — experiencing the same thoughts and feelings and emotions that we've experienced. It's startling and it's magical. Suddenly, we feel connected to this person we've never met before and probably never will, and in turn, to all people. The idea that we all share the same universal emotions and experiences — that we're all connected – strikes me as profoundly beautiful.

Some finds feel incomplete: They hint at a story but withhold important details. The things you don't know are often as fascinating as the things you do. Part of the joy of finding something is the imaginative process that ensues, trying to piece together a narrative that will make sense of things. There are questions to be answered: Who wrote this? What do some of these strange, cryptic phrases mean exactly? How did this thing end up here? Was this note trashed by the person who wrote it or the person who received it? It's up to the finder to guess at these riddles, knowing they will never truly be solved.

Folks ask me where the best places to find stuff are. Certainly, some spots are more fertile than others. I like sidewalks and bushes, all forms of public transportation, elementary school playgrounds, the recycling bins at Kinko's and university computer centers. While I appreciate the efforts of determined finders who prowl through Dumpsters looking for troves of abandoned letters, I think it's a mistake for folks to believe that you have to go far out of your way to find things. It's more a matter of simply keeping your eyes peeled during your everyday wanderings through the world. On your way to work, on your way to school, be aware of what's around you. And if you see a piece of paper lying there with writing on it, take a second and a half to pick it up and check it out. Four out of five notes you pick up might not be anything too interesting, but that fifth one will always be a real gem.

I always tend to get consumed with my little daily problems. I worry about girls and money and what the hell I did with my dang keys. Looking for found stuff is good for me because it brings me back to the present moment. I'm brought out of my own head and into the world around me. I start listening to conversations between strangers, gazing at people's faces, feeling them. Even if I don't find any wonderful notes on the ground, my day is far richer for having deeply experienced my surroundings.

Thank you *so much* for peeping this book and becoming a part of this. On the pages that follow is stuff people found. I implore you to join in — finding is fun! I can't wait to check out what *you* turn up.

All right, enough bullshit, let's get this fuckin' party started. Read on, my friends, read on — and for goodness sake, keep your eyes to the ground and send in your finds!

Much love, and peace out for now—

**Davy Rothbart**

point guard, *FOUND* Magazine

photo by Dorothy Gotlib

Helen loves me more than I love her. ♡

Bobby's love ♡ compared to Helen's love

Aaron —

I really can't see the humor in explaining to my professor why my homework has pornography taped to it, or having parts of an equation ripped out of my book because of taped man porn. Please make sure that these kinds of things stop. :(

Ticket for funny story Starting in 5 m

notes on this page FOUND by Susannah Felts, Nashville, TN, John Kovacs, Ann Arbor, MI, Jordan Morris, Santa Cruz, CA the **FOUND** book!

brought to you by

*FOUND Magazine*'s

*point guard*

**DAVY ROTHBART**

&

*power forward*

**JASON BITNER**

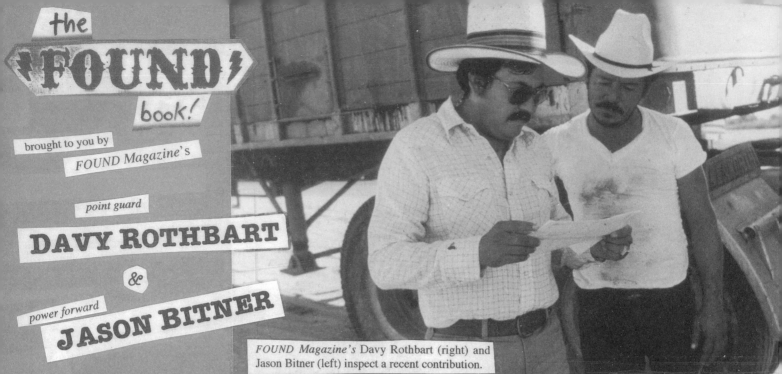

*FOUND Magazine's* Davy Rothbart (right) and Jason Bitner (left) inspect a recent contribution.

this photo FOUND by Katie and Nina, St. Louis, M

this photo FOUND by Benn Ray, Baltimore, MD

with

**BRANDE WIX**

**BETH KILLIAN**

**ROSEMARY DARIGO**

**MIKE KOZURA**

**AARON WICKENDEN**

**MALKAH SPIVAK-BIRNDORF**

**BROTHER MIKE ROTHBART**

&

millions of

**FINDERS**

worldwide!

this photo FOUND by George Stevens, Winston-Salem, NC

this flag FOUND by Mike DiBella, Philadelphia, PA

*The finds in this book come from many countries, but the bulk of them come from the United States. Check the handy guide below to see which pages contain finds from your home state!*



*FOUND Magazine*. Made in the U.S.A.

this photo FOUND by Katie and Nina, St. Louis, MO

MAY 23, 1996

DEAR RON,

THE LONGER I THINK ABOUT WHAT I'M DOING THE SICKER I FEEL. RON I'M SORRY BUT I DON'T THINK THAT WE SHOULD CONTINUE TO HAVE A RELATIONSHIP TOGETHER; AT LEAST NOT AS A COUPLE. I LOVE YOU BUT THINGS HAVE NOT BEEN THE SAME SINCE WE FOUND OUT THAT WE WERE RELATED. IF YOU NO LONGER WANT TO SPEAK TO ME BECAUSE OF THIS, I WILL UNDERSTAND. I WILL STILL COME VISIT YOU ON SUNDAYS IF YOU LIKE, I JUST DON'T KNOW WHAT TO SAY TO YOU.

LOVE ALWAYS,
ALISHA

**READ LAST** FOUND by Mark Stevens, Durham, NC

I found this note in my front yard, folded up, soggy and dirty. On the outside of the note it said, "Read Last."

—M.S.

# I DID NOT TAKE ANYTHING

FOUND by Kyatta Robeson

Los Angeles, CA

Jessie
I did not take anything.
I know there's no
convincing you once you've
made up your mind. And
although I cannot offer
you any other explanation
as to what happened to
it. That doesn't mean I
did it. How could I have?
You say your car was
locked and Katie had the
keys.?
Anyway I dont need
to take something of yours
when I can get my own.
I doesnt make sense.
So here is a replacement.
Cuz I can't stand it when
you think I've wronged you
—mom

FOUND MAG
3455 Charing Cross Rd.
Ann Arbor, MI 48108-1911

FOUND
N/R
JESSIE—
I DID NOT TAKE ANYTHING
—MOM

BUSINESS REPLY MAIL
FIRST CLASS MAIL PERMIT NO. 3906 SAN JOSE, CA 95134
POSTAGE WILL BE PAID BY ADDRESSEE
SONY ELECTRONICS INC
12451 GATEWAY BLVD
FORT MYERS FL 33913-9972

NO POSTAGE NECESSARY IF MAILED IN THE UNITED STATES

By believing
passionately
in something that still
does not exist,
we create it.
The nonexistent
is whatever we have
not sufficiently
desired

Dear Friend,

I found this note on the ground while I was delivering mail in Tahlequah, Ok. on May 31, 2002.

Name: Would that it were so

Sincerely,
Wallace Blue
Wallace Blue

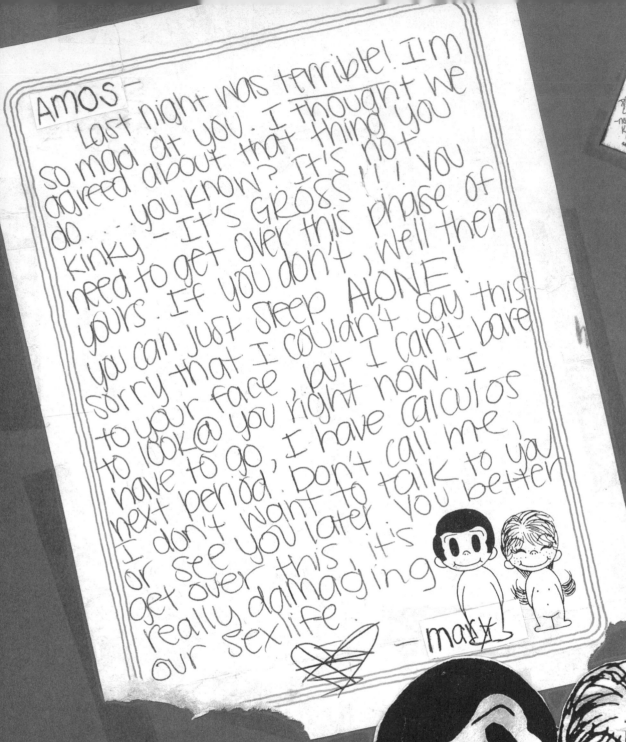

Amos -

Last night was terrible! I'm so mad at you. I thought we agreed about that thing you do . . . you know? It's not kinky - It's GROSS!!! You need to get over this phase of yours. If you don't, well then you can just sleep ALONE! I'm sorry that I couldn't say this to your face, but I can't bare to look@ you right now. I have to go, I have calculos next period. Don't call me, I don't want to talk to you or see you later. You better get over this. It's really damaging our sex life.

— mary

Melissa Brown

Elle

Yes

-not Kinky Gross!!

Found Magazine/Ellegirl Coll.
3455 Charing Cross Road
Anne Arbor, MI 48108-1911

***THIS PHASE OF YOURS***

FOUND by Melissa Brown

Hoffman Estates, IL

NOVEMBER 21

# NOVEMBER 22, 1963

FOUND by Sharon Vanorny

Madison, WI

Friday NOVEMBER 22 1963

Dear Tammy,

Today the president was killed! isn't that terrible! At school everyone was crying, except the republicans. President Kennedy was killed by a guy named Harry Oswald. He says he didn't do it but he did. Tomorrow's Joe's birthday. I hope they crusify Oswald. Everyone's very broken up about it. President Kennedy was such a nice guy to. President Johnson will be president now. I really don't think he'd make very good president but it's only for a year. Nadine

Saterday NOVEMBER 23 1963

Dear Tammy,

There will be no school Monday because Presidentt Johnson has declared it a national day of morning for President Kennedy. I stayed over night at Jerri's today becaus it was Joe's birthday. We babysat for the nextdoorneighbors until 12:30. Boy the babie's a brat. There hasn't been much news about the assasunation of President Kennedy. I don't think it'll be much fun having an extra day off because you can't watch T.V. or radio because it's all news. Nadine

Sunday NOVEMBER 24 1963

Dear Tammy,

Guess What! The assanater got assacinated! Yes! Harry Oswald got killed. I think it serves him right. After all an eye for an eye a tooth for a tooth. Some people say that he's entitled to a fair trial. But I would just waste moor time. Why not get it over and done with? Today on T.V. they played the national anthem on a program which was dedicated to the late President Kennedy and I ran into the kitchen cause I was crying. Nadine

# FINDS FOR THE HOUSE

It's always seemed a shame to me that all of the wonderful finds you've sent in—which someone at some point spent time and care to create—have been stripped of their original purpose. So, I thought, why not put some of these FOUND notes to use around my own house? —DAVY

Ladies "Please" Keep Restroom Clean "Please" Put Tissiue Where it Belong After it has been Used that is not the floor. We do have a larae Trash Can "Putt" this door and Look to Your Left. I did say LADIES

Thank You

FOUND by Leccia Manning, New York, NY

I share my house with three women—Dorothy, Helen, and Shawna. I figured this one was appropriate to post in the bathroom.

The FOUND "office" is in the damp, stone-and-dirt basement of our house. With all the low ceilings, pipes, and doorways, I thought I'd put this one up in a few places to keep Brande and Mike and the rest of the FOUND crew safe from injury.

WATCH YOUR HEAD

FOUND by Candida, San Francisco, CA

I taped this one to the shelf next to my alarm clock

YOU BETTERDO SOME SITUPS AND WORKOUT TODAY!!!!!!!!!!!!!!!

FOUND by David Wysocki, Berkeley, CA

Okay, you know how you put your leftovers from some amazing meal away in the fridge, and then the next day you've got this smug contentment going all day, knowing that great snack is waiting for you when you get home—and then you get home, and it's gone?! Well, this note's been very handy.

I will **Kill** you if you Touch!!
Don't make me do it, I don't like violence... but I will kill you if I have to.
Thank you
P.J.

FOUND by Mike Montedoro, Jr., North Versailles, PA

Before Entering & when you enter
focus - on the task
Knock and wait -
Introduce My Self & Identify
Explain - why I here.
~~get~~ place Supplies
Wash My hands
Gather & prepare persons own things if they have them
ajust bed
provide PRIVACY

I posted this for visitors on the door to my room.

FOUND by Stephen Cramer, Detroit, MI

Thanks for everything! I had so much fun last night ☺
♡Heather

FOUND by Jordan Small & Nick, San Luis Obispo, CA

I leave this one rumpled casually on the floor by the foot of my bed, so that anyone who's hanging out in my room will think I'm some kind of player.

*FOUND Magazine*. I did say LADIES.

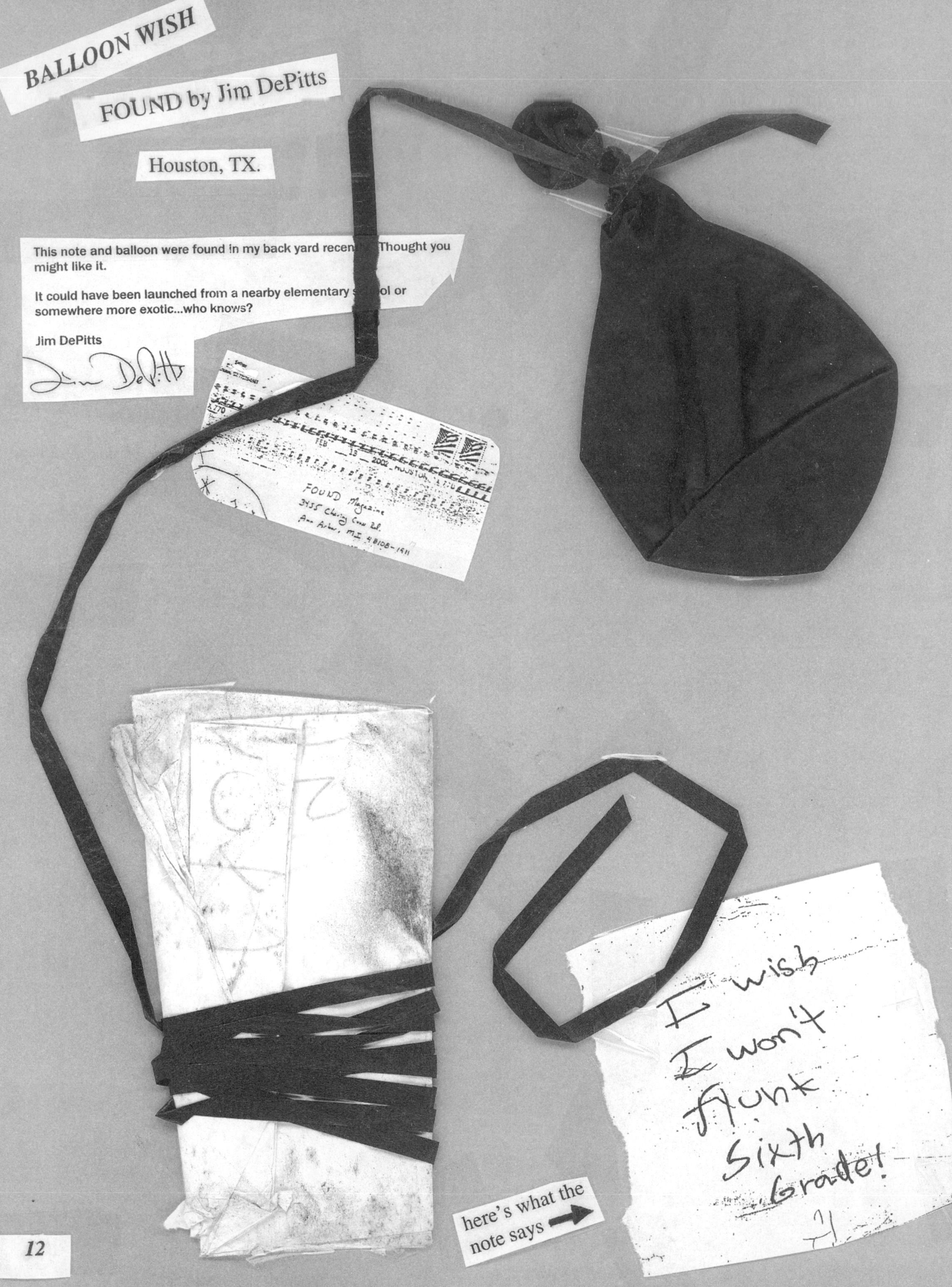
BALLOON WISH
FOUND by Jim DePitts
Houston, TX.
This note and balloon were found in my back yard recen Thought you might like it.
It could have been launched from a nearby elementary s ol or somewhere more exotic...who knows?
Jim DePitts
Jim DePitts
FEB 13 2002 HOUSTON
FOUND Magazine
3455 Charing Cross Rd.
Ann Arbor, MI 48108-1911
here's what the note says
I wish
I won't
flunk
Sixth
Grade!

Stuff I would put into safe

~~passport~~
CD
birth certificate
will

~~3~~ 1/4 lbs. butternut squash
whipping cream
~~[illegible]~~
~~[illegible]~~
bread M. pepperidge farm crountons
~~potatoes~~
sugar, flour
oatmeal

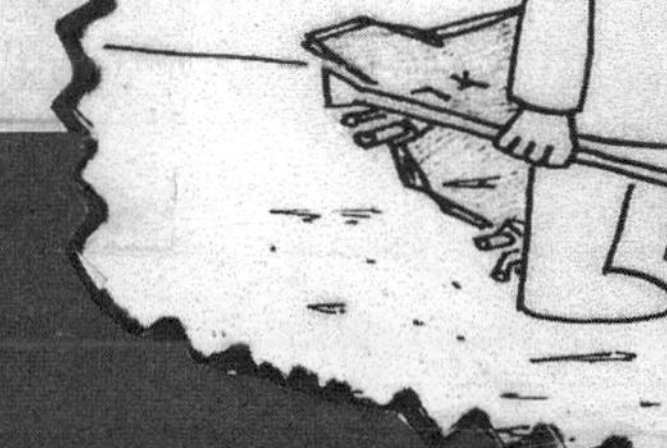


VALUABLES

FOUND by Jainee

Hinsdale, IL

www.ingredientx.com

## A GAME OF CATCH

FOUND by John Moriarty

Sacramento, CA

I found this behind the drawer of a dresser I bought at a garage sale.

## PRACTICE ON THE CAT

FOUND by Cara Lynn van Kleid

Edmonds, WA

I found this in a thrift store inside a book called *The Husband's Cookbook*.

Dear Tim, 7/23/81

The bride-to-be is "showered" with gifts galore,
While the groom-to-be stays home and walks the
floor.
Since I am "strange"---(YOU KNOW THAT!),
I'm sending you a "shower gift" --,
Practice on the cat!!!!!

XOXO
Mom

illustration by Lev

www.ingredientx.com

## STACKS

FOUND by Kevin Dole, Jr.

Ypsilanti, MI

On July 31st I found in the library stacks one live cat. The two hippies playing with it denied ownership, so I collected the cat and gave it to a friend whose landlord allows pets. We have named him Stacks. After debate, we decided that it would be inappropriate to submit him to your magazine. He is far too cute to part with anyway.

—K.D.Jr.

illustration by Lev

# CUPCAKE

FOUND by Sandy Ferrier

Grand Rapids, MI

the real Cupcake! →

My mom is a librarian and one morning she discovered a kitten that someone had deposited in the overnight book drop. Cupcake moved in with us that afternoon.

—VALERIE F.

# WORLD DOMINATION FORMULA

FOUND by Andrew Demcak

West Oakland, CA

7 · 3 = 21 + 1 = 22 ÷ 2 = 11 · 3 = 33 + 1 = 34 ÷ 2 =
17 · 3 = 51 + 1 = 52 ÷ 2 = 26 ÷ 2 = (13 · 3) + 1 = 40 ÷ 2
20 ÷ 2 = 10 ÷ 2 = (5 · 3) + 1 = 16 ÷ 2 = 8 ÷ 2 = 4 ÷ 2 = 2 ÷ 2 =
(1 · 3) + 1 = 4 ÷ = 2 ect.

1004
One Thousand and four
18
eighteen
8
eight
5
five
4
four
4
four

Some day, cats will rule the world.
27
Twenty-seven
11
eleven
6
six
Three
5
five
4
four
4

drawing FOUND by Debbie Steinberg, A² MI

Goals

1. Go to church. Find God, thats find myself through him. Get Baptised.

2. Party a lot. Meet new people. Start drinking once a week. Be social. My Mom met my Dad at a party... Don't forget that.

3. Start exercising with my Mom this week (March 10th - March 14th)

4. Spend a lot of time alone. Find myself. Figure out a way to be happy alone. I need to know that I can be content by myself. I know that I am beautiful. I know that I have a wonderful personality. I know that I'm smart. I know that I'm worthy of being loved.

5. Find a new job. Tomorrow, I will call back all my places that I applied to. I will turn applications into new places.

6. Go to the 200 Bar alone; get soaked into the music. Go to a lot of small concerts alone.

7. Take one class at SCC on March 31st Debt Free Living. $45 Sec: SA. Monday, Ma 31, 2003. 7-10pm Rm A-1. Inst: Meyer

8. Go home and visit w/ family more ofte At least 3x/week.

9. Send in my finds!!

## FIND GOD, START DRINKING

FOUND by Fil

Lincoln, NE

I went to take out the trash and found this in the bushes just outside my apartment complex.

FOUND Magazine. Find myself.

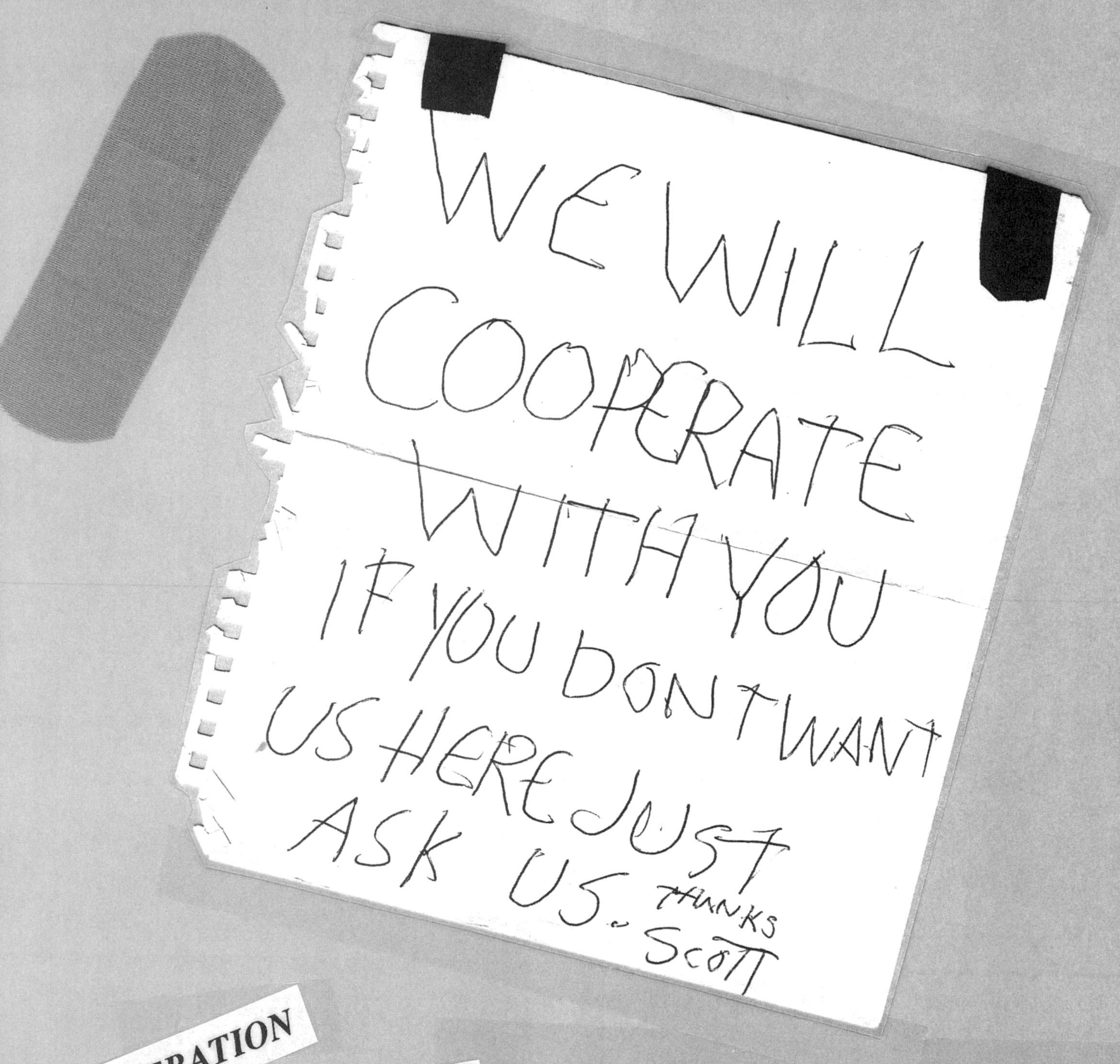


# COOPERATION

FOUND by Stacey Rubin

Oakland, CA

*I* was doing Street Outreach for a local needle exchange program in a *Mad Max*-type neighborhood in West Oakland , lots of people living in cardboard shanties and huts made of rough wooden pallets. We had a nurse with us on this Outreach team, and she was concerned about one guy we met named Scott who had a particularly bad abscess on his leg—he couldn't walk well or move around much because of its location. Scott and another guy were living in a cardboard and tarp shelter in a loading area behind a warehouse.

A few days later I went out with another medical team doing Street Outreach again. When we went to check on Scott's condition, his shelter had disappeared and this note was in its place, tacked to the brick wall.

—S.R.

Steve

Steve

Steve

Steve

Steve

Steve

STEVE

FOUND by Seth Meisels

Brooklyn, NY

This was on the floor of the laundry room in my apartment building in Bed-Stuy. More baffling than the flyer itself is the fact that five people have ripped off names.

—S.M.

7-18-99

I have had a sense of foreboding regarding this trip for some time. I have been left with the impression that I shall not return from it… in this lifetime. Understand that if I am taken it is somehow necessary and should be viewed as merely a delay. I have prepared myself for the journey, do not fear because I am indestructible.

My possessions do not mean a great deal to me only my work. However, I would like 2,000 dollars from my savings given to Rita Brau with the hope that someone will also explain my feelings to her. The balance of my money should be given to Brian Keith Lennigan for the purpose of completing the mission.

All of my rifles and ammunition should also be transferred to Brian Lennigan as well as my writings. All handwritten manuscripts, computer disks, printed copies and electronic copies of both *The Immortal Remains* and *Vae Victis* should be transferred to him on the condition that he finishes the manuscript to the best of his ability. Save for spelling and grammatical corrections the text should be left unaltered. I regret more than anything not finishing this text. One half of all proceeds from their publication should go to help poor and hungry people throughout the world and the other half should be split between Tess Emczek and Brian Lennigan with the hope that he receives a formal education.

The rest of my possessions can be split up in any way seen fit under the provision that Evelyn Santelli and her family in no way receive anything and do not profit by my passing. For legal reasons I have explicitly stated this.

I retract and ask apology for any bad remarks made about any people or groups except for Barbara Allison Jo Devereaux and her family who have forever earned my enmity and for whom I may return.

I make these statements in full control of my rational faculties and in complete mental and physical health.

7/18/99

Jon Leo Trespian

**SENSE OF FOREBODING**

FOUND by Dave I., Lakewood, OH

This living will was nestled in the pages of an Adolph Hitler biography. —D.I.

I TALK TO ALIENS

they tell me to tell you that you are loved! —Terry

FOUND by Elena Leonard, Seattle, WA

VISITORS

FOUND by Brande "Short Line" Wix, Ann Arbor, MI

FOUND by Jeff Thompson, Minneapolis, MN

FOUND by Shaun Williams, Ann Arbor, MI

**Tom Snyder Productions®**

*Software for Teachers Who Love to Teach™*

Time of the Attack
7:00 AM est.

1-800-342-0236 • Fax: 1-800-304-1254

YMA Y398

**www.tomsnyder.com**

FOUND by Matt Samford & Jason Affolder, New Orleans, LA

"it was a lizard." – in response to "what's the awful smell in my truck? the heater core leaking?"

Satire, although I know it to be,
isn't funny. Nothing's that funny, or exciting,
or anything. Night is tough when sleep cannot
be welcomed without the requisite number of tears.
Morning's no cupcake either, waking alone, knowing the
day hold's only sorrow and more crying before I
can get up.

I've had the whole existential problem going on forever, as well, and I
guess that I've just figured that life would go on, + things
would happen, and I'd just go with whatever. And eventually, I'd be
old, and die, or just die, and that would be it. But I'm not
content to wait around for death, after you. I don't care what I do
when I'm with you, just so long as I can live every second
knowing that I have you to tell whatever hilarious, ridiculous, stupid,
mediocre, and/or boring shit I've heard. Or better, just hear or see
it with you, so we can look @ each other, smile (at least), laugh, and,
not saying anything, know. I want to do thing's I've never done, and
have never desired to. Like when I said I've never wanted to go to NY before, and then
I did. I still do. I want to live in cities, get the fuck out of Indiana, and
see the States, and the world. With you. I can't do it alone, you recall
my timidity @ advancing on the boardwalk/Lagoon. But I feel I can
do anything with you. And I want to.

# IT WAS A LIZARD

FOUND by Chirag Thakkar

Brooklyn, NY

I found this note on the corner of North 2nd and Berry in Williamsburg.

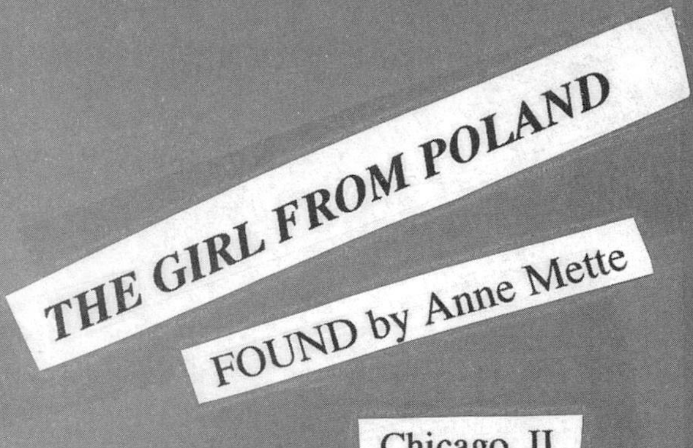

# THE GIRL FROM POLAND

FOUND by Anne Mette

Chicago, IL

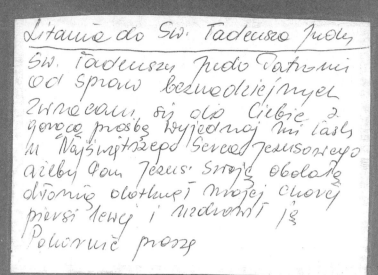

Litanie do Św. Tadeusza Judy
Św. Tadeuszu Judo Patronie
od spraw beznadziejnych
zwracam się do Ciebie z
gorącą prośbą wyjednaj mi łaskę
u Najświętszego Serca Jezusowego
aiby Pan Jezus swoją obolałą
dłonią dotknął mojej chorej
piersi lewej i uzdrowił ją
Pomóż mi proszę

*I* found this note tucked in the bushes in front of the little Polish church in my neighborhood. I wasn't able to find someone to translate it for some time. One day I walked to a local park where many new immigrants from Poland gather. An older man I showed it to began to cry when he read it, but could not speak English well enough to explain what it meant.

I kept finding more notes, all folded exactly the same, all saying the same thing. They were in the bushes and tucked in the church's window sills. In all, I found over forty identical notes.

Finally, I found a friend who could read it for me and also read between the lines. It's a prayer request. In Poland, it's common for people to leave their requests tucked in little nooks and crannies all around churches.

This woman has breast cancer. She has lost one breast to the disease and is in danger of losing the other. From the writing and word usage, it seems that she is young and very scared.

My friend wrote her a bunch of notes in Polish, telling her that we would pray for her, and we left them in the bushes on bright-colored paper for her to find. She never picked them up and as often as I lurked nearby, hoping for a glimpse, I never saw the woman who, for a time, continued to leave notes.

I have found no more notes in six months. I don't know if her prayers—and ours—were answered.

—A.M.

this drawing FOUND by Debbie Steinberg
Ann Arbor, MI

EVER CUT YOUR SKIN FOR FUN?
SELL YOUR ASS?!
SLEEP ON THE STREET?
DO YOU LIKE PAIN? TAKE HEROIN?
IF SO LETS START A BAND
CALL 246-0882 AND
LEAVE A MESSAGE WITH
INNOCENT BYSTANDER JESSE

FOUND by Rachel Racecar, Vancouver, B.C.

BASSIST WANTED

DARK GLAM DYED STRAIGHT HAIR
CONCRETE GYPSY STREET TUFF IMAGE

No free ride Hollywood hype dream
no money gettin' Yeah I'll be there and not show up
looser fat my girlfriend won't let me play Kids using
a band as an excuse to wear mommie's make-up.

We're Image Image Image, We have the look
and the songs. You've heard all the lies,
and met all the flakes, We're sick of it too.

(818)

FOUND by Chris Rush, Tucson, AZ

HELP US BRING THE DARKNESS!!
Needed:
—Guitarist
—Bassist
—Drums
—Lead Singer
—Death Metal
—Speed Metal
—Horror Core
—Must have musical experiences
—Must have car or bike
Call Tony
#630-


FOUND by Katherine Raz, Chicago, IL

MUSICIANS WANTED

Front man looking for a Band

Neo Pop Rock

NEEDED FOR OCTOBER PERFORMANCES

Guiterist, Keyboardist, Drummer
And Bass Player

Men or women 18 to 35

For upcoming Band you must be:

+ Dedicated to the Band +
+ Be able to understand you would be a part of a inner circle +
+ Expect to practice 3 to 4 times a week. +
+ Musicians who are looking for a career in music +
+ Musicians who are looking for this new style of Rock +
+ Open minded to now this new style of Rock +
+ Cannot lie in any way to the band +
+ Believers of your own talent and self worth +
+ and expect nothing but reaching the big time!!! +
+ a believer of God if not please don't reply +

Interested please call Frontman Solid at (917)
Leave only name, instrument you play, and best time to call you.
And I will

~~~~~~~~Many are called Yet few are Chosen~~~~~~~~

FOUND by Christa Neu, Hoboken, NJ

FOUND by Matt Rotter, San Francisco, CA

LEGENDARY TEENAGE DRUMMER AVAILABLE

16, seeks other YOUNG, CRAZY, REBELLIOUS rockers to
start the BIGGEST, most OUTRAGEOUS, fucking WILDEST
party band to come SCREAMING out of the strip!!! With
the BEST, CLASSIC, BONE-CRUNCHING songs that'll blow all
these fucking poseurs AWAY!!! It's time to bring back the
image and spirit of KISS and MÖTLEY and kick some FUCKIN
ASS, like only the YOUNG can do. None of this rehearsal every
week BULLSHIT!! This is FOREVER, every waking second of every
DAY! I have a lifelong commitment to Rock N' Roll, and I sure
as hell can't do anything else. I've gotten call after call from
the same BORING BOZOS who just DON'T get it, and aren't willing
to FIGHT their way to the TOP. So if you wanna continue
playing the same BORING, TIRESOME NOISE—FINE—But the
BIGGEST sin in Rock N Roll is being BORING!!! I'm gonna do
it the AMERICAN WAY! SEX, DRUGS, and ROCK N ROLL FOREVER
IF this add describes you 100% then call me!!!
DEVIN-(310)
Fi- KISS, OZZY, CRÜE - THE WORLD NEEDS THIS...
~~~~~~~~

COLON HOLE

WILL NOT BE PERFORMING TONIGHT

WE APOLOGIZE FOR ANY DISAPPOINTMENT

THANK YOU

FOUND by Craig F., Hollywood, CA

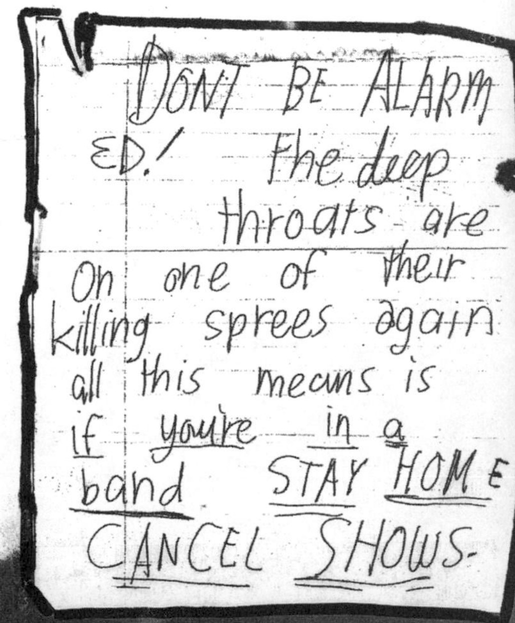

DONT BE ALARMED! The deep throats are on one of their killing sprees again all this means is if you're in a band STAY HOME CANCEL SHOWS.

FOUND by Micque Li, San Francisco, CA

Dear mommy + daddy

I know its hard for you to stop. I know you love me but when you keep bringing that stuff in the house it feels like you dont. I don't want to be rude but I really want you to stop. Please for me mommy and daddy. Dont bring it in the house. It makes a greater chance of us getting kicked out of here. I do get scared. Please mommy and daddy I love you. (I dont like it when you do it)

love, Eliza

FEELS LIKE YOU DON'T

FOUND by Liam Bahneman

Seattle, WA

Justin Gotlieb

What I Know about US History

Betsy Ross sewed the first american flag.

George washington was the first american president.

George washington was a general in the war.

martin luther King was a civil rights leader

Chris columbus discovered America.

George washington cut down his fathers cherry tree with an axe his Father gave to him for his birthday.

The Black Panther was started During the Vietnam war.

the sputnik sattelite was launched

man went to outer space

Malcolm X began His Quest For Freedom

The constitution was sighned

The Boston tea Party Happened

the anti government group, the anarchy was started

King Tuts tomb was discovered

the stop light was invented

the 1967 Ford Mustang Shelby SS was introduced

nitrous oxide was allowed to be used in muscle cars show cars, and modified racing cars, for use in Drag racing in 1978

Black people won the right for freedom

Hitler began the Nazi clan

Ted Bondy was sentenced, then commited suicide.

Richard chase was murdered

JFK was assasanated

Richie valins died in a plane crash

Edgar Allem Poe's short stories and Poems were Published

Elvis Died of a D.O.D.

Jimi Hendrix died

Jim morrison died.

Paul mcartney was Knighted

Justin Gotlieb was Born

# WHAT I KNOW ABOUT U.S. HISTORY

FOUND by Rona Miller

South Bend, IN.

FOUND S.R.

Found Magazine
3455 Charing Cross Rd.
Ann Arbor, MI 48108-1911

Please get gas

1 bag of Peppermint Patties

1 bag of Hershey's miniatures

1 bag of lollipops or something fruity

HEALTH NUT

FOUND by Joe Principe

Oak Park, IL

Beer meat.
Dog Food
boloney
Bread
sanka

FOUND by Sarah Boudreau, Edina, MN

Sleeping bag
extra blanket
Towel etc
pillow
raingear
hiking etc
scope
flashlight

FOUND by Brandon Barnes, Denver, CO

## SHOPPING LISTS

this photo FOUND by Katie and Nina, St. Louis, MO

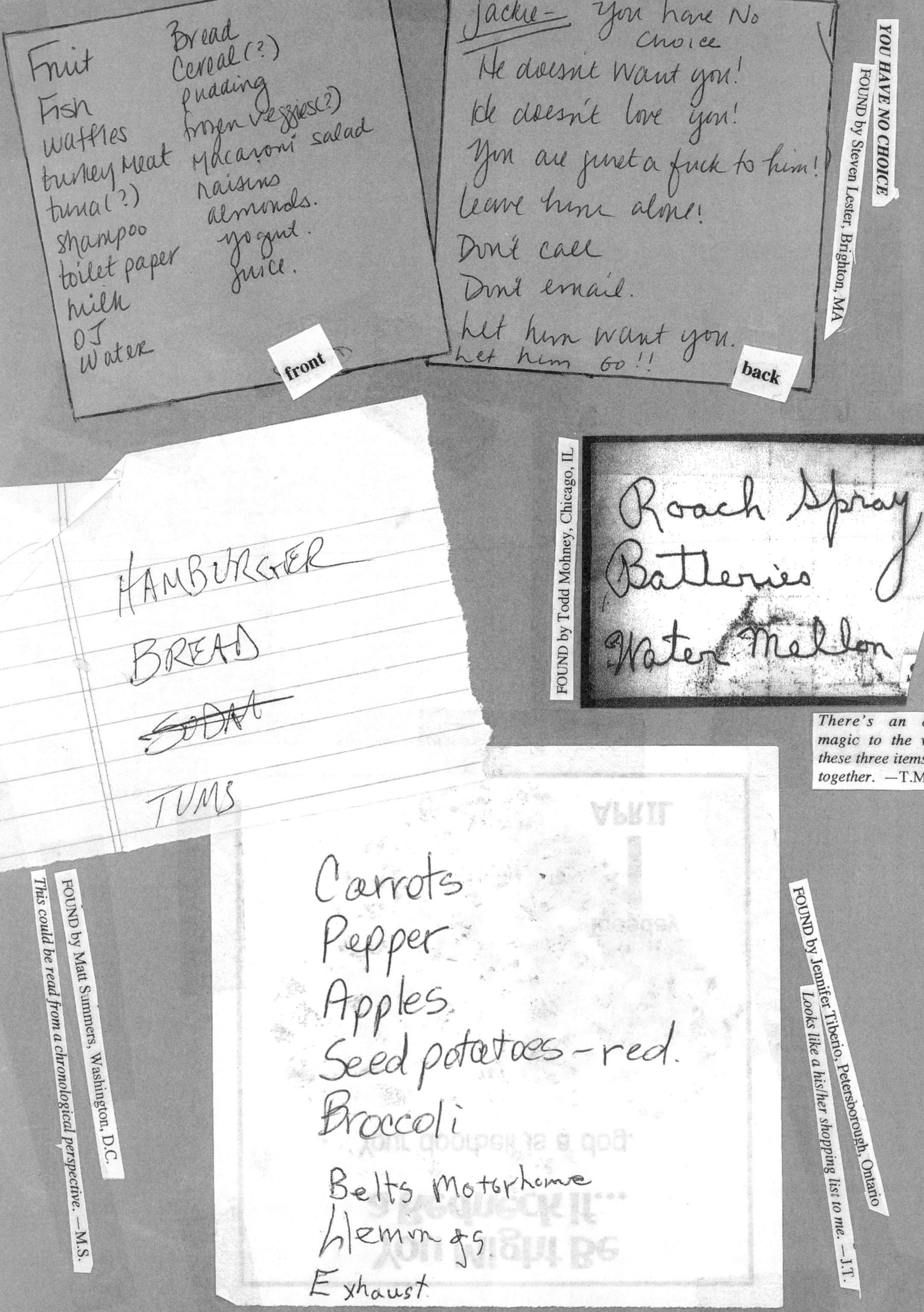

Fruit
Fish
waffles
turkey Meat
tuna(?)
shampoo
toilet paper
milk
OJ
Water
Bread
Cereal(?)
pudding
frozen veggies(?)
Macaroni salad
raisins
almonds.
yogurt.
Juice.
front
Jackie— You have No choice
He doesn't want you!
He doesn't love you!
You are just a fuck to him!
Leave him alone!
Don't call
Don't email.
Let him want you.
Let him go!!
back
YOU HAVE NO CHOICE
FOUND by Steven Lester, Brighton, MA
HAMBURGER
BREAD
SODA
TUMS
FOUND by Matt Summers, Washington, D.C.
This could be read from a chronological perspective. —M.S.
Roach Spray
Batteries
Water Mellon
FOUND by Todd Mohney, Chicago, IL
There's an odd magic to the way these three items go together. —T.M.
Carrots
Pepper
Apples
Seed potatoes - red.
Broccoli
Belts Motorhome
Lemmings
Exhaust
FOUND by Jennifer Tiberio, Petersborough, Ontario
Looks like a his/her shopping list to me. —J.T.

# Adventure Club

How to get in the Club!
you need to know how
to climb a fence. Need
to like Adventure.

**Club Members**
Shane
Ethan
Carlos
Brandon

Rules
- can't tell ~~anyone~~ were or what it is.
- No messing up the club
- Don't bring anything ~~in whith~~ out pelmisson from Shane or Ethan.
- You have to be nice to squrills

## CAN'T TELL ANYONE

FOUND by Laurie Carvalho

East Providence, RI

**I found this in my backyard, apparently it blew in from one of the neighborhood kids. It looks like a rough draft of rules for the "Adventure Club".**

**A day after I found it, I called the group of neighborhood kids over (approximate ages 5-8) and inquired about the "Adventure Club." They looked surprised that I was aware of this newly formed club, then they looked shocked when I began reciting the rules. They insisted that I tell them how I knew this top secret information. I told them my dog "Kismet" overheard them making the rules. They were speechless and perplexed. As they were walking away I could hear the youngest one exclaim "Wow! Kismet heard us"!**

—L.C.

illustration by Dylan Stryzynski

## More Respect

*by Joe*

Respect is needed towards MARILYN MANSON,KORN and TOOL which are all
underground bands which means they want to make it to the top without being
supported by the t.v or the raido but there not the only ones doing this.
Then theres MARILYN MANSON a man of his word in my eyes because I respect him
alot because MARILYN MANSON stands for your good side and your bad side like
Mariyln Monroe and Charles Mason and thats allhes tring to repusent along with him
being the ANTI CHRIST SUPERSTAR which means your against god and the devil
but you wirshop yourself. MR. MARILYN MANSON is very racist because his music is
intended for whites only and im glad its for white people only because its about time
theres something for one race only .
MARIYLN MANSON made over two million dollars alone just by going on the 1996
DEAD TO THE WORLD TOUR.
KORN and TOOL are among alot of other underground bands like THE DEFTONS
and PANTERA "but the fans are great to us" says Jon Davis the leader of the five man
band KORN. Then theres TOOL a band that tours alot with KORN but both bands feel
that there getting the respect they need but in my eyes theres no respect for them
where i live but i hope that will soon change.

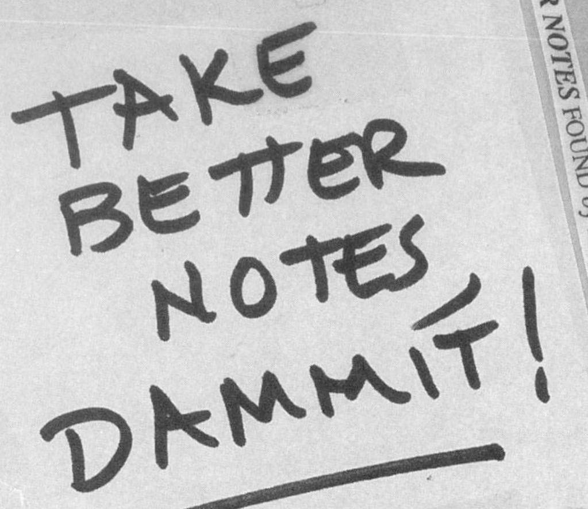


**BETTER NOTES** FOUND by Prentiss Riddle, Austin, TX

I hate Alton!
I hate Alton!
I hate Alton!
I hate Alton!
I hate Alton!
I hate Alton!

**ALTON**

FOUND by Will Golden & Kate Kirkpatrick

Houston, TX

In a long line at the supermarket, we watched the cashier—a girl in her late teens—write furiously on the back of a receipt, then crumple it up and drop it on the counter. At last we got to the register, and after the cashier rang up our groceries she wandered away for a half-minute, just enough time for us to grab the balled-up receipt and read the back of it. We were still laughing over it when she came back. We paid, and thanked the boy who'd bagged our groceries; then Kate grabbed my arm suddenly and pointed out his nametag: ALTON.

—W.G.

BE RIGHT BACK
-GODOT

MAY 1978

**STILL WAITING** FOUND by Jonas Westover, Plymouth, VT

***THE GIRL WHO WASN'T THERE***

FOUND by Laura Geuskens and Damon, Phoenix, AZ

This fascinates me because you can press your thumb over the girl in black, and it looks like she was never there. Nobody noticed her. The watermelon truck still turns the corner, the man still passes on his bicycle, the woman still crosses the street.

—*L.G.*

(16)

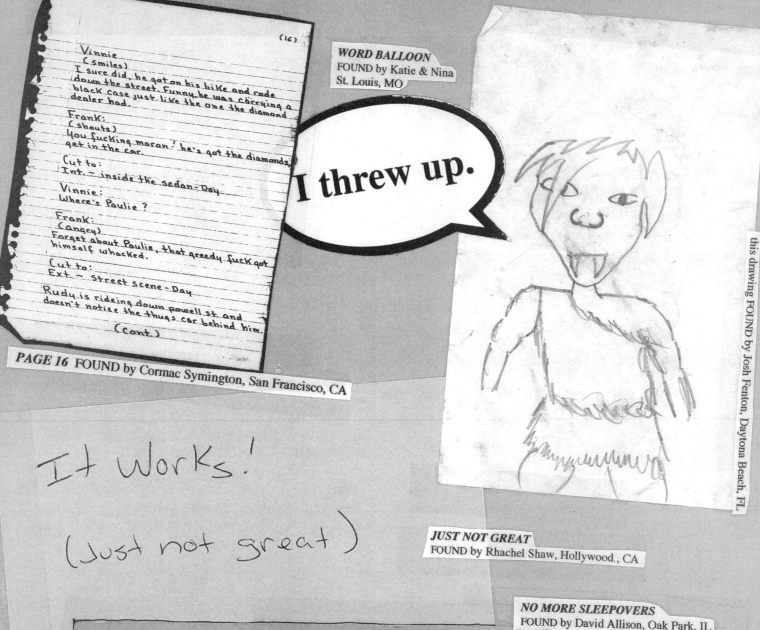

Vinnie
(smiles)
I sure did, he got on his bike and rode down the street. Funny, he was carrying a black case just like the one the diamond dealer had.

Frank:
(shouts)
You fucking moron! he's got the diamonds, get in the car.

Cut to:
Int. - inside the sedan - Day

Vinnie:
Where's Paulie?

Frank:
(angry)
Forget about Paulie, that greedy fuck got himself whacked.

Cut to:
Ext. - street scene - Day

Rudy is rideing down powell st. and doesn't notice the thugs car behind him.

(cont.)

***PAGE 16*** FOUND by Cormac Symington, San Francisco, CA

I threw up.

***WORD BALLOON***
FOUND by Katie & Nina
St. Louis, MO

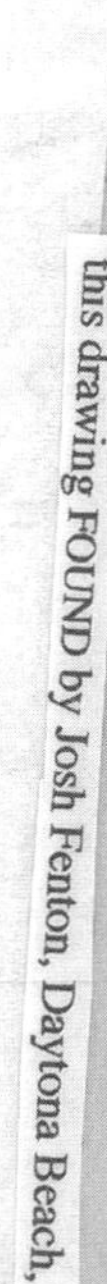
this drawing FOUND by Josh Fenton, Daytona Beach, FL

It Works!

(Just not great)

***JUST NOT GREAT***
FOUND by Rhachel Shaw, Hollywood., CA

***NO MORE SLEEPOVERS***
FOUND by David Allison, Oak Park, IL

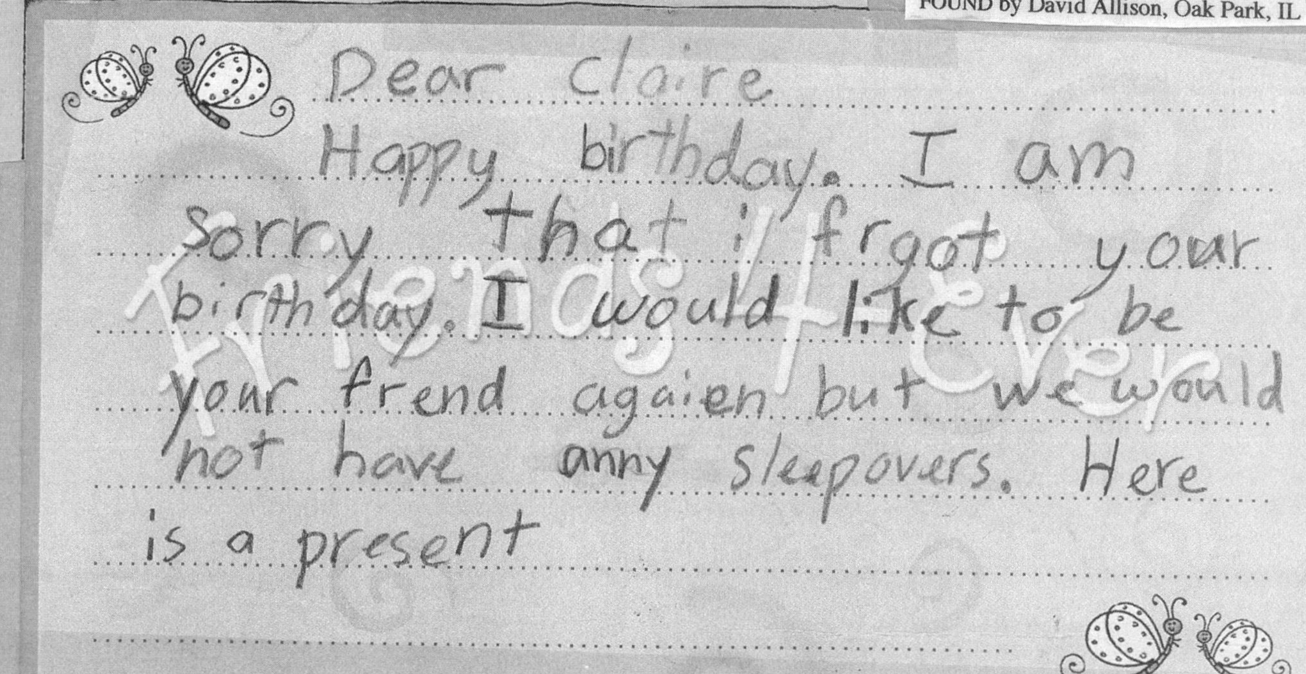
Dear claire
Happy birthday. I am sorry that i frgot your birthday. I would like to be your frend agaien but we would not have anny sleepovers. Here is a present

**ABLE GLASS NOTE**

FOUND by Maureen

San Francisco, CA

# ABLE GLASS COMPANY

380 E. Evelyn Avenue, Sunnyvale, CA 94086
**(408) 739-8829 • FAX (408) 739-7818**
www.ableglass.com
Contractors License #690198

Since 1969

I really hope that you get this. I also hope that you read this. It's now been 9 hours since your friend dropped me off in Burlingame and I'm somewhere between Mountain View and San José, on my way to Santa Cruz where I intend to get a job and get my life on track again, in hopes that you might have a change of heart & mind.

Maybe, if I can support you with a job & a roof over your head, then you just might want to spend some time with me again.

And, why? Why tell your family that I'm some kind of psychotic who keeps stalking you? I'd rather leave you on a more friendly basis. Bumper, kept telling me that you still like me and that you still consider me a friend. Friends don't

**WINDOWS • PATIO DOORS • SHOWER DOORS**
**COMPLETE GLASS SERVICE • SCREENS • TABLE TOPS**

## *HALLOWEEN GEM*

This true story takes place on October 31st, 1985, in Roseville, California, which at the time was a sleepy little railroad town. I was attending Roseville High at the time. The school is near a few sets of railroad tracks, so there were a lot of train hoppers who got on and off the trains as they slowed to stop in town.

I had stayed late after school and was walking home in the evening twilight. A full moon shone through the brooding clouds. There were hardly any cars on the road so it was really quiet, and off in the distance I could hear the strange whine and grind of train breaks. I knew it was shaping up to be a creepy Halloween.

As I got close to the train tracks I noticed an old bag lady on her hands and knees. As I approached she stood up, looked at me, and flashed a toothless grin. "It must be my lucky day!" she said. "I found a diamond!" She held it out for me to see: a small piece of clear broken glass in her dirty hand.

*—M.A. Ross*
Sacramento, CA

illustration by Dylan Stryzynski

**WITH JOE**

FOUND by Aimee McDonald

Dexter, MI

Rejoice In His Love!

On that first EASTER, darkness turned to light, despair gave way to joy, and death to eternal life... as the Christ of the cross arose, Savior of the world.

Dear Mother Pat,

God gave His only Son that the world might witness His perfect love.
May God's love bring you joy at Easter and always.

Love,

Janette

I almost died this past November, I thought I would be with my beloved Joe again.
Hope all is well with you I miss your smiling face
I would love to have you over for supper if, and when I get back on my feet.

Dear Jesus,

Thank you for not making me cut my dick off and suck yours. Today I am one cool sober mother fucker.

Amen

**COOL**

FOUND by Rachel Jacobs

I found this slip of paper in a copy of *What to Expect When You're Expecting* that I borrowed from Bernal Heights Library in San Francisco.

San Francisco, CA

## RAPPIN' FOR THE LORD

FOUND by Carly Sommerstein
Weehawken, NJ

This is just one page from a yellow pad completely filled with rhymes about Jesus Christ. —C.S.

The pen is mighteir than the ~~sword~~ Sword, while you lift weapons to wage war, I lift up my pen ~~to~~ in the name of the Lord To Be a ~~never seen~~ never Reviled to your eyes before, ~~like~~ Soilder in a war ~~like~~ what come's out of your weapon is to penatrate Kills, what come's out of mine hearts By the Lord So By his Chosen ~~is to fill~~ They will. Be filled. ~~The~~ To become followers of Spirt The Teacher of teacher - The preacher of all preaches ~~By him to know the truth~~ who has Relived The troth to the touth seeker ~~to~~ to do the will of God, to Carry out his command against all odds. while you sit in high places and order innocent lives ~~are sent~~ to ~~be~~ slayed And you at the comfort at your home growing more wicked every day. While mony and power are your God, keep this path and problems will grow that your money and power can't solve. Repent Now and follow the King ~~for~~ or when he come to take his kingdom and those who don't acept him Now a wrath the is unbearable to you he will bring. Thou shall not Kill but every day blood is spilled against God will, ~~I see my lord's propechy for filled~~ You dare call your selves Just. While your hearts are filled with selfish...

## RESERVED FOR JESUS

FOUND by Min Suh Son
Cambridge, MA

You Are Obviously Illegally Parked.

We cannot come in and out of the Antioch Church Parking area when you do this.

If this persists, we will have you towel.

Thanks,
IN Jesus' Name
Min. E. B. Carnini

this card FOUND by Brad Smith, Cincinnati, OH

# BAD CRAZINESS

FOUND by Joe Gainer

Portland, OR

Hello Bonehead –

Now that you have completely fucked up the program and alienated everyone since firing me, you should know what the hell is going on.

Your idiotic decisions have lead to the demise of a great team. You have not got the slightest idea how to manage a team and never will you stupid fuckweasel.

To give you an idea of how little you know about what the fuck is going on – try dialing up your own office phone and when your shitbum voice comes on the answering device, punch in '0505' and then punch in '1' followed by '1' and then when some important message comes on, (like someone who wants to join you worthless program) punch in the number '0' and it will be erased!. I'll bet you didn't know that you fucking moron! I have been doing that for the past six months!

I went to see a voodoo lady recently and paid with $$ from your team to have her put a hex on your pitiful life. Be prepared for a scrotum infection that slowly, painfully and irreversibly creeps up your ass to the point where you shit fire continuously until your balls disintegrate culminating in your dick shriveling up and falling off!!

So while you still have a dick, go take a flying fuck at a rolling donut you shitpig cop!

Have a nice day, fuckwit!

From you know who.

P.S. Why don't you take a flying fuck at the moon too!!

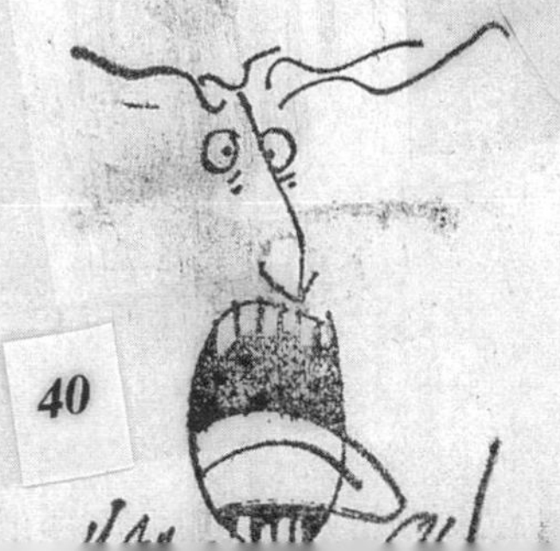

**NEED / HAVE**

FOUND by M. Adler

Novi, MI

Need

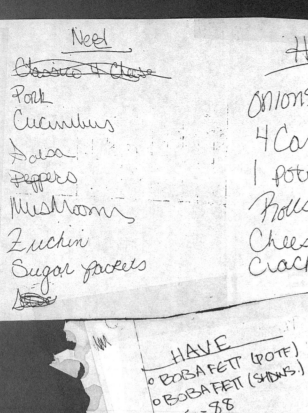

~~Classico & Cheese~~
Pork
Cucumbers
Salsa
~~Peppers~~
Mushrooms
Zuchini
Sugar packets

Have

Onions
4 Carrots
1 potatoe
Rolls
Cheese
Crackers

**HAVE / NEED**

FOUND by

Christa and Mike

Providence, RI

HAVE

- BOBA FETT (POTF)
- BOBA FETT (SHDWS.)
- IG-88
- GREEDO
- HAN SOLO
- X-WING LUKE
- CHEWBACCA
- R2-D2
- BEN KENOBI
- LEIA (BOUSHH DISG.)
- TUSKEN RAIDER
- JAWAS
- DARTH VADER
- TIE FIGHTER PILOT
- DEATH STAR GUNNER
- SANDTROOPER
- HAN SOLO / STORMTROOPER
- R5-D5
- 2-1B SURGEON DROID
- BOSSK
- JEDI LUKE
- YODA
- HAMMERHEAD
- IMPERIAL DROID
- C-3PO
- LANDO CALRISSIAN (BESPIN)
- HANSOLO IN ENDOR GEAR
- HOTH LUKE

NEED

- ~~BOSSK~~
- ~~2-1B (SURGEON DROID)~~
- ~~LANDO CALRISSIAN (BESPIN)~~
- ~~JEDI LUKE~~
- HOTH HAN SOLO
- HOTH REBEL TROOPER
- ~~YODA~~
- DAGOBAH LUKE
- TATOOINE LUKE
- ~~HAMMERHEAD~~
- AT-AT COMMANDER
- HAN SOLO IN CARBONITE
- ~~C-3PO~~
- PRINCESS LEIA (WHITE DRESS) $20-
- * SPIRIT OF OBI-WAN $13 EA.
- FIGRIN D'AN (MAIL OFFER) ~~$20~~
- * ~~IMPERIAL DROID~~ $20-
- * ELECTRONIC R2-D2
- BIKER SCOUT / SPEEDER BIKE

NEED (SHADOWS)

- LUKE / IMPERIAL GUARD
- DASH RENDAR
- SWOOP TROOPER + SWOOP $10-
- PRINCE XIZOR
- CHEWBACCA / BOUNTY HUNTER
- GRAND MOFF TARKIN
- ~~HAN IN ENDOR GEAR~~
- LUKE IN STORMTROOPER DISG.
- BIB FORTUNA
- LANDO IN PALACE GUARD DISG.
- EMPEROR PALPATINE
- ENDOR LUKE w/ SPEEDERB

**FOUND Magazine.**

**The booty don't NEVER stop.**

# HI DAD, WHAT'S UP (LETTER FROM ERIE)

FOUND by Raspberry Rosen

Erie, PA

( 1/24/01 )

Hi Dad what's up. Not much here just working
to save money. I'm working at old country Buff
starting at $6.50 an hour 'cooking' Dad is there
any cooking jobs down there let me know when
you write me back. I gave Robert your letter. ok.
without mom knowing. ok. I can't wait to come down
there. Erie sucks Dad there ain't nothing to do too
cold the weather sucks too. Dad I drink too beer
~~Bud~~ Budweiser, but I don't drink alot and I do a
little drugs too I smoke joints and I got bowl that
is cool I'll let you see it ok. I talk to
grandma chapman she said that she going to send
you a letter and some money. Dad I don't know if
Robert or Jill is coming down but I'll talk to
them and see. If not it will just be me only

Dad your going to rent a mobile home that's cheap
hundred a week that's cheap. Dad try to see if
there's any apment's for rent and let me know
how much 'ok'. Dad I'm going to take a greyhoud
because it's cheap only $49 dollars but you to call
ahead of time. Dad all of the money I'm saveing
from working at my job and my income tax check
I should have a lot ok with the money we should
be able to get a places for us ok! Dad I can't
wait to come down there pretty soon.

Turn over ↘

Dad I'm A cook I CAN cook some shit up
cook some meals up for us get a grill and cook on that
Also I got A lot C'ds Like AC/DC, Led Zeppelin
OVER Kill, METALLICA, Pink Floyd, THE DOORS,
Jimmy Hendrix, Judus Priest, black sabbath. And ALL
Kinds. And we can jam out and have lots of fun.

(IMPORANT DAD)

I'm going to send you some stamps so you
can wright me back and I'm going give you a calling
Card so you can call me.

Dad when you get your place give me your
Address and let me know where your at.
I miss you and I can't ~~what~~ wait to see
you we will have lots of fun

Keep in touch so I know what's
going on ok.

Dad I'm still coming down there
I can't wait
So let me know what's
going on ok.
Take care and I love you!
Take it easy. ok. Dad

W/B/S!!



This letter was found in the street after a rain; its envelope was addressed to a man in Arizona. I count it among the most moving and affecting FOUND notes I've seen. —DAVY

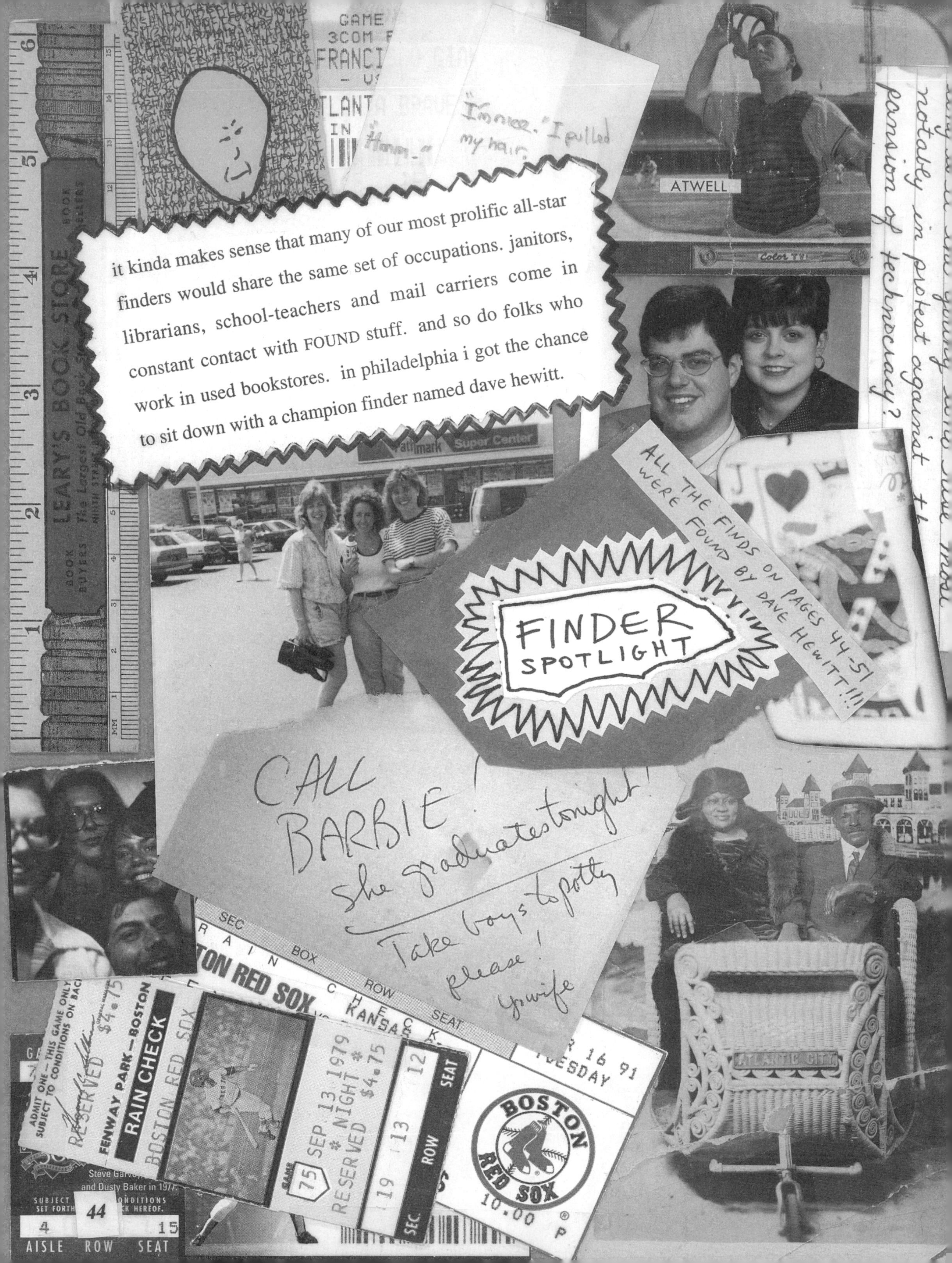

it kinda makes sense that many of our most prolific all-star finders would share the same set of occupations. janitors, librarians, school-teachers and mail carriers come in constant contact with FOUND stuff. and so do folks who work in used bookstores. in philadelphia i got the chance to sit down with a champion finder named dave hewitt.
FINDER SPOTLIGHT
ALL THE FINDS ON PAGES 44-51 WERE FOUND BY DAVE HEWITT!!!
CALL BARBIE! she graduates tonight!
Take boys to potty please!
Yrwife
"I'm nice." I pulled my hair.
"Hmm..."
ATWELL
LEARY'S BOOK STORE
BOOK BUYERS
BOOK SELLERS
RAIN CHECK
FENWAY PARK—BOSTON
BOSTON RED SOX
SEP 13 1979
NIGHT
RESERVED $4.75
ROW
SEAT
SEC
BOSTON RED SOX
TUESDAY
10.00
AISLE ROW SEAT
ATLANTIC CITY

**davy:** *what up playa. i hear you've got a crazy collection of FOUND stuff.*

**dave hewitt:** yeah. i've worked at used bookstores for a bunch of years. one of my jobs is to flip through every used book that comes into the store – check the condition of the binding, see if there's any writing inside, make sure no one's marked it up too bad with a highlighter. and inside the books i find all kinds of phenomenal stuff.

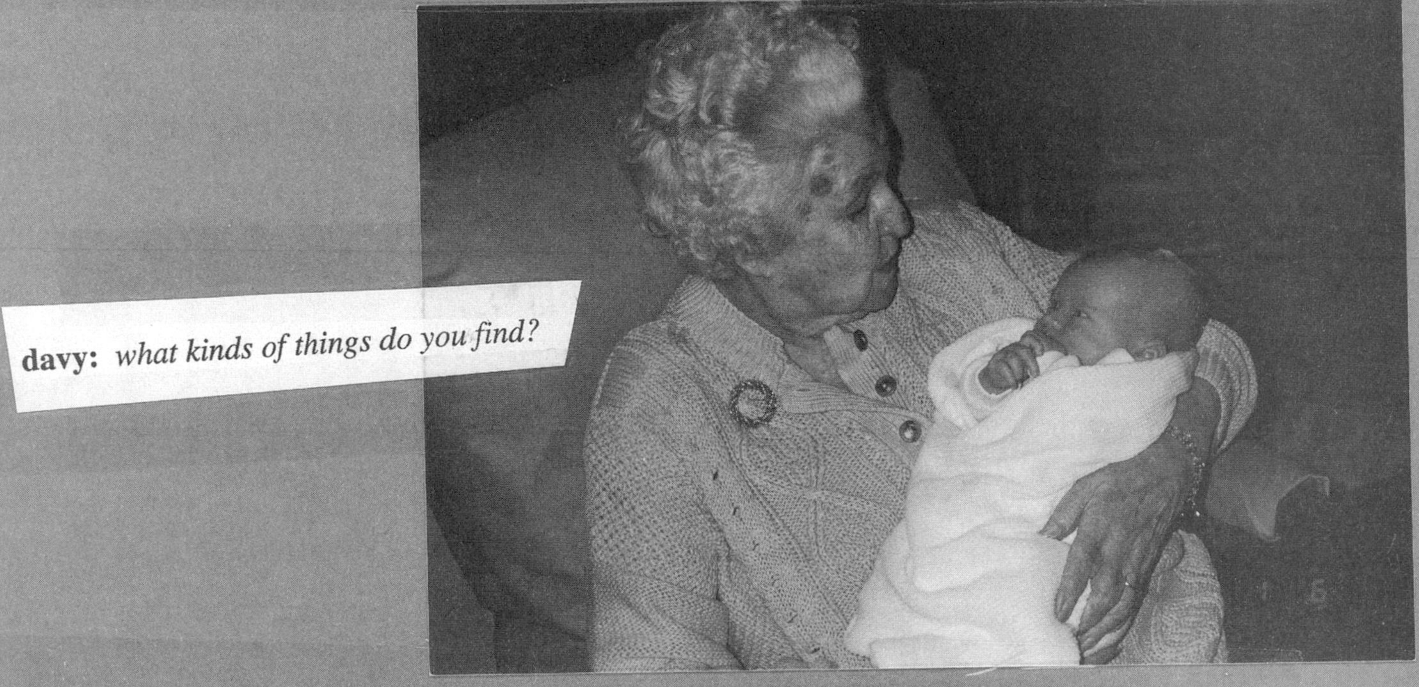

**davy:** *what kinds of things do you find?*

**dave hewitt:** well, i've found photos, letters, journal entries, postcards, bookmarks, birth announcements, death certificates, a handwritten will, sketches, drawings, ticket stubs, poetry attempts, wallpaper samples, bills, credit card statements, cancelled checks and uncancelled checks, including one from january 1986 made out to "*people for the american way*." i've found money, play money, baseball cards, baseball schedules, playing cards, bumper stickers, subway passes, passes for the premiere of the movie *song remains the same*, *archie* fan-club membership cards, business cards, including wolf blitzer's when he worked for the jerusalem post, christmas gift tags, pocket calendars, to-do lists, old coupons expired in the 1960's, cootie catchers, parking tickets, tongue depressors, emery boards, and an envelope with a lock of hair in it. that's one of my favorites.

Hi Bill - (that was said in a very sexy voice.) May I watch you wash? (Hot!) Be sure & scrub behind your ears. And between your toes, too. Scrub hard.
Love,
Cassie
RYAN SIAS

**davy:** *dang! all stuff folks used as bookmarks.*

**dave hewitt:** right. it's all flat in nature. actually, i don't think the $600 i found was used as a bookmark. i think they were just hiding it in the book.

**davy:** *you found 600 bucks in a book?! how come you didn't send* that *to FOUND magazine?*

**dave hewitt:** i should have. at the time, i was working in this gigantic warehouse for a company that sold out-of-print books. i was way off in a remote corner of the building going through a box. well, i can't pick up any book without flipping through it. inside the pages of beryl markham's *african stories* were six crisp hundred-dollar bills. it would've been the easiest thing in the world to stash them in my front pocket. but a week before i'd dented up the company van pretty badly and they'd been really generous and let me keep my job. besides, i was excited and had to tell someone! so i went to the boss and said, "what's the most money you've ever found in a book?"

of course, he had to outdo me. he said he'd found $700 once. but that was in one of those book safes, you know, a book with a carved-out inside where you can store money and valuables. i showed him the 600 bucks and he said, "we gotta try and find this person." but he was just saying that – we both knew the box of books had come from a guy who was moving to bolivia and that we'd never be able to find him. later, the boss gave me $60, he called it a finder's fee. i was a little pissed off and sad about the whole thing. i wished i'd never seen the money, or that the thing with the van had never happened. if it hadn't, i would have tucked the cash in my pocket and run off whooping and hollering to the nearest record store.

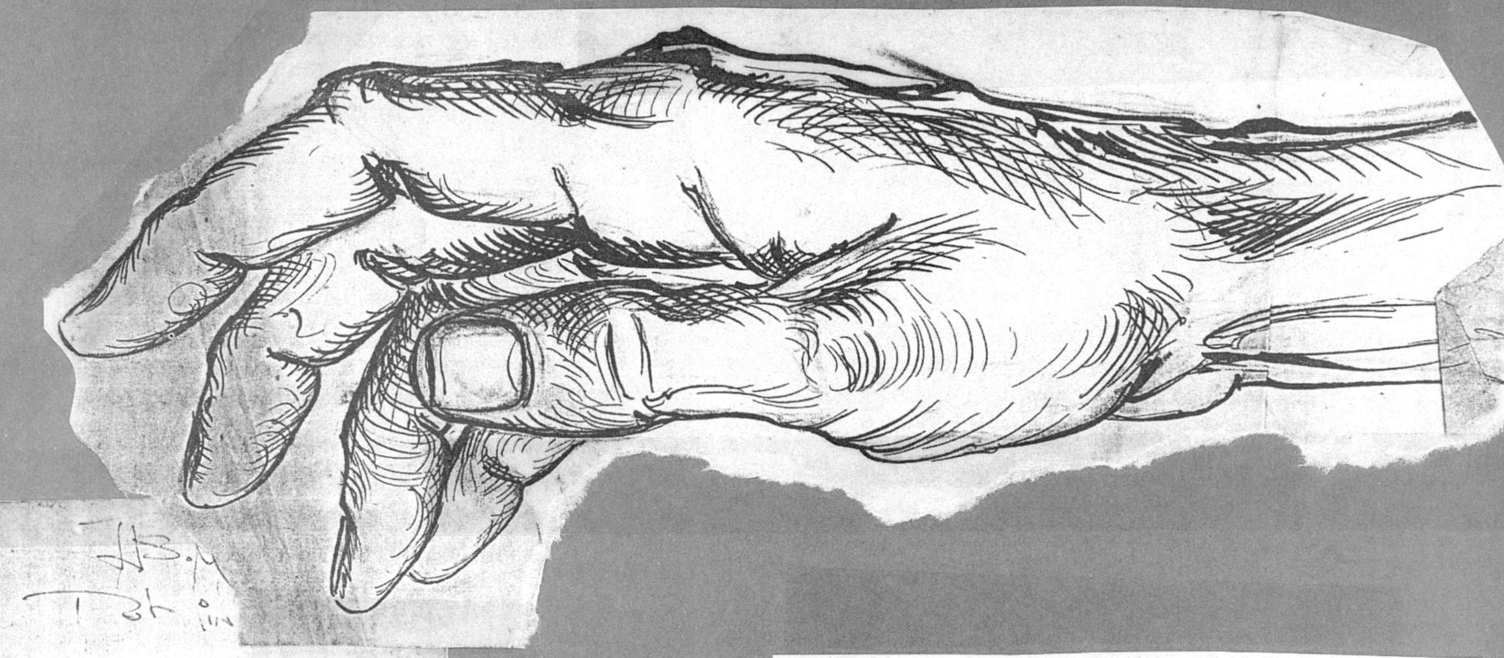

FOOL FOR LOVE
AND
THE SAD LAMENT OF PECOS BILL ON THE EVE OF KILLING HIS WIFE

March 1987
Sweet One,
Over a year
since first you
daringly touched
my knee, and
the magic just
soars higher daily.
Feel very much like
you're here with me,
which puts a bound
in my step
7 stories high....
I love you,
Skip

**davy:** *when did you start saving the stuff you found in books?*

**dave hewitt:** a few years ago, i worked in the used department at the harvard bookstore in cambridge. one time a woman came in to sell a bunch of old books and a picture fell out of one of them; it was a picture of her, naked, in the midst of a strip poker game. she slammed her hand down on the counter and covered it, then took it and ripped it up and threw it in the trash can – *our* trash can! so of course once she left we plucked it out and taped it back together. that was my first big find. i was working with a woman named hillary and i'm indebted to her for encouraging me to start a collection.

**davy:** *what are some of your favorite finds?*

**dave hewitt:** oh, there's so many. i've got a lot of favorites. there's a picture of a very old woman with a newborn baby. that one's nice. there's a picture of an old lady sitting at a table, writing, with a bunch of balloons hanging above her and a big dog at her feet. a lot of beautiful pictures and a few really bizarre ones. the will, that's a good find. it ends abruptly, like the guy was closer to death than he realized. there's someone's itemized list of reasons they want to break off a relationship, like they were preparing for a difficult talk. one book had an inscription in it, which is a kind of find: *sweet one, over a year since first you daringly touched my knee, and the magic just soars higher daily. feel very much like you're here with me, which puts a bound in my step 7 stories high....i love you, skip.* the funny thing about that one is the book in which it was written; the book's called *the sad lament of pecos bill on the eve of killing his wife.* and there's some drawings i love. this comical one of a kid with a knife and everyone around him is butchered up, the t.v. is broken, and the kid's got a big happy expression on his face. and this drawing of an extremely beautiful woman.

**davy:** *hey, let me take a look at that. damn, she fine! she looks sad and tough. i think i'm in love.*
**dave hewitt:** i want that back eventually.

**davy:** *but don't you ever wonder about a find like this. like who drew it? and who's the girl in the drawing? don't you wonder if the fact that you found it, you specifically, if it means you and this girl were meant for each other or something?*

**dave hewitt:** i don't know. this one was in a really old art book. the person who drew it is probably in her sixties now. here, let me have that back. there's a kinko's down the street. we can go make a color copy if you want.

Bobby -
You are the
one who has
been my true
friend. I know that
I can always count on
you, and it's a good
feeling. There are so
many things I feel
in my heart that
I am unable to
express here. You know
how I feel, Bobby.
Thankyou for everything
Someday we'll be
married, you know.
Love,
Mollie
'69

**davy:** *why do you collect all these FOUND things?*

**dave hewitt:** you can learn so much from just the smallest fragments of people's lives. someone's essence emerges from these tiny details, notes and lists and things never intended for other people's eyes. that makes it sound like it's a purely voyeuristic thrill, but the appeal extends much farther than that. yeah, it's fun and it's amusing, but it's also really poignant. within each of these finds – especially the letters and the photographs – something universal is revealed, something that offers insight into the human experience, the human condition.

**davy**: *i like seeing that people who seem to be leading very different lives from me are still experiencing so many of the very same emotions and rafting through so many of the same triumphs and sadnesses. it makes me feel powerfully connected to them – and i don't know who they are really, just this single anonymous person whose note i've found. they end up standing for all people and so by extension i begin to feel a sense of powerful connection to everyone.*

Dre I love you
Tree

Rosie Ro-3

Rozy Rosy

Rozy Rosy

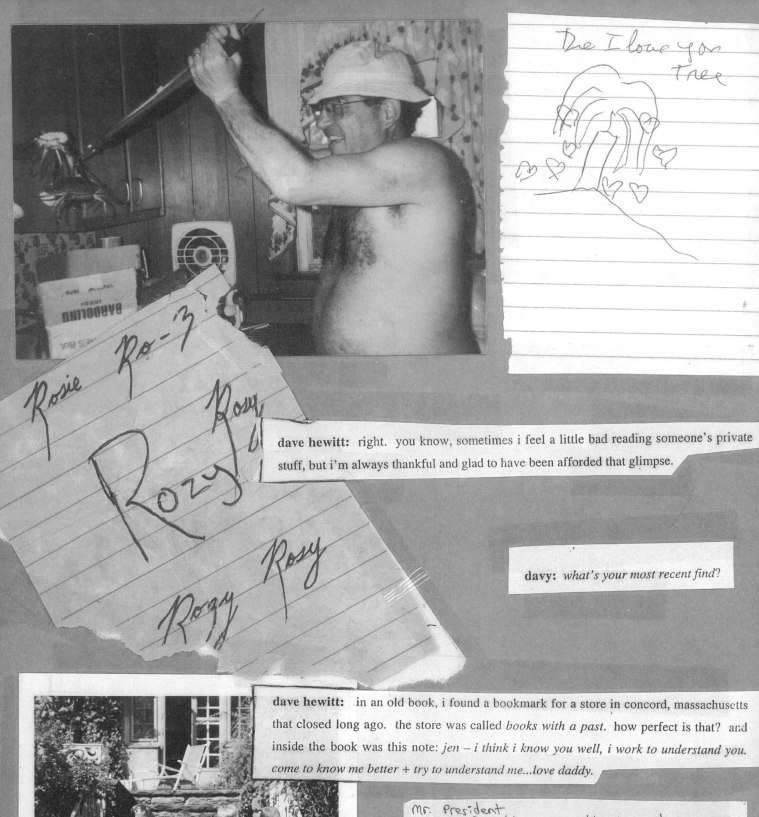

**dave hewitt:** right. you know, sometimes i feel a little bad reading someone's private stuff, but i'm always thankful and glad to have been afforded that glimpse.

**davy:** *what's your most recent find?*

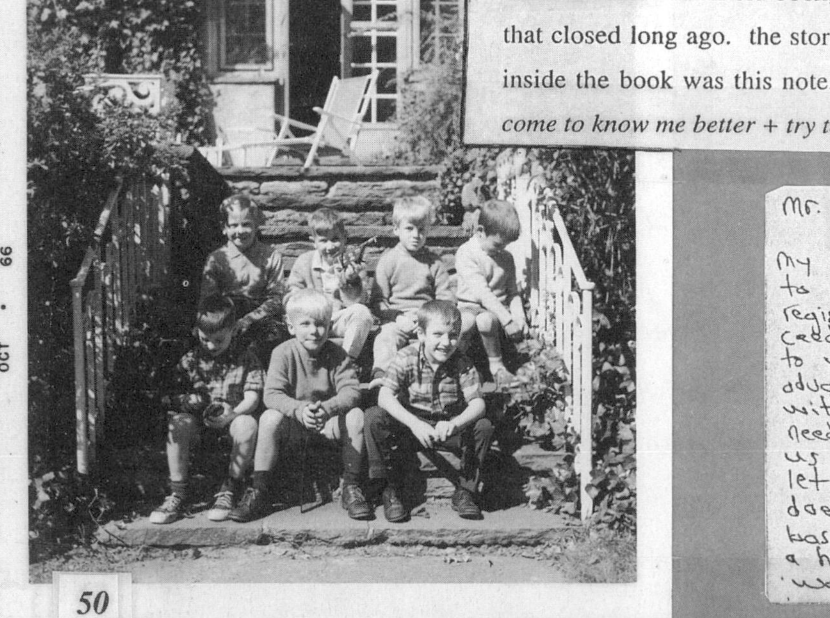


**dave hewitt:** in an old book, i found a bookmark for a store in concord, massachusetts that closed long ago. the store was called *books with a past.* how perfect is that? and inside the book was this note: *jen – i think i know you well, i work to understand you. come to know me better + try to understand me...love daddy.*

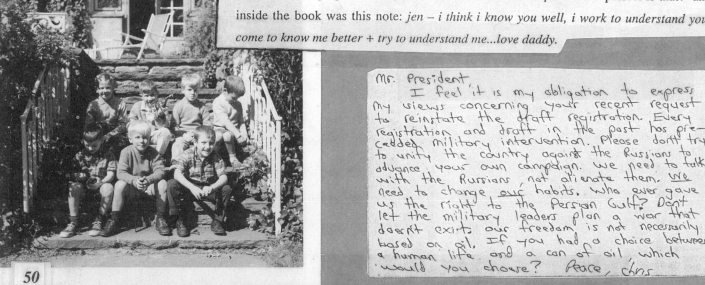

Mr. President,
I feel it is my obligation to express my views concerning your recent request to reinstate the draft registration. Every registration and draft in the past has preceeded military intervention. Please don't try to unify the country against the Russians to advance your own campaign. We need to talk with the Russians, not alienate them. We need to change our habits. Who ever gave us the right to the Persian Gulf? Don't let the military leaders plan a war that doesn't exist. Our freedom is not necessarily based on oil. If you had a choice between a human life and a can of oil, which would you choose? Peace, Chris

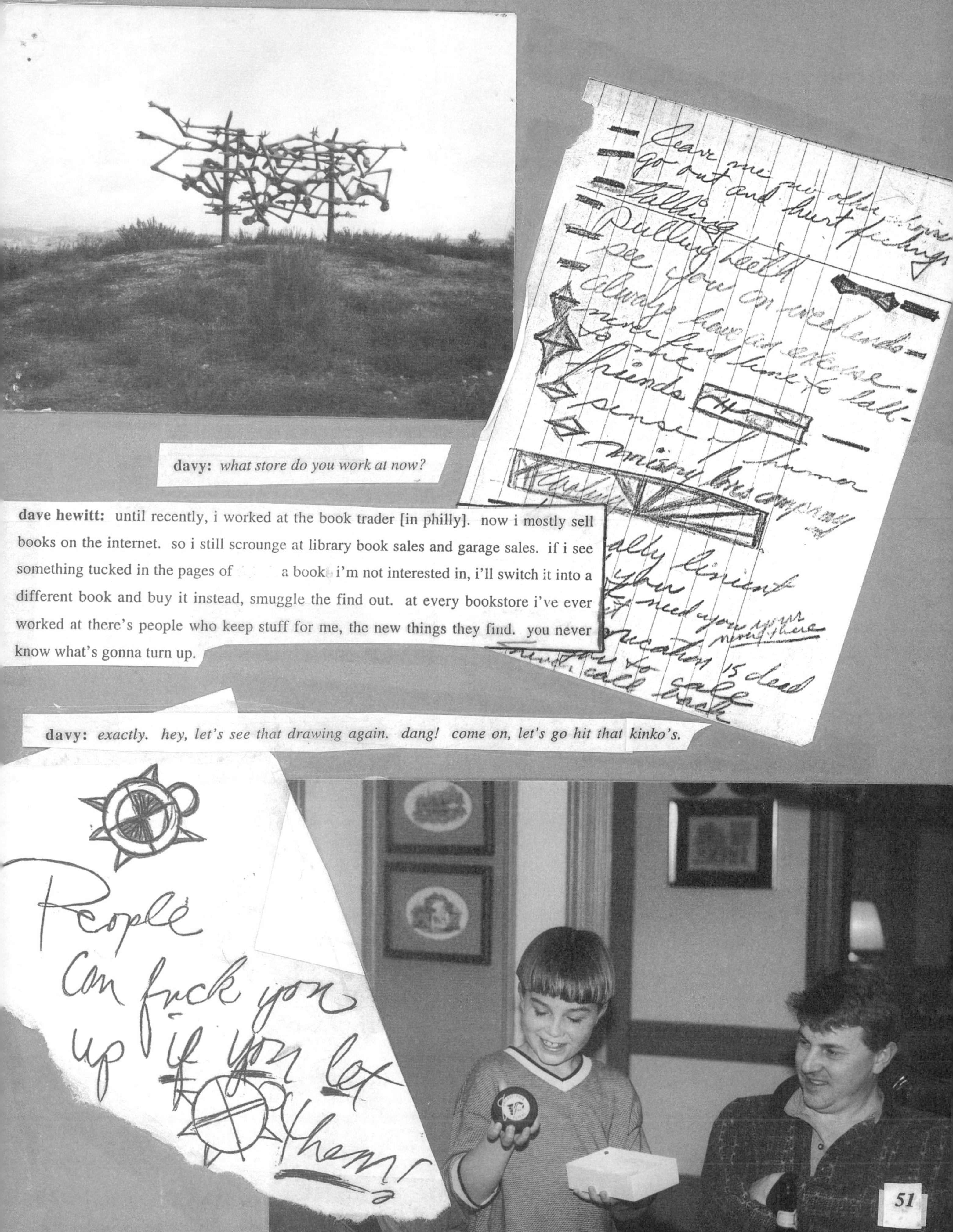


**davy:** *what store do you work at now?*

**dave hewitt:** until recently, i worked at the book trader [in philly]. now i mostly sell books on the internet. so i still scrounge at library book sales and garage sales. if i see something tucked in the pages of a book i'm not interested in, i'll switch it into a different book and buy it instead, smuggle the find out. at every bookstore i've ever worked at there's people who keep stuff for me, the new things they find. you never know what's gonna turn up.

**davy:** *exactly. hey, let's see that drawing again. dang! come on, let's go hit that kinko's.*

David, my mountain man of summer rain, my fantasy lover on the night train!

You left me happy, David, and I thank you. You made my journey complete and I'll never forget. Even if I never see you again, ever, I'll always remember the little wrinkles by your mouth that show when you're smiling, your deep, passionate gentle eyes talking to me in silence, and your strong, smooth shoulders. The skin on your neck in the dim light of a godforsaken Bahnhof in the middle of nowhere; the two of us on foreign territory, safe in unknown surroundings, with no destination in mind but living instantly. Lying there half naked in bed under thin cotton sheets while the motion of the train put me in a state of lust and delight I turned my gaze on you and saw someone who made me feel instant desire... I wanted to crawl down and lie in your arms, inhaling the scent of your skin, caressing your back, your neck, your hands while the fantasies of what I wanted you to do to me if we were alone and the rhythm of the running train would make me come in a way that would make it really hard not to scream out loud.

When the German lady, whom you earlier had entertained for so long and treated so respectfully, complained that my having the lights on at this late hour made her sleepless I imagined myself asking her in a calm, innocent voice whether she would, then, object to my having a wild and uninhibited sexual intercourse with the nice, young man below? This cracked me up and made it difficult for me to go to sleep...

I'm grateful that you were sleepless too that night. It was a pleasure breathing your air, feeling your firm body against mine, listening to your voice, and knowing you slowly. Yet, when I close my eyes I sense your softly spoken words in my ear.

I cherish my fantasy about you. A fantasy accidentally come true. I remember your face, I remember that your lips were chapped, that the skin on your shoulder was burnt, and the structure of your hands; I fear to lose these images. Will I still remember when time has passed? And your scent? I want you to be with me. I feel so alive, so happy! and I want to share with you. I hope we will somehow find a way to be together again although the geographical distance between us might be a reason not to.

Love and thousands of wet everlasting kisses

STRANGERS ON A TRAIN

FOUND by Line Brandt

Copenhagen, Denmark

What do you think Jesus looked like?
Draw His picture here.



**YOUR OWN PERSONAL JESUS**

FOUND by Davy Rothbart

**New York, NY**

**SUCCESS STORY**

Comments: [redacted]

12-19-02 Wal-Mart 84 Camdenton, Missouri
Masterfoods, Pedigree pouches + dry,
After placing shelf strips for all Kal-kan
products, the department manager was very
pleased and asked if I had more, I did and
we used them on a endcap that had cat litter on
it and replaced it with little champion pouches
and 22# bags of dry ped, S&B. The level
of service (Advantage gave) convinced him that we deserved a long
term display.

***SUCCESS STORY*** FOUND by Trevor Harris, Columbia, MO

this photo FOUND by Nick Johnson, Minneapolis, MN

Dear Maggie.

This is a note about stuff.+

a. { how much stuff there is

b. { what i think of stuff

why am I here?

there is a lot of bullshit stuff.*

—Cameni

\+ Stuff: notes not having to do with us
* bull shit used in all due respect

***A NOTE ABOUT STUFF*** FOUND by Kate Croft, NYC

this photo FOUND by Nick Johnson, Minneapolis, MN

# THINGS TO DO TODAY

- Dear Dad I love
- you so much Just
- so you no
- I cry for
- you evry
-
- night. I love
-
- you so much
-
- dad.
-

***EVRY NIGHT*** FOUND by Andrea Marchyok, Hamtramck, MI

You have to make up your mind
Mr. Dickens. It was either the best
of time or the worst of time
it could scarcely be both, the
[illegible] was never [illegible] and

***MAKE UP YOUR MIND*** FOUND by Claire Reichstein, San Francisco, CA

*FOUND Magazine.* We deserved a long-term display.

# SWOOSH (THE JIMMY DONOHUE EXPERIENCE)

FOUND by Matt Kuehl

Providence, R.I.

-1-

6/20/85

Yeah, happened to me just this evenning. It was gauche, obscene, taboo; it was downright lewd. Sure, it happens to everyone. It happens to me, you, my dad, your dad. Christ sakes! But it has even happened to Leila, god forbid. "What the hell is it?" you ask. Welp Bud, I'll tell you. I guess it takes a "real man" to own up to his faults, confront them (you know, take the bull by the horns), and deal with them. So here goes. I was in my room minding my own business, just minding my own business you see, and I heard Wanda whisper to me; Donohue was pummelling my insides. I knew I was going to have to get rid of him. So I'm in the bathroom taking a Jimmy Donohue, minding my own business, just minding my own business. Donohue was at the port, ready to leave via a 4 inch pipe. I tore the Charmin off the roll (didn't squeeze it) and with one calculated, determined 'swoosh,' I wiped my ass. Then it happen.... A thing more private than picking your nose and eating your gritty snot, more private than masturbation. Yes after that swipe, I felt It's presence. Warm, creamy, like well kneaded clay. It was shit, right on my fuck finger.

Other than that, nothing big going on here. I was at my Grandma's today meticulously washing and waxing her car. My shirt was off and in the window's reflection I could see a small, but distinct layer of fat ringing my body. I thought of barnacles clinging to a ship's hull, then fish that ride on the dorsal side of a whale. They're nature, but they don't belong. So my mind got to wandering and I got real deep. Theorizing, you know? Here's what I came up with. The world is spontaneously becoming flabby. Sort of like the shift towards higher entropy, but I'm talking flab. Now by world, I mean you, your second cousin's friend, his pet hampstir, the hampster's food, the plants that the food came from, the earth that the plants grew in: the soil, bedrock, and

## LOOKING FOR BEARS

FOUND by Fred Nocella

Chicago, IL

Bears
About
Talking
Assholes
Dumb
Keep
Can
You
Long
How
Look.

REMOVE BEFO...

## TALKING ABOUT BEARS

FOUND by Brian Thompson

Fayetteville, AR

This fell out of a cookbook of homespun recipes I saved from the dumpster.

—B.T.

To me Spiders and Trains are very similar
They both are hard workers, They both are very strong.
They both get "bum deal" reputations as being the "bad guys" when in Fact, we'd be in trouble without them.

**SPIDERS AND TRAINS**
FOUND by Therese & Heather
Boston, MA

I ♥ U
Zoloft (sertraline HCl)

***ZOLOFT*** FOUND by Miriam, Madison, WI

Displaced southern Belle looking for Heathcliff. Tired of wearing my curtains. - ~~Financially secure~~ / ~~and healthy~~ ~~sexuality~~ appealing. ~~Understands~~ ~~Goethe's Couplets~~. Knows Madame Butterfly isn't a stripper in Vegas.

Secure enough to know what he wants and to handle a woman who does as well.

You can be a gentleman and understand the qualities of partnership.

Recognizes at least some of the following: Van Gough, Guttenberg, Arch 'd Triumph,

***BELLE*** FOUND by Anna Belden & Jim McKay, S.F., CA

FOR MAILMAN: PLEASE MAIL

***RAIN, SLEET, SNOW*** FOUND by Danielle Hummel, Philadelphia, vent your frustration on us.When your as far away as you are it is not so easy for you to take care of

If the ball is too loud, take it up when you sleep & put it back down when you get up.

:) -K

*NOISY BALL* FOUND by Clare Brennan, Ottawa, Ontario

We ~~So~~ are here today to praise God for a life well spent—I thought I had it all—But now my perception of life has changed.

Papa Williamson was a good man that commend respect from his peers—May ~~his~~ his Soul rest in peace.

*EULOGY* FOUND by Chris Goodwin, Washington, D.C.

*NOT SO EASY* FOUND by Philip G. Muzzy, Holland, MI

I'M Stupid Kick ME

*KICK ME* FOUND by Pete Cropley, New Orleans, LA

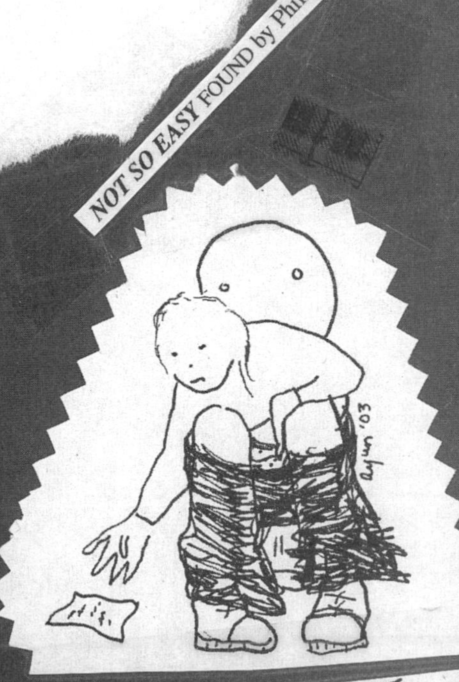


illustration by Ayun Halliday

Do we ever return FOUND stuff that's sent in to us to its original owners? Occasionally, if the items seem especially important and the owners are easily identifiable. Here's a story I really love of a find being returned.

—DAVY

Dear FOUND magazine,

I'm not sure this qualifies as a FOUND item since the actual things I found were returned to their rightful owner. However, I've enclosed the thank you letter I received, which turned out to be almost as good as the goods themselves. Here's the story.

Upon looking for a map to the LA airport as we drove out of Joshua Tree National Park, my friend Eric and I happened upon a stash of someone's personal belongings in the glove compartment or our rental car. At first, I noticed a pair of tan leather gloves sticking out from a small stack of papers. (Wow. Who actually keeps gloves in a glove compartment!?) How sad, I thought, the last renter had left her church gloves behind, never to be worn again. But as I rifled through the Budget-rent-a-car documents, I began to uncover a handful of other personal things. I put them all in my lap and sorted through them delicately, fascinated by this odd collection of items which included the following:

- A wad of coupons collected from all sorts of places, paper-clipped together
- A tiny cloth change purse, which held a tube of used-up lipstick, some mismatched buttons, a foreign coin, and a few small seashells
- A stack of mail, all addressed to Kay "Jones" (not actual name), Joshua Tree, CA. Some of it was junk mail, but there were also some unpaid utility bills.

Then I struck gold. There was a handwritten letter in an envelope. I felt guilty opening it – this was someone's private letter after all – but my curiosity got the better of me. The words, written in a swoopy (yet sloppy) cursive, just about broke my heart.

"Dearest Brother,
I heard you was having a hard time with money and I know I don't have much, but maybe this twenty dollars will help out.
Your Loving Sister, Kay."

This woman - who saved coupons for laundry detergent and had a pile of overdue bills - was sending her brother twenty dollars. The letter was complete and the envelope had been addressed, but there was no money in it.

Well, it was a done deal. We decided to send this woman her belongings (so she could use her coupons, pay her bills, hold onto her seashells, and send that letter) – after all, we had her full name and address. And we'd been so touched by that letter she'd written, we decided to include some money for her brother. Once I returned to Chicago, I put everything in a padded envelope - along with a humble little note of explanation and a twenty-dollar bill - and took it to the post office.

A month later, this letter arrived in the mail. I treasure it - every word (especially the "wept for about 3 to 5 minutes" part). Kay and I now write each other on occasion – she even sent me some photographs of her dogs (enclosed).

Meredith Siemsen
(and Eric Robbins)

3/12/02

Hi you two receive the return of my things on 3-9-02 I set in my bed at about 8:00 pm reading my mail then I looked at the big envelope and said who do I know in Chicago then I said no one opening the package and pulling out the zip lock bag and seeing my things and your letter and the twenty dollar bill I set in my bed and wept for about 3 to 5 minutes Praise God on high, how He had use you honest and godly people to take time to return my things which was not anygood to anyone but me and then for the two of you to donated the money to someone you had never seen nor talk to. I knew God hands was all in this no one but children of God would have done what you two did. I love you two, Please keep me and my family in your prays who knows maybe God will make it so that one day we might meet that would be a blessing. Please keep in touch if you will my phone number is 760-...
address 87...
Ca 92252 ... Joshua Tree
Would love to become pen pal
(over)

P.S. I pray God will multiply back 100 fold in return to the two of you. gave this testament in church on sunday 3/10/02

Thanks!
Kay ...

DUKE

TONY PROTECTOR

FOUND Magazine. God hands was all in this.

GETTING TO KNOW YOU BEFORE I FUCK YOU APPLICATION

Personal
Name________________________________ AGE__ D.O.B________

Address________________________________ Phone____________

Do you have boyfriend/girlfriend yes or no______________
(If yes is it the person you having sex with now____)

How do you like it fast, medium, or slow? ______________

*Fast is it rough and hard.
*Medium is you like to take your time but still like it rough.
*Slow is when you wont to take your time and make sure you are doing it right.

How low can you go? ______________

Do you like to have four play before you have sex? __________

Do you know where there spot is? ______________

How long will you last? ______________

WHEN YOUR FINISH RETRUN TO THE PERSON THAT GAVE IT TO YOU.

I ____________ list all the following information above is the truth the whole truth and nothing but the truth.

***NOTE*** Any information you gave above in not true you will be severely punish. You will be fine and sent to jail

**GETTING TO KNOW YOU**

FOUND by Pat Kambitsch

Dayton, OH

I found this in a high school.

Dear Hot Boys,

Hey, my name is Joshua Whitaker. Can you give me one of your chains and $1,000. If you can mail it to 8013 S. Kedzie Chi., IL, 60620.

Thank you your #1 fan,
Joshua

# *FAN LETTER (SPECIAL REQUEST)*

FOUND by Tim McIlrath

Chicago, IL

www.kaganmcleod.com

illustration by Kagan McLeod

My Pretty Little Miss: I must write you thus because I havent yet found out what your name is but I know where you live for I followed you home last night.
Say- if you are married tear this note up and don't tell your husband. If you are single and long for a life partner I am ready to leap without looking so long as I will find you where I land. If you want to meet me carry a newspaper under your arm tomorrow. I'll arrange it. Expectantly.
© 1926 by Ex. Sup. Co., Chgo.
oford Paxton
ALBANY OREGON
POST CARD
THIS SIDE FOR ADDRESS ONLY
CRONISE
160 STATE ST. SALEM, OR.

these two old photos FOUND by Kevin Sampsell
Tillamook, OR

CARRY A NEWSPAPER

FOUND by Cynthia Piper

Lakewood, OH

I found this postcard inside the wall of a demolished barn. The 90-year-old woman who lived there didn't remember this suitor, though she had three other sisters.
—C.P.

this photo FOUND by Mimi Paquette, Montreal, QB

## SAN FRANCISCO POSTCARD

hi davy + jason + friends!

some of my best finds are now only memories but funny nonetheless.

in sixth grade while waiting for the bus in a field by my house, i found two polaroids of a grown man's erect penis. the photos had not been there the day before and showed mist and fog around the "subject" so we could tell they were shot early in the morning. my friend got on the bus and handed them to this prissy girl and said, "can you identify the man in this photo?!" the thing i always wondered about was what this guy was doing there next to a house in a field, with a hard-on and a camera by himself early in the cold morning. it just boggled my mind!

one windy day i was broke and walking downtown to buy a nickel-bag of weed when something hit me in the chest. i looked down and there was a twenty-dollar bill stuck to my shirt—cha-ching, make that a twenty sack!

on the bay area subway once i found a bag under my seat and opened it. inside was a camera, shirts, and some letters to the owner. it turned out he was a d.j. in this super-hip club and had shined his old hometown friends and become some big drug-obsessed rave club kid star. what was so weird was that just from these letters and a couple of shirts and flyers i got such a vivid look into this kid's life. he had transformed into something else and his old friends were really sad about it. it was a trip.

but probably the best was when my wife and i were up visiting my dad one year in humboldt. my mom had passed away when i was young and i never got the chance to know her that well or ask her about my childhood. so one night bored i was rummaging through some old trunks when i found a book i had never seen before. i opened it and was blown away. it was a whole scrapbook my mom had written in for me with hopes that one day i'd find it in just such a way. she said i was a "happy mistake" and once i was born i was loved more than any kid could want. the book was full of pictures and mementos of my first steps in life, things i had never seen or remembered. i felt like i was granted part of that wish to talk to her again and the book was packed to bring home with me, proof of what a great a family i had landed in. i got pretty choked up that night. and that's the story of my favorite find.

—DREW LAWSON

# EATING YOUR PUSSY "2001"

FOUND by Brenda Coultas

New York City

Hi Karen!!

I hope this letter
finds you well and in the very best of health
and Spirit, and As for my-self I'm doing very well
but to tell you the truth I'm very much home sick and I'm
missing you Soooo very much.. each day I think of you
and I wish I knew you longer.. in the Short time we
met we became friends and I wanna thank you for that
you gave me a chance to open my-self to you and to let me
feel comfort (thank you) Soooo I write to you today to
tell you Something else, when I first seen you I knew
you was in the life, the way you dress and carry yourself and that turned me on I love gay women As for
my-self I go both ways I eat Pussy and Suck dick
and this you already know.. to tell you the truth I would
love to go to bed with you, I dream of this all the time
I even masterbate when I'm thinking of it..

Turn over

#2

You know when we was at Cosmetics Plus
and each time I went to the bath Room
I would masterbate and Pictures of you would
come to my mind I would see you eating out the other
female who work with us. I forgot her name but you
know who I'm talking about the one who goes to clubs with you
there's times when I wish if I can watch the two of you
while I Play with my dick.. I even thought about sucking
a dick for you while you watch colleen I'm nasty like
that what I want is Two #2 women something I never
had and I wish Right now for that to come true..
I have something to say when I come to New you will
you give me that.. Picture this me eating your Pussy
while you eating the other Pussy "Dool" Tell are you fucking
her and is it gooooood.. if you can "send" me some pictures..
This Place is beautyful. and the train Ride here was
very nice it took me four #4 and a half 1/2 days to
get from New York, to Seattle wa.

Next Page

FOUND *Magazine*. Send me some pictures.

Hey you—kind reader! Forget the bathroom at Cosmetics Plus.
For a real charge, check out www.foundmagazine.com!

IT WAS SET UP

FOUND by Matthew Schwartz

New York, NY

ATTENTION ALL AMERICANS

THE MONICA LOWINSKI TRIAL IS A FARCE. IT WAS SET UP BY A GROUP CALLED THE ILLUMINATI. THESE ARMOURED CHRISTIAN SOLDIERS WHOS LIFE EFFORT IS TO ~~FULLFIL THE BOOK AND END TIME AS~~ WE KNOW IT. ONLY THEY BELIEVE THEY SHOULD SURVIVE AND WE THE PEOPL SHOULD DIE. CLINTONS A GOOD MAN AND IS IN THEIR WAY. IN 1994 MEMBERS OF THIS ORGANIZATION CONTACTED ALEX GROSS (OF 197 10th AVE Apt 10B - 247-3131 FAX 247 3138) IN EFFORT TO FIND A WOMAN WHO WOULD BE CAPABLE OF SEDUCING THE PRESIDENT AND THE TURN HIM IN FOR SO CALLED IMORAL BEHAVIOR. ~~THIS MAN~~ GROSS WHO DOES NOT VOTE CLAIMES HE IS A MULTINATIONAL IS ALSO A MEMBE OF A CUT CALLED NANYOHERIGKYO. ONE CAN ONLY WONDER WHAT WAS PROMISED HIM. MAYBE KEYS TO THE MOUNTAIN SHELTER IN UTAH WHERE THE 72 FAMILIES THAT OWN THIS COUNTRY BY METHODS OF INTIMIDATION WILL GO ONCE THEY FIGURE OUT A THOUROGH WAY TO GET RID OF US. WHERE GROSS FOUND MONICA GOD ONLY KNOWS!

PICTURES OF BILL

FOUND by Nina and Katie

St. Louis, MO

## IT STAYED

FOUND by R.J. Sidwell

Charleston, IL

IT STAYED
ON THE
GRILL BITCH!

this photo FOUND by Matt Summers, Omaha, NE

LOSS Cat

SPEckLES, Does not cabd witten come, LIMPS, DIRty, Not tAG. REWURD Needs medicines. FOAM. CALL WARD 404-

FOUND by Tim Speeld, Atlanta, GA

REWARD
LOST CAT

ANSWERS TO THE NAME
BITCHY
LAST SEEN AT THE CORNER OF
JUNE and DE LONGPRE
12/8/2002
IF FOUND, PLEASE CONTACT US AT:
323/

FOUND by Jay Koivu, Los Angeles, CA

MISSING
CAT
GREY AND WHITE
FAT CAT

ANSWERS TO
JACK AND FOOD

IF FOUND PLEASE CONTACT:
LESLIE
CAMBRIDGE
734-

FOUND by Cat Lardas, Ann Arbor, MI

FOUND: BUNNY

WHITE FUR → ← PINK EYES

FOUND 9/9 ON
BERNAL HILL
CALL: 697-7746

FOUND by Carole Okolowicz, San Francisco, CA

If that's what the little guy really looks like he couldn't have roamed too far! — DAVY

LOST COBRA
Color: brown, black, yellow, red (on teeth), blue ( color of tongue)
Snake has been known to bite off heads.
Snake is not house trained.
ANSWERS TO "PSYCHO".
Length: 7'
Weight: 45 lbs
Warning, snake is deadly.
Will bite if provoked.
IF FOUND, CALL (510) 3
Psycho has strong scottish accent

FOUND by Anne Gunnison, Oakland, CA

MISSING
A
CHICKEN?

If you or anyone you know is missing a chicken please call:
848-9669

Date:
10/11/98

FOUND by Mack Reid, Harper's Ferry, WV

LOST &
FOUND
PETS

For those who find this

dedicated to Chris Daymore 276-8982

This place is sacred, the very grounds upon which you stand on was once where a love, more powerful than anything, ~~a friendship, more~~ deeper than anything grew. COA camp is a great place to go to. There is an unknown magic to it. This garden was once where Chris and I stood. Our secret place like our hearts. We stood there starring at eachother proclaiming our love for one another without words. You could see our love for one another pouring forth like a fountain in our eyes. We vowed right then and there that we would always love and be friends forever. This place was where we always met even when it had been years we could come back and find the other. A magical unknown force drawing us together. We have been to this camp together since 2nd grade. Now we are in highschool and our love ~~is just as powerful.~~ We aren't friends anymore but I know that I will always love him and carry his love for me always and forever. No one knows what the future holds but I know I will meet him again for we are destined to be together

Love - Chan

FOUND *Magazine.* For those who find this.

# DESTINED

FOUND by Ian Mohler and Maeve Turner

Bar Harbor, ME

Found this while cleaning up the grounds of the College of the Atlantic.

—I.M. & M.T.

To whoever Finds
this I hope your
life is perfect or perfecto.
my father + step mom was
killed while I was in the
house.
My Grandma Aunt,
unkle All turned
their Back on me
my dream is to become
A modle someday I hope

# PERFECT OR PERFECTO

FOUND by Jelly Helm

Richmond, VA

This note was on the street for a week before I picked it up.

Good luck to your
your
dreams
Stranger
& monique

Radisson.
HOTELS WORLDWIDE
The difference is genuine.℠

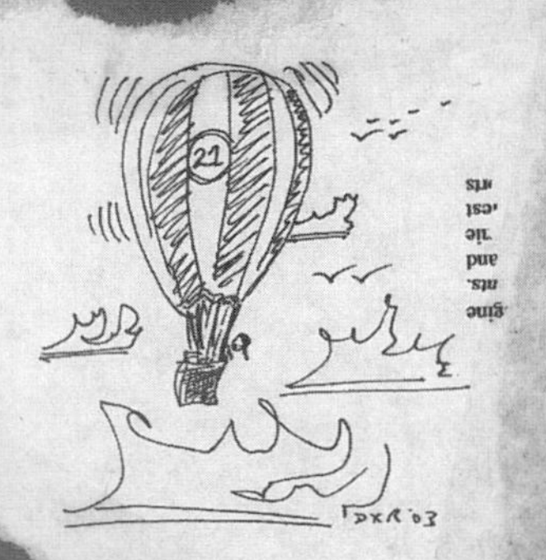

**AN ACCIDENT** FOUND by Mike Jackson, Seattle, WA

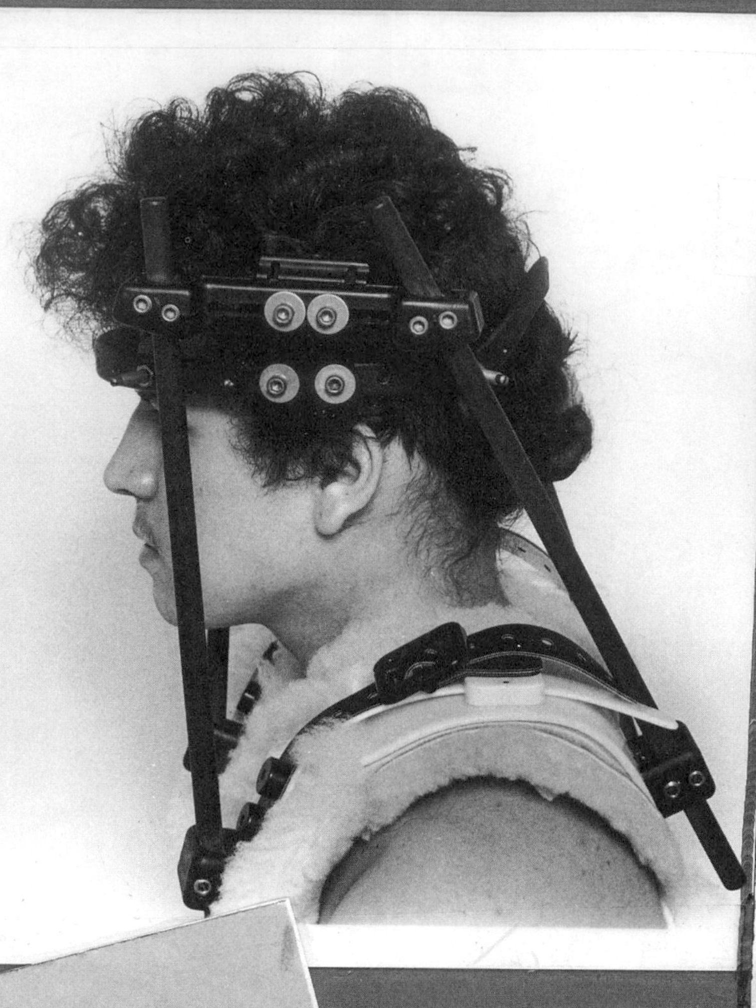

**NO SMOOCHING!** FOUND by Gary Singh, San Jose, CA

SAFETY

1. NO RUNNING
2. LOOK FOR PALLETS & PALLET JACKS
3. NO WALKMANS
4. NO PUSHING
5. KEEP AISLES CLEAR
6. LOOK OUT FOR YELLOW SIGNS & WET FLOORS
7. STAY WITH SUPERVISOR DURING DRILLS
8. PICK UP TRASH
9. CLEAN UP SPILLS
10. REMIND OTHERS OF THE RULES
11. NO FIGHTING OR NAME-CALLING
12. NO HITTING

SAFETY

13. TELL SUPERVISOR ABOUT HEALTH ISSUES LIKE SEIZURES
14. WEAR HELMETS
15. NO WANDERING
16. NO SMOOCHING
17. BE AWARE
18. NO TALKING DURING DRILLS
19. LISTEN CAREFULLY TO INSTRUCTIONS
20. CHECK BATHROOMS DURING DRILLS
21. PUT ITEMS BACK IN PROPER PLACES
22. NO CLIENTS SITTING IN CHAIRS w/ WHEELS
23. WASH YOUR HANDS
24. LIFT WITH YOUR LEGS

We've posted these Safety Rules at *FOUND Magazine* headquarters and we suggest you put them up at your place of work as well. Remind others of the rules!

—DAVY

**LENSCRAFTERS** FOUND by R. Goodwin, Plainfield, VT

Pattie—

Please take Juan to Lenscrafters (or someplace that is a one-stop eyeglass place) and get him a pair of glasses.

It is not good for him to be driving your car without glasses, especially with student in the car!

Thank you—

Juan's Mom

KEEBLER ELVES

FOUND by Julie Gerstein

Philadelphia, PA

May 20, 1997

Dear Larissa

There may be some things left over for Mary, Like why do I even bother lying to you? Of course I ate the rest of the chocolate covered graham crackers. When Joc passed on them because they melted, I thought to myself, well here finally is an opportunity to be rid of them. I'll just toss them into the trash like I said I was going to do at Larissas' We were outside, however, and I had to get started for Harrisburg. No trash can was close by, and I really don't wish to go further. Don't ask about the Limburger.

Its like this Mary, I wanted to please Larissa by eating some form of chicken at almost every meal, but she wasn't feeling well and she didn't have any chocolate. The closest we came was strawberry shortcake with whipped cream, which she spooned from the tub, Into her mouth. I'm not judging, but she tells me about pouring cocoa mix onto the whipped cream. Do I ever see any of the cocoa powder? I'll answer that, no. She puts the lid back on and the meals over. Now the chocolate coated graham crackers come out when she turns in for the night. I could have hidden the remaining crackers, but I didn't.

She reads the ingredient label to me. They're not good for me, three is a slice of cheesecake. Mary, I really like this woman, but she sits there pointing out the dark side of the keebler elves. I have no rebuttal. And I eat them anyway. Now its all a plastic hassle because I distinctly told her on two occasions that I had tossed my cookies when I hadn't.

Yes, she is far more important to me than what I eat. I believe I can get with the program. I've lost some weight already, and I'm not missing it at all. At the center of this is our hearts. She is fragile and I want to give her my heart without guile or omission. I want to give it freely and lovingly, and I don't want her to puzzle out what I say from what I do. To win her love, I'll have to drop the elves.

Did I say fragile? Not you, rather your threshold of patience. Tonight I thought about things I wouldn't tell your mother on Memorial Day. I would not tell her that the face and shape of her daughter excites me. Nor would I tell her I was foolish in not asking her to be my wife several years ago. Your mother does not want her daughter connected with a fool. Neither do you for that matter. What was done has ended. I was preserved from my own folly. Ms. Wood, my lessons came hard, I love Larissa, if she'll have me, our lives will be rich and your daughter will be cared for. Is that a cheesecake?

Frank

## MY OWN PRIVATE LIBRARY

FOUND by Bill van Sickle

Casper, WY

**Thank you for the One-Cent #12!**
**Let us know what you are thinking. . .**

*Family, travel, community, literacy, spirit, dreams, business, future, puppies, hope, careers, hobbies, music, goals, news, recipes, fantasy, genealogy, tigers, employment and more!*

**Today in the library, I wanted to find** life, and it more abundantly...

**When I listen to music, I prefer** to be able to hear.

**I want to learn more about the following topics or subjects** the wombats' mating habits.

**It would be easier to use the library if** you moved it directly to my house.

**I wish my library had more** free money to give away.

☑ Yes, please share my comments with other library patrons!
Name (optional):

☐ No, please hold my comments in confidence.

Natrona County Public Library

(307) 237-4935 • http://library.natrona.net/

illustration by Paul Koob

THE SIGNAL

FOUND by Megan Hutchison

Bloomington, IN

Roseanne

I miss you so much honey. I feel so horrible that I had to leave. I know that I couldn't help it but still. I hate knowing that I came into your life and made everything perfect. I made you feel like you were loved. I made you feel like you were cared for. I made you invincible. But I, the one that made everything right, am also the one that took it all back when I left that Sunday night. I want so much to be there every aching second to make sure that nothing or no one will harm you. The one thing in this world that I want is for you to be happy. If you're not happy then I feel as though I have failed you and God. I do my best to make sure that my girl is loved and cared for. And recently I have felt closer to you than ever before. We have bonded on such a level that I never thought possible. There is a quote that says "Absence makes the heart grow fonder." And quite frankly, I think its 100% right on the money. Being away from you for just one day has made me realize even more just how much you do mean to me, how much I do care about you, and how much I do love you. You are my everything baby, and that's something that will never change. You're mine till the end! And yes that's a promise! There has also been a recent occurrence that has really and I mean REALLY showed me that you are just as serious when you say "I love you" as I am. Don't get me wrong or anything. I thought you meant it before but now its like there isn't any possible way that you don't mean it with all your heart. Does that make any sense? Sunday afternoon, when we "napped", that had more meaning to me than you could possibly imagine. It really hit me that you love me THAT (*arms spread as far as they can go*) much. You want to be with me till the end and I know it, boy do I ever. Even now, I'm not positive of what you had in mind when you grabbed my hand...heck I have no idea what you



THIS FIND CONTINUES ON THE NEXT PAGE!

*I like how this letter—in its love and its longing—is so similar to the handwritten one over to the right, while the reasons behind the separation are so different.* —DAVY

# APART ON VALENTINE'S DAY

FOUND by Samantha Morgan

San Francisco, CA

THIS FIND CONTINUED FROM THE PREVIOUS PAGE. DANG!

wanted....you may have just wanted to hold my hand and I misinterpreted the signal. But I do want to know if that's what the signal was for, that is if you don't mind. You can be honest with me. I promise. But no matter which, I do know that it was a big step...maybe even a bigger one for me. I know that you have a fear and maybe it was a sign that you are meant to be with me. For instance, maybe it wasn't just a fear of it but rather a fear of the wrong it. I guess I really have no idea but it was just a suggestion. But for me, I have already fallen because of this. This in a way may make it a bigger step for me rather than you. But then was for all the wrong reasons and it was wrong from the beginning. But with you and I, things are completely different. It isn't all about that. In fact it isn't lust at all. Its just telling each other that "I'm committed no matter what till the end". And you just had to lay all these feeling on my heart right before I go away to college. Why did you have to do it? I just hope that I didn't do anything that you are going to regret anytime in the future. If so, then just talk to me about it and if not then, I guess that's it. You mean the world to me baby and you've convinced me that I mean the world to you. I love you with every bit of my heart and nothing is going to change that. I know this whole college thing is going to be hard but once we get through it, it's all going to pay off. I promise.

I love you baby

* * * * * {[(xoxoXoxo-x)]}.....

-Your Macky Doo

*FOUND Magazine.* You may have just wanted to hold my hand and I misinterpreted the signal.

control over the situation, I can't see, hear, or even touch you. No one has came and visited me, or put any money on my books, I've been here since last Wednesday that has been eight days I've been in jail. Have anybody came and seen you? I hope somebody has. It can be lonely if you have nobody in your corner. Whenever I get out I know it will be before you I hope. I will come and get you on the 24th I hope with a fresh pair of shoes, a High Life beer, a fat blunt, and a pack of Newports. Being in here has made me want more out of life and in the game. So when I touch down on the streets no more playing with this shit, I'm going for the goal!! EVERYTHING!! you and I want will be reality. Extra hours and overnites will be in affect. You probably would want to leave me but I don't see it any other way Baby! I want more for you and me, I see it in my dreams, and feel it in my heart. Class is over I will write you tomorrow. ♡ U baby with my mind, body, and soul. Sweet dreams and goodnite.

Friday 14, 2003

Happy Valentine's Day sweetheart. I know it is not much but don't worry, this is the last time you and me will not be together on any holiday. I got a little cold right now it be a fuckin freeze shop in here. I miss #647. Have you missed me like I miss you. I sorry I couldn't get my family to bail me out to take care of your storage fee's, I hope you found someone to take care of that on the out's. The food in here is treahous, I don't know have the time what I am eating. I need a coka cola so bad I'm drying without it. At least I've been clean and sober for a minute now. And you said I couldn't stop smoking. :) I have not sleep with my lighter in two weeks, now that's a record! :) I hope when we get out nothing has changed about how you feel about me. I've been calling the public def to find what's up with this and he has not came to see me or nothing. Damn, baby I →

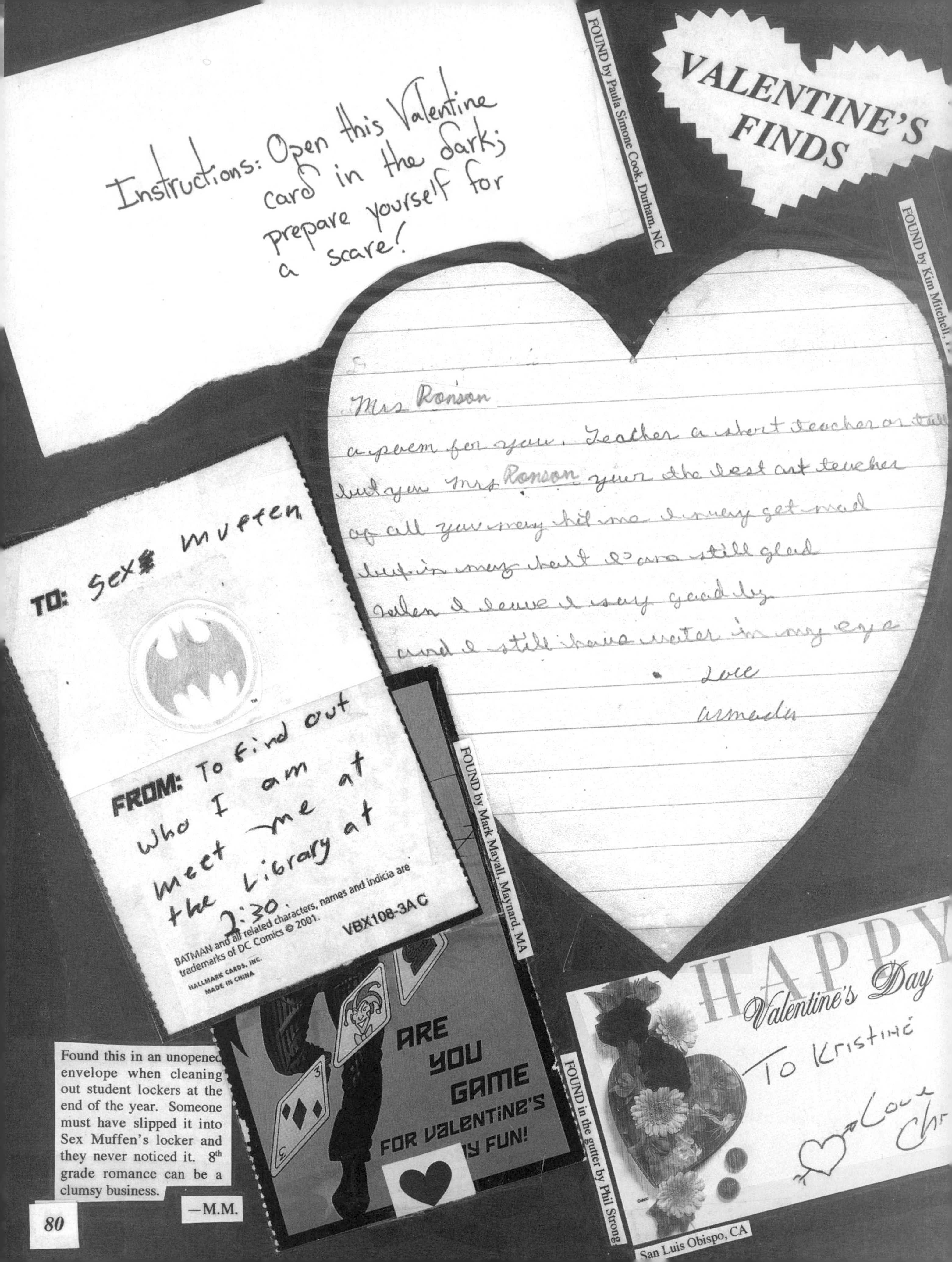

Instructions: Open this Valentine card in the dark; prepare yourself for a scare!
Mrs Ronson
a poem for you. Teacher a short teacher or tall
but you Mrs Ronson your the best art teacher
of all you may hit me I may get mad
but in my heart I'm still glad
when I leave I say goodby
and I still have water in my eye
Love
TO: Sex Muffen
FROM: To find out who I am meet me at the Library at 2:30.
BATMAN and all related characters, names and indicia are trademarks of DC Comics © 2001.
VBX108-3AC
HALLMARK CARDS, INC.
MADE IN CHINA
ARE YOU GAME FOR VALENTINE'S
FUN!
HAPPY Valentine's Day
To Kristine
Love


# VALENTINE'S FINDS

FOUND by Paula Simone Cook, Durham, NC

FOUND by Kim Mitchell

FOUND by Mark Mayall, Maynard, MA

FOUND in the gutter by Phil Strong
San Luis Obispo, CA

Found this in an unopened envelope when cleaning out student lockers at the end of the year. Someone must have slipped it into Sex Muffen's locker and they never noticed it. 8th grade romance can be a clumsy business.

—M.M.

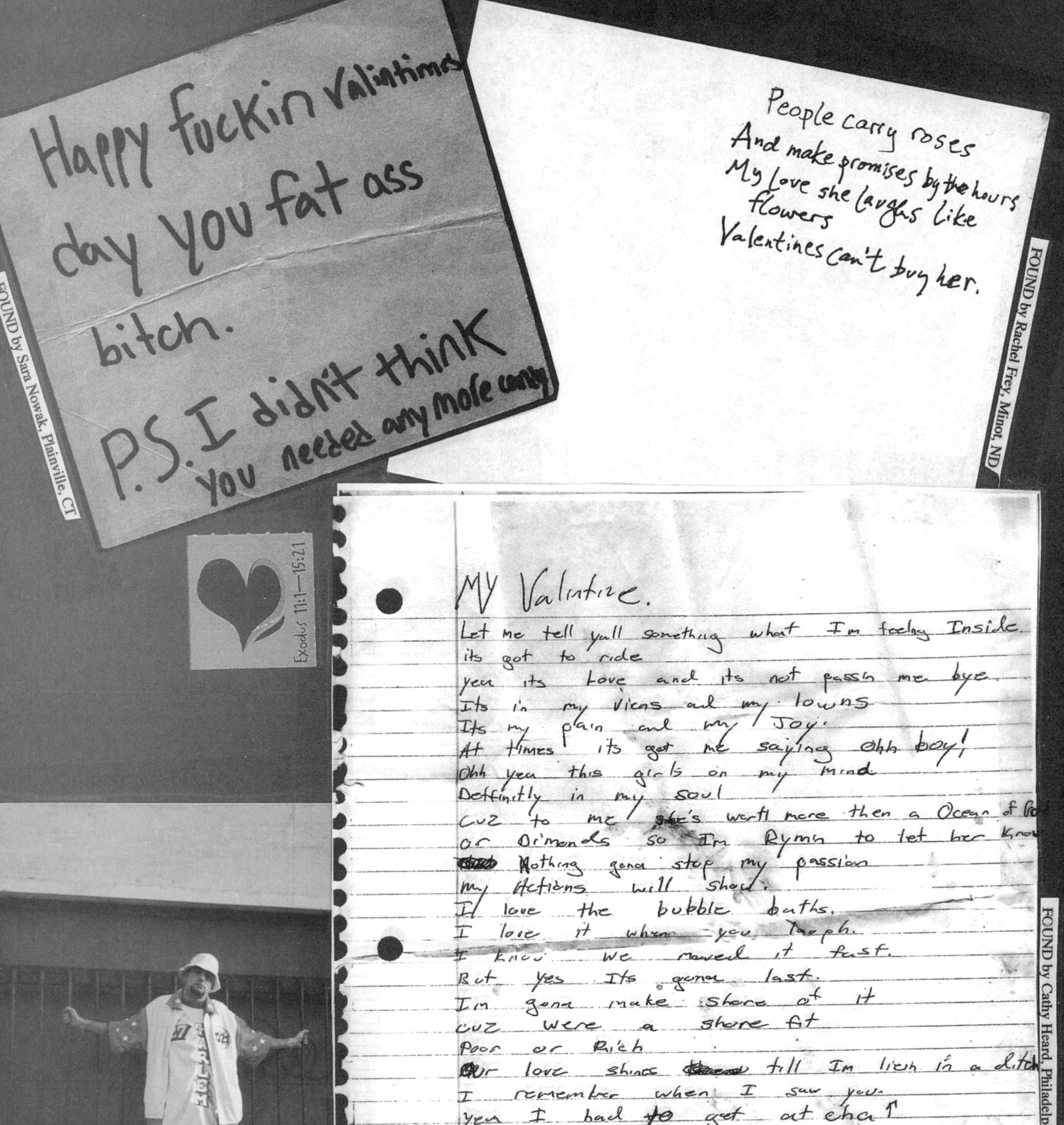

Happy fuckin valintimes day you fat ass bitch.

P.S. I didn't think you needed any more cand

FOUND by Sara Nowak, Plainville, CT

People carry roses
And make promises by the hours
My love she laughs like flowers
Valentines can't buy her.

FOUND by Rachel Frey, Minot, ND

Exodus 11:1—15:21

My Valintine.

Let me tell yall something what I'm feeling Inside.
its got to ride
yea its Love and its not passin me bye.
Its in my Vicns and my lowns
Its my pain and my Joy.
At times its got me saying Ohh boy!
Ohh yea this girls on my mind
Deffinitly in my soul
cuz to me she's worth more then a Ocean of Gold
or Dimonds so I'm Rymin to let her know
Nothing gona stop my passion
my Actions will show.
I love the bubble baths.
I love it when you laugh.
I know we moved it fast.
But yes Its gona last.
Im gona make shore of it
cuz were a shore fit
Poor or Rich
Our love shinc till Im lien in a ditch
I remember when I saw you.
yea I had to get at cha
Dream was Packed up
But your Number I raped up
gave you a call to let you know Im No Actor
Then god made us click
And Then I knew we would Match up
My Hearts been pumpin every since its been Gravy
Im Happy cuz thats my girl
And Im her baby.
she reads my letters.
yea she peeps what I write
And untill I talk to her man
I can't sleep at night. My Valintine.

FOUND by Cathy Heard, Philadelphia, PA

FOUND by Kevin McGuire, Mt. Pleasant, MI

1

IM sorry about last friday... I thought it was you!! I swear

2

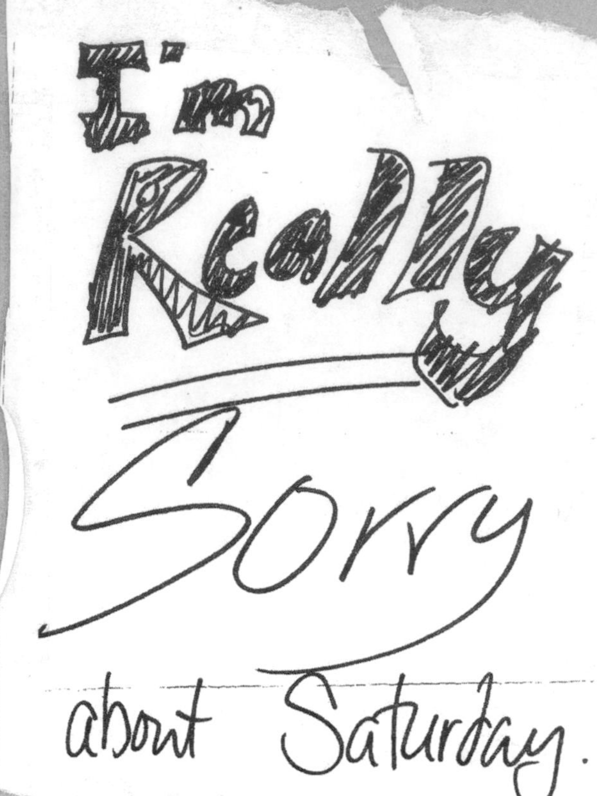

I'm Really Sorry about Saturday.

3

Reasons **NOT** to love me:

- I'm an ass hole ☑
- I slept w/ your Best friend ☑
- I never pay ☑
- Opening doors is for wussies ☑
- I'm clingy (really, you may need scotch guard!!) ☑
- I HATE CHILDREN ☑

P.S. I want to build a life together.

# A LIFE TOGETHER

FOUND by Sindhu Zagoren

Boston, MA

I found these three notes nailed to three different trees on the way from my house to the subway station in Jamaica Plain. The first tree explained Friday, the second Saturday, and the third had the handy checklist.

—S.Z.

It Devours From Beneath!!!

SMALL CRAFT WARNING

FOUND by Scooter Burch

Brighton, MA

illustration by Lev

# CHOICE NEVER TASTED SO GOOD!

FOUND by Dave Shelton

Boulder, CO

I was eating lunch at Schlotzky's and noticed that the little table display had a list of pros and cons on the back.

—D.S.

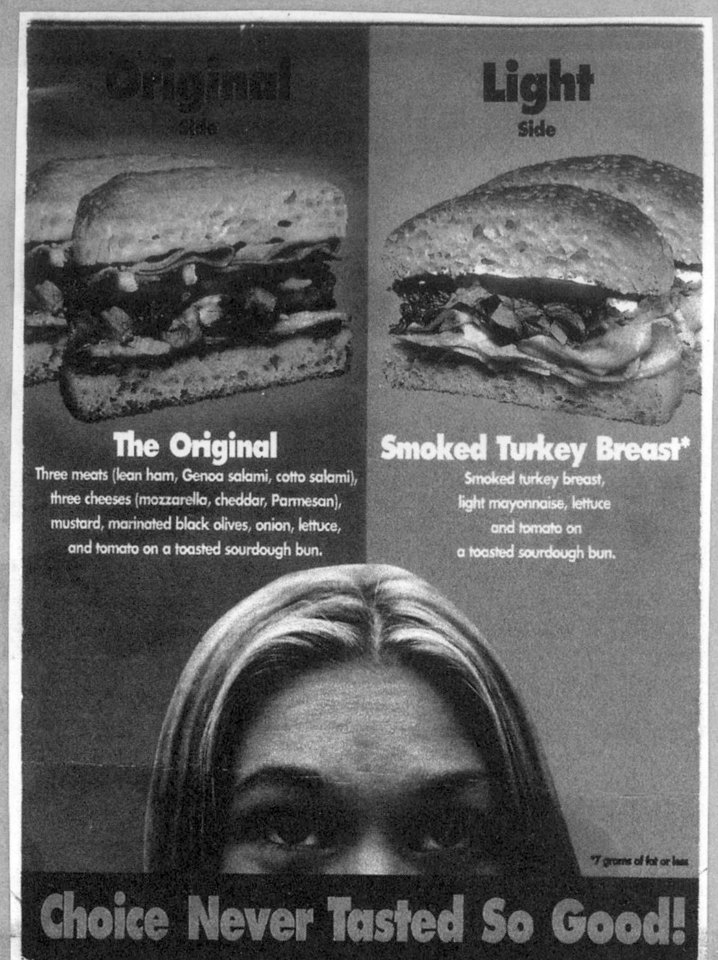


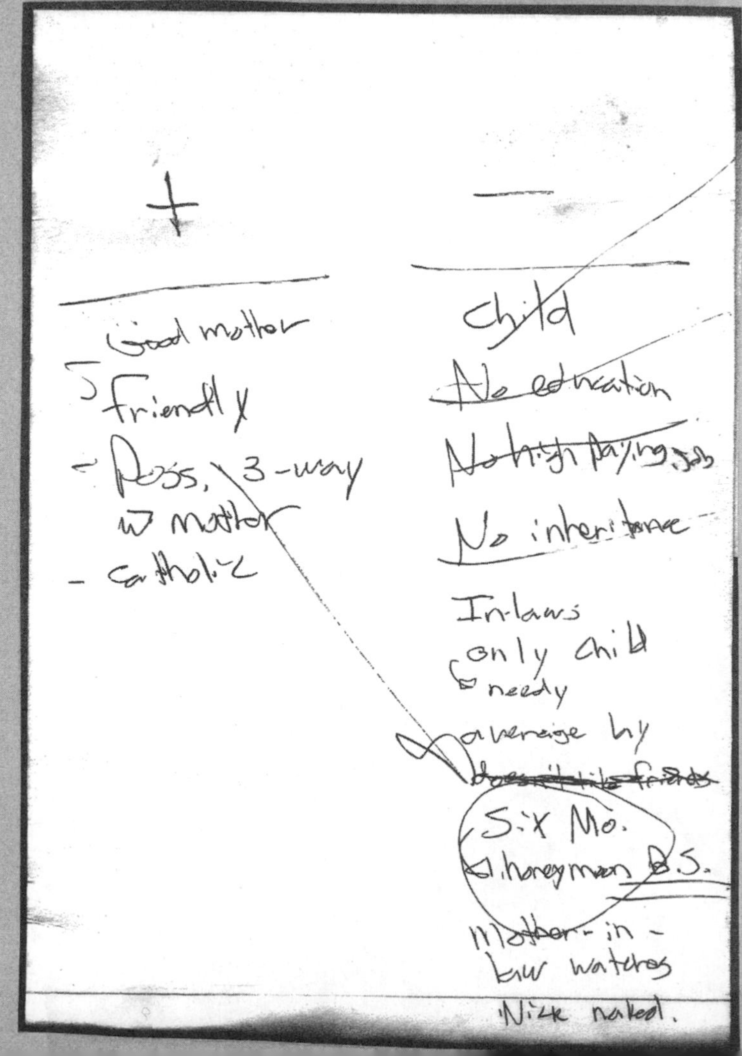

| + | — |
|---|---|
| - Good mother | Child |
| - friendly | ~~No education~~ |
| - Poss. 3-way w mother | ~~No high paying job~~ |
| - catholic | No inheritance |
| | In-laws |
| | only child |
| | needy |
| | average lay |
| | Six Mo. honeymoon D.S. |
| | Mother-in-law watches |
| | Nick naked. |

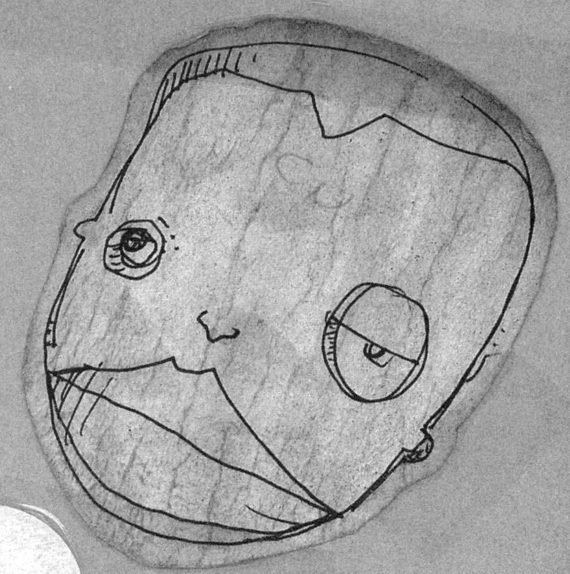

Bad things

| Andrew | Paul |
|---|---|
| crazy | crazier |
| has issues w/ fat people | too loud |
| torn between Stacy & I | too childish |

Good things

| Andrew | Paul |
|---|---|
| married him | child |
| always been good friend | house |
| sex (?) | money |

**ANDREW VS. PAUL**

FOUND by Ivy Tominack

St. Charles, MO

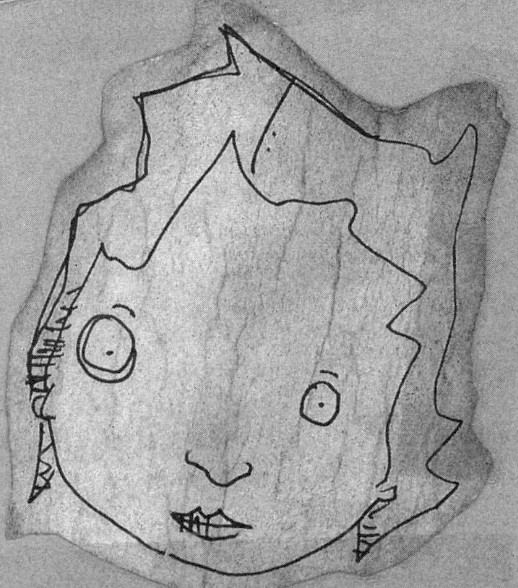

these drawings *FOUND* by Alisha McKinney, Rochester, NY

KEYS
Fo d by Heidi Swillinger
Berkeley, California
I've had a thing about keys for as long as I can remember. The first thing I ever lost was a key – a tiny gold charm that slipped out of my hand and disappeared down a floor vent when I was 5.
USA
My favorite keys are the ones that show evidence of their journey through the world. Some have been run over and over and the wear and tear makes them sparkle. Others, like the key bent in half, double back on themselves. And with enough exposure to elements and time, some – like the key eroded by battery acid – simply wear away.
I walk part way to work each day, and whenever I find a key, it's a big event. I've trained myself to note what I was thinking the instant I spot one; sometimes the thought proves to be a key to a door inside that needs opening.
—H.S.

Los Angeles, CA

REWARD for copy of video that George Bush and Congress had taken of me engaging in sexual intercourse

(213)

-2-

George Bush and Congress sought to thwart my fraudproof nat'l telephone voting system invention, with which AT&T offered assistance, & which allows voters to vote on or veto any issue before Congress. The video was taken to discredit me & the voting system

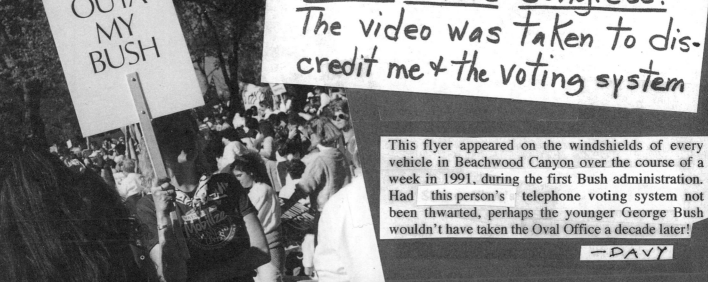

this photo FOUND by Nat Antman, Manhattan, NY

This flyer appeared on the windshields of every vehicle in Beachwood Canyon over the course of a week in 1991, during the first Bush administration. Had this person's telephone voting system not been thwarted, perhaps the younger George Bush wouldn't have taken the Oval Office a decade later!

—DAVY

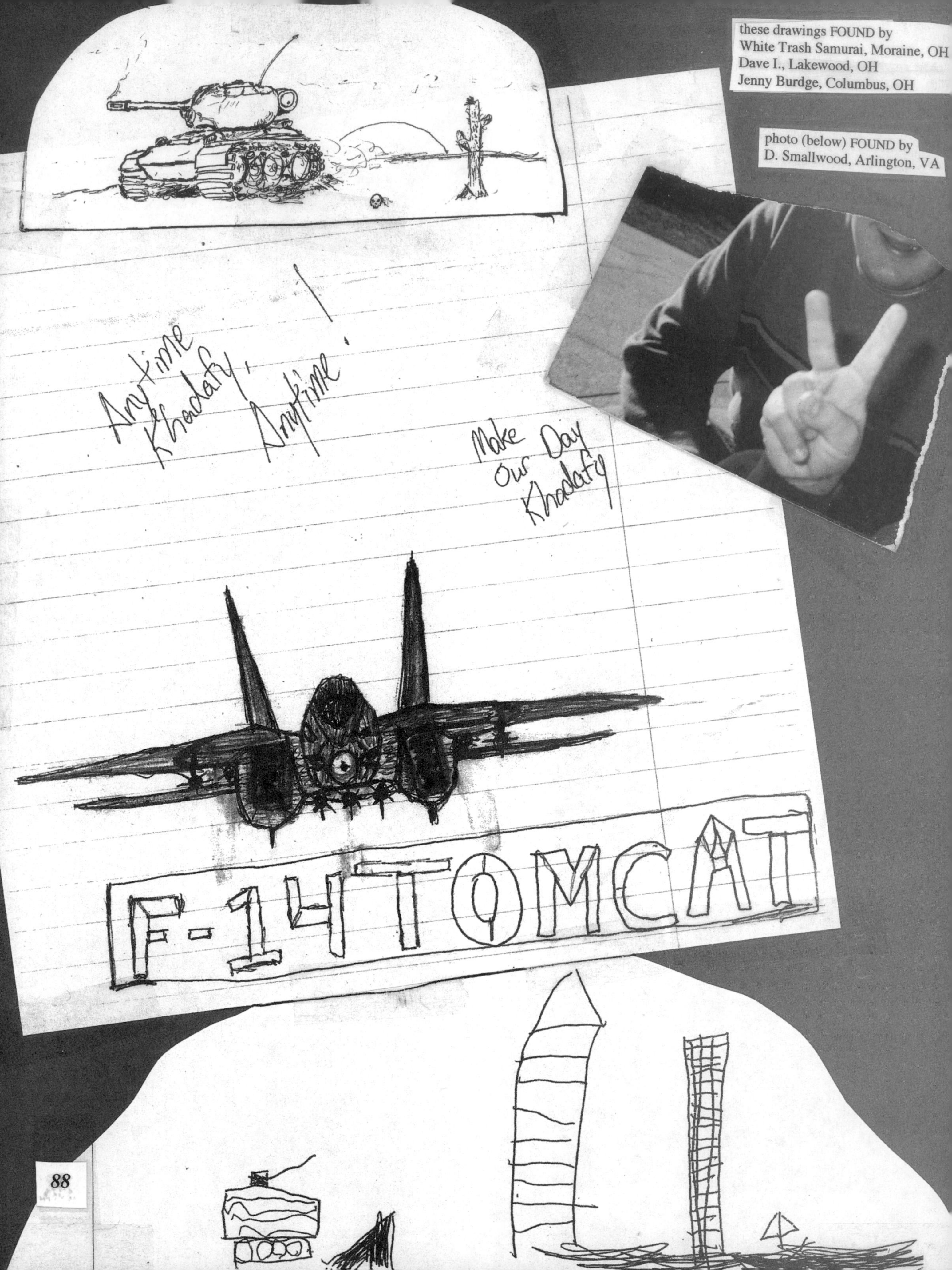
these drawings FOUND by
White Trash Samurai, Moraine, OH
Dave I., Lakewood, OH
Jenny Burdge, Columbus, OH
photo (below) FOUND by
D. Smallwood, Arlington, VA
Anytime Khadafy, Anytime!
Make Our Day Khadafy
F-14 TOMCAT

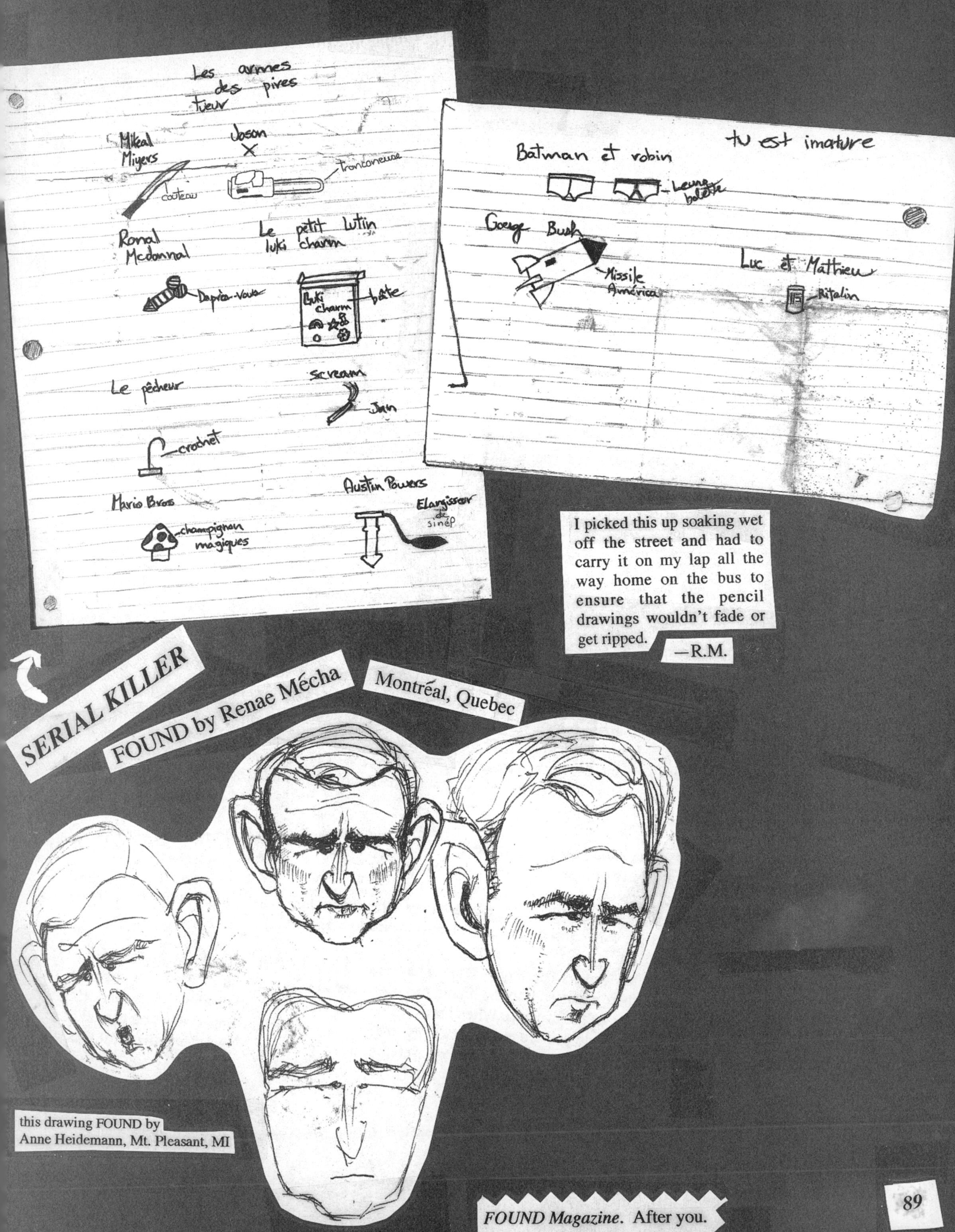


I picked this up soaking wet off the street and had to carry it on my lap all the way home on the bus to ensure that the pencil drawings wouldn't fade or get ripped.

—R.M.

SERIAL KILLER

FOUND by Renae Mécha

Montréal, Quebec

this drawing FOUND by
Anne Heidemann, Mt. Pleasant, MI

*FOUND Magazine*. After you.

Lynn K Madge
950 N United Ave #202
Coconut Creek, Fl 33066
954-

General Manager
Clark's Restaurant
Santee, S.C.

Dear Sir:

My wife and I visited your restaurant in March 2000, when we happened to stay at the Hampton Inn in Santee. We asked the desk clerk about a good restaurant and the clerk stated "You can't beat Clark's" which was seconded by a second party sitting in the lobby. We, indeed, had dinner that evening and found the ambience and the cuisine out of this world.

This year my wife and I again traveled to upstate NY and made it point to stop both on the way North (7-19) and on the return trip (7-31). We opted to stay at the inn and got the breakfast special deal.

The first night we arrived at about 7 P.M.. We were greeted by Tyrone. He was most gracious and asked if we were there for the "Evening of Jazz." We indicated that we were going to the bar and that we would have dinner in about half hour. David, the bartender, made us cocktails which were perfect- a Perfect Manhattan on the rocks and a Beefeater martini straight up. He explained about the jazz night and introduced a couple of the musicians.

Tyrone sat us and our waitress was Melanie. We sat at the exact table as we did in March of 2000. I had the fried green tomatoes and the fried chicken. My wife also had the chicken and we shared bottle of Mystic Cliffs Merlot. The dinner was out of this world. We so totally loved the taste of that chicken and fried green tomatoes. Reminded me of my days as a kid as my mother would fry up green tomatoes. The meal was superb and doubly so with Melanie tending to our every need.

We returned to the bar and listened to the Talk of the Town. What an enjoyable group. They played quite a variety of music and we totally enjoyed it.

Next morning we had breakfast in the garden room. Frances took our order and was so gracious. She was right there with extra coffee and whatever we needed.

On the return we arrived on Tuesday 7-31. The bar was closed but Tyrone made us our favorite drinks. We were then escorted into the dining room and David was our waiter. We noted that it was a very busy time of the evening. When David came over we ordered the Mystic cliffs merlot. We told him "we can see you are busy, we'll enjoy the wine and when it calms down you can take our order!" He seemed so appreciative that we were not in a big hurry. As per usual the meal was superb. We totally enjoyed the evening.

Next morning we had breakfast with Frances. Again all went so well- the eggs were perfect and the ham was wonderful.

We stopped at the desk before leaving and my wife remarked about the wonderful background music. She stated it really adds to the ambiance. We learned that you sell the C.D.'s. The lady was so nice to figure out which CD was playing the night before at the time we entered the restaurant as my wife's favorite song "What a Wonderful world" was playing. We purchased the CD.

I noted the book "The Black Bag" written by Robert Holman MD. I read a few excerpts and asked about it. I bought it and am in the process of reading it. What an interesting collection of remembrances. He must be a wonderful person-just the way he writes and how he expresses himself. I understand that he comes to your restaurant on occasion. After I have read it I am going to send him a letter relative to my thoughts and address it to him in care of Clark's.

I don't write letters to often. However, my wife and I just love stopping at your dining establishment. The people are so nice and the ambiance of the main dining room is wonderful complemented by that background music. I just had to write a note and let you know.

Tyrone, Frances, Melanie, and David were just wonderful and wanted to bring their names to your attention. They made our stay so memorable on two different evenings.

Sincerely

Lynn and Patty Madge

## WHAT A WONDERFUL WORLD

FOUND by Hannah Berman

Providence, R.I.

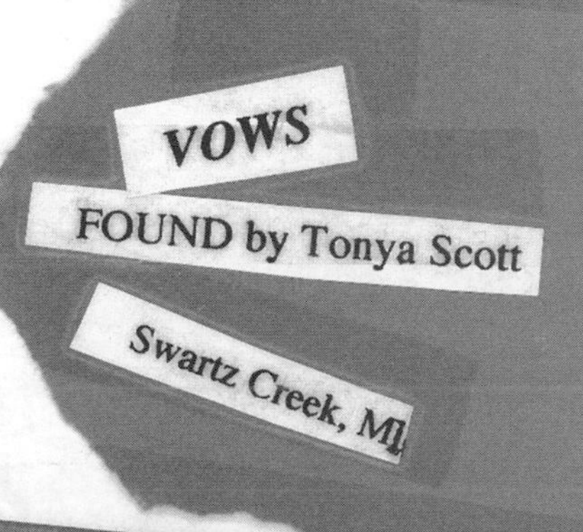

## VOWS

FOUND by Tonya Scott

Swartz Creek, MI

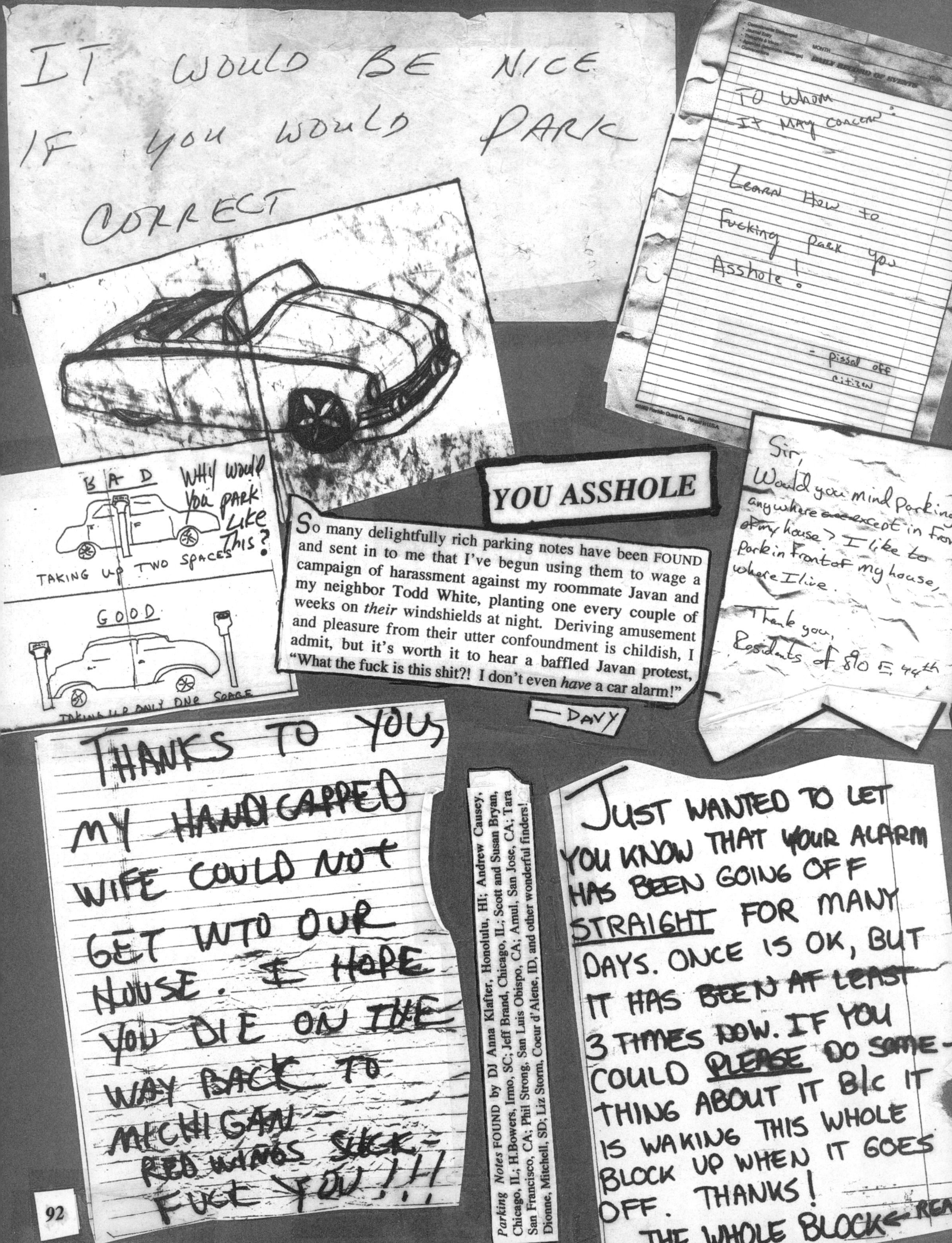

IT WOULD BE NICE IF YOU WOULD PARK CORRECT
TO WHOM IT MAY CONCERN:
Learn How to Fucking park you Asshole!
- pissed off citizen
BAD
WHY WOULD YOU PARK LIKE THIS?
TAKING UP TWO SPACES
GOOD
TAKING UP ONLY ONE SPACE
Sir,
Would you mind parking anywhere except in front of my house? I like to park in front of my house, where I live.
Thank you,
Residents of 890 E. 44th
THANKS TO YOU MY HANDICAPPED WIFE COULD NOT GET INTO OUR HOUSE. I HOPE YOU DIE ON THE WAY BACK TO MICHIGAN
RED WINGS SUCK
FUCK YOU!!!
JUST WANTED TO LET YOU KNOW THAT YOUR ALARM HAS BEEN GOING OFF STRAIGHT FOR MANY DAYS. ONCE IS OK, BUT IT HAS BEEN AT LEAST 3 TIMES NOW. IF YOU COULD PLEASE DO SOMETHING ABOUT IT B/c IT IS WAKING THIS WHOLE BLOCK UP WHEN IT GOES OFF. THANKS!
THE WHOLE BLOCK

**YOU ASSHOLE**

So many delightfully rich parking notes have been FOUND and sent in to me that I've begun using them to wage a campaign of harassment against my roommate Javan and my neighbor Todd White, planting one every couple of weeks on *their* windshields at night. Deriving amusement and pleasure from their utter confoundment is childish, I admit, but it's worth it to hear a baffled Javan protest, "What the fuck is this shit?! I don't even *have* a car alarm!"

—DAVY

*Parking Notes* FOUND by DJ Anna Klafter, Honolulu, HI; Andrew Causey, Chicago, IL; H.Bowers, Irmo, SC; Jeff Brand, Chicago, IL; Scott and Susan Bryan, San Francisco, CA; Phil Strong, San Luis Obispo, CA; Amul, San Jose, CA; Tara Dionne, Mitchell, SD; Liz Storm, Coeur d'Alene, ID, and other wonderful finders!

BLACK CORVETTE MOVE IT!

Thanks for taking 2 spaces, you clueless piece of shit.

INCONSIDERATE MUST COME TO THE MINDS OF ALL THAT THINK OF YOU

This was my parking 1st space they stupidly squeezed in ticket them not me

It would be Nice if you Fucking was the one Who Clean this Fucking Space for your car move it or loose it. paul Redmond Resident

Van owner—

Do you have any courtesy for people's autos? Thank you for scratching mine w/ your bumper. I have your license plate number asshole.

Must be your lucky day next time I call the police. + got your car off mine

Michigan Department of Corrections
**PRISONER STATIONERY**

4835-311
CSJ-11

| TO: | | | FROM: | |
|---|---|---|---|---|
| NAME | | | NAME | |
| NO. AND STREET OR R.R. | | | NO. | LOCK |
| CITY | STATE | ZIP | INSTITUTION | DATE |

**IN CORRESPONDENCE, USE NAME AND NUMBER ON YOUR LETTER AND ENVELOPE.**

IN 1979, I WAS residing When I was in SanFransico. Given the pristenLey beautiful weather, I opted To Traverse hone on Foot one Evening.

The sky WAS ArrestingLy beautiFul; The Night breeze carried the exotic fraygrance of A CINNAMON Tree. The crisp, Soothing Night Air Served to remind me of other times-other place. I WAS ELated because I had just got paid.

SuddenLy, I reached the Golden GAte Bridge. I had the SubLime feeLing that something WAS Askew. upon closer inspection, I observed A MAN reading to Jump. I Approached with caution.

"What's the matter, Sir," I Asked. "I have No incom NO Job, Life the desoLete man ExcLaimed.

Being A SmalL business man, I offered him A job.

That WAS 3 years ago. Now Bob works gainfuLLy For me. Last week I promoted him to ASSistant manager.

I WAS gLad that I opted To wALk that Night.

The End

By: D. Argero

**PROMOTION**

FOUND by Shorty Smooth Dawson

It was February of '62' colder than a witches tit ina brass brassiere, and the ship I was aboard was anchored in the harbor of a small coastal town, that was the asshole of the world.

I had recently made PO3 (Petty Officer 3rd Class), and was also on the Chief's (Chief Petty Officer) shit list for what I don't even remember now. So I got stuck with Shore Patrol duty for a replentishment detail that was to meet the trucks full of fresh meat, milk, veggies at the fleet landing for loading into the utility boats.

The wind that day was like a knife that cut right through our heavy winter blues and peacoats. The water in the bay had been whipped into a nasty chop into which the bow of the boat would plunge, thus throwing up an icy spray, that found its way into the boat. It was a bitch of a ride, that made every soul in that fuckin' boat's life miserable.

The boat tied up at the quay and the sailors unassed it to stand around pissin' 'n moanin', and lightin' up smokes. Naturally the trucks were'nt there yet, so we all stood out in that cold wind freezin' our asses off.

Finally the goddamned trucks showed up and the sailors begun unloadin' 'em, 'n loadin' ~~the~~ up the boat. I was busy freezin' my ass off, 'n watchin' the sailors work, when I happened ta spot a couple a ragged assed kids over by one of the old shacks by the quay. They sure were a sad sorry lookin' bunch, but its a sight sailors see all over this mudball we call Earth.

One of the little fuckers hollered to me, "hey Joe ya got american cigarette for me?" So I motioned the little shit over and gave 'em one of my Humps (what we called Camels), the little shit could'nta been 8 or 9, but he could hack that fuckin' Hump. Me 'n the little fucker stood there smokin' for a bit 'n he looked up at me 'n said "I hungry Joe", shit I didn't have nothin' ta give that poor raggedassed kid. I looked over at the trucks and saw the workin' party unloadin' cartons of fresh milk in cases 'n frozen beef, 'n got me an idea. I told the kid ta go stand by the shack 'n wait for me, then walked over ta one of the trucks 'n grabbed a case of milk 'n one of beef, I toted 'em over ta the side 'o the shack 'n gave each 'o those sorry lookin' rugrats a hunk 'o beef 'n a carton a milk, 'n before each one scamppered off they thanked me.

Givin' those kids that food was a courtmarshel offense, but fuckit I was'nt caught, 'n it made me feel good!

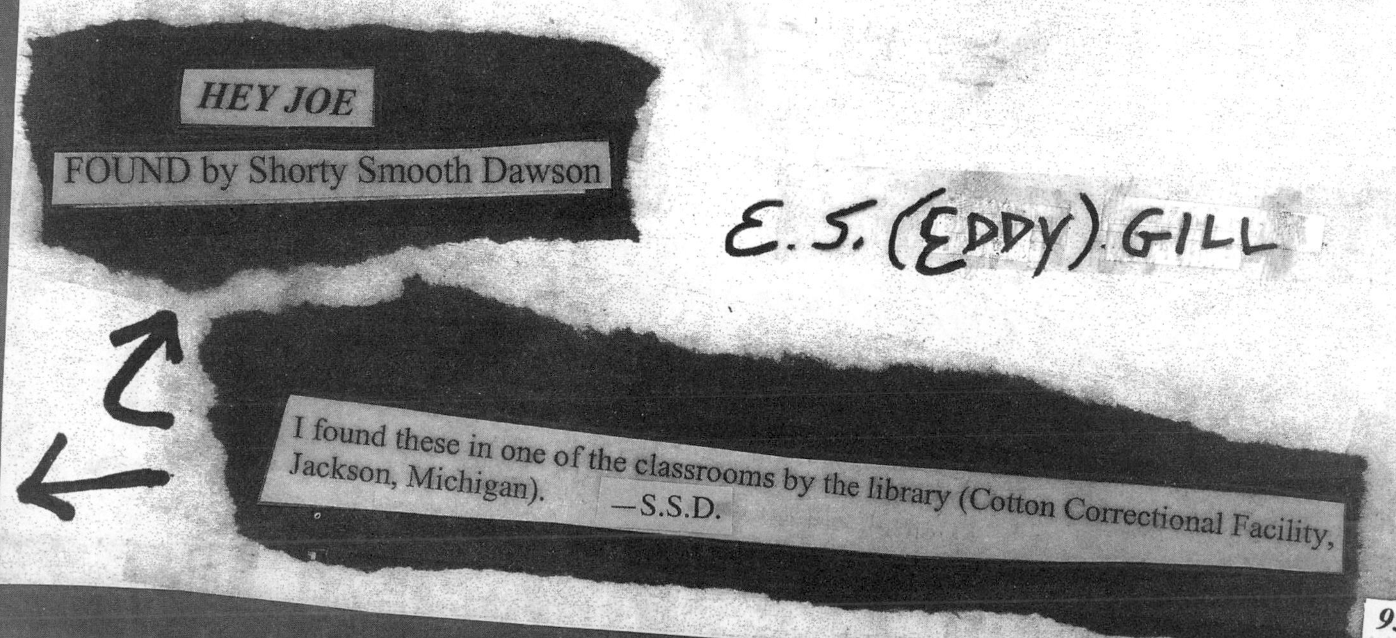

HEY JOE
FOUND by Shorty Smooth Dawson
E. S. (EDDY) GILL
I found these in one of the classrooms by the library (Cotton Correctional Facility, Jackson, Michigan). —S.S.D.

Hello Rudy, it's Deon Jan 1, 2003

I'm writing you because I have something important I'de like to discuss with you. It has nothing to do with me, it has to do with my parents. This has nothing to do with the house in Italy or the relationship you have with them or anything you can possibly infer. I don't know how you feel about me or my parents right now but I'm just asking to sit down and talk with you for 15 minutes. I'm working Friday 11-4PM
Saturday 2-9PM
Sunday 5-10PM
Monday 5-10PM
Tuesday 10-4PM

back →

**PLEASE DON'T TELL ANYONE EXCEPT FOR MAYBE LISA ABOUT THIS**

FOUND by a junkie on Polk Street and given to Ryan Schude

San Francisco, CA

*O*ne misty night not too long ago I was sitting in my car on Polk Street reading *FOUND Magazine* when this guy walks up and starts talking to me outta nowhere. He is deathly skinny and talking fast and impatiently, asking questions and continuing before he gets the answers. He tells me his name is Jasper and that it's his 28th birthday; when I wish him a Happy Birthday, I find out he isn't having a very happy one. He explains that he's addicted to heroin, and due to the speed he's consumed to alleviate his depression, he hasn't slept in three days. "That's nothing, though," he tells me, "I've gone at least thirty days before!"

Jasper expresses his desire to get out of the streets, how he wishes someone would just take him away from San Francisco for good. He tells me he is a Photoshop fiend but is careful to point out that the program works better when you start with a photo instead of a blank canvas. A man walks by and Jasper says, "Look at the way he's shaking his ass," and does that fast tongue gesture you might see some cheeseball in an '80's flick use to pick up girls. I let him page his buddy from my cell phone, and when he gives my phone back he sees the *FOUND Magazine* in my hands and asks about it. I explain the whole idea of *FOUND*, and Jasper nods vigorously, then all of a sudden dashes away down the street. He picks up a piece of paper that's gusting across the next intersection and walks slowly back toward me, reading the note.

Our entire conversation up til then he's been lost in rueful despair but something changes when he starts reading this letter. He stands next to my car, both amused and amazed at the details that we, as outsiders, are missing—every couple of sentences he looks up to point out to me the moments when he is simultaneously the most confused and the most intrigued. Finally, he folds up the piece of paper, hands it to me, and says, "Show this to your friends, they'll get a kick out of it." Then he wheels off again and disappears into the fog.

—R.S.

If you can e-mail me at d_olomite[illegible]7@yahoo.com (underscore) to set up a time and place at your discretion I'de greatly appreciate it.

Thanks,
Deon

P.S - please don't tell anyone except for maybe Lisa about this.

**A b s c h r i f t**

Ther esienstadt d.20 .4.
43-

Meine Lieben!
Hoffentlich seid Ihr gesund. Unserer Schwester Johanna und mir geht es Gottseidank gut. Mein geliebter Ehemann Otto ist leider nach dreiwöchentlichem Krankheit an Altersschwäche gestorben. Ihr könnt Euch denken wie traurig ich bin darüber. Meine Arbeit als Fürsorgerin im Gesundheitswesen - Siechenfürsorge - befriedigt mich sehr und lässt mich über den Schmerz einigermassen hinwegkommen. Habt Ihr etwas von Hans und Gretel gehört? Ich würde mich sehr freuen von Euch bald zu hören. Briefe Postkarten, Pakete und Päckchen kommen hier an und werden uns zugestellt. Teilt bitte Maria und Paul unsere Adresse mit und grüsst alle unsere Freunde herzlich. Hoffentlich sind unsere Freunde dort gesund. D ie Luft ist sehr gut hier, Theresienstadt liegt erhöht und wir haben schöne Sonne und meine Tätigkeit führt mich viel in die Luft. Habt Ihr auch von unserer Schwester Eugenie etwas gehört? Ich hoffe bald von Euch Allen zu hören und grüsse Euch recht herzlich, in alter Treue,

Wwe Frieda Baum
L. 42
Theresienstadt Böhmen.

# LETTERS FROM THERESIENSTADT

FOUND by Aaron Hurst

New York, NY

translated by Helmut Puff

My dears,

Theresienstadt, April 20, 1943 [Hitler's birthday]

I hope you are well. My sister Johanna and I are doing well, thank God. My beloved husband Otto unfortunately passed away after three weeks of illness. The cause was age-related infirmity. You can imagine how saddened I am by this. I enjoy my work as welfare worker in the health system – on the ward of the sick – greatly. It helps me some to get over the pain. Have you heard from Hans and Gretel? I would be delighted to hear from you soon. Letters, packages, and small parcels arrive and are delivered to us. Please, communicate our address to Maria and Paul and say hello to all our friends. I hope that they are well there. The air is very good here; Theresienstadt lies elevated. We have nice sun and my job gets me out into the air frequently. Have you heard something from our sister Eugenie? I hope to hear soon from you all and greet you warmly; in old loyalty,

Wwe. Frieda Baum
L. 42
Theresienstadt, Bohemia

5 h

POSTKARTE
DOPISNICE

*Theresienstadt, am* 24 Sept *1943.*

Meine sehr Lieben

*Ich bestätige dankend den Empfang Ihres (Deines) Paketes vom* September *1943.*

*Brief folgt.*

Baum Frieda

*Unterschrift.*

My very dears,
(with thanks, I confirm having received your package of) September (1943. Letter will follow.)
Your grateful
Baum Frieda

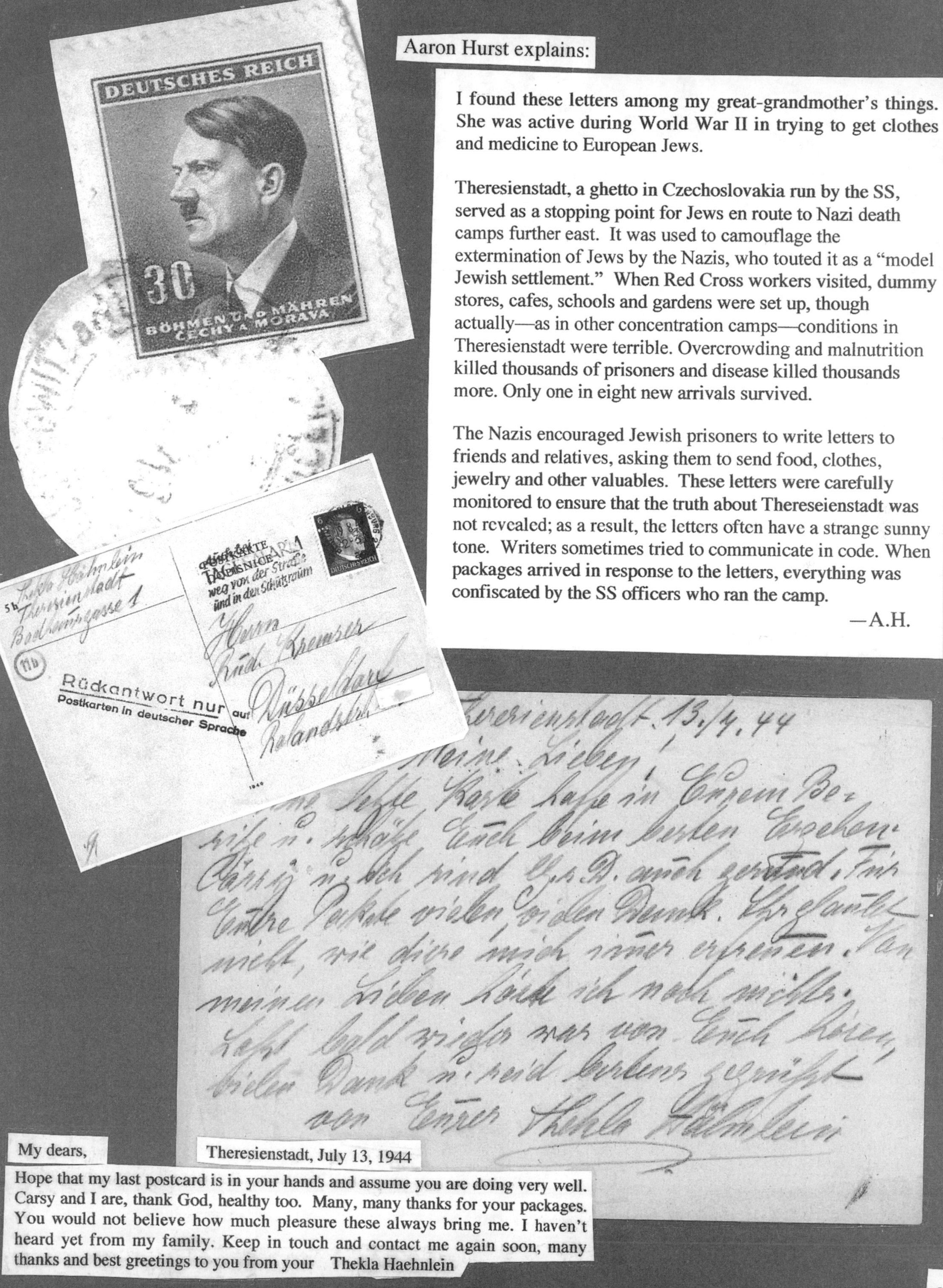


Aaron Hurst explains:

I found these letters among my great-grandmother's things. She was active during World War II in trying to get clothes and medicine to European Jews.

Theresienstadt, a ghetto in Czechoslovakia run by the SS, served as a stopping point for Jews en route to Nazi death camps further east. It was used to camouflage the extermination of Jews by the Nazis, who touted it as a "model Jewish settlement." When Red Cross workers visited, dummy stores, cafes, schools and gardens were set up, though actually—as in other concentration camps—conditions in Theresienstadt were terrible. Overcrowding and malnutrition killed thousands of prisoners and disease killed thousands more. Only one in eight new arrivals survived.

The Nazis encouraged Jewish prisoners to write letters to friends and relatives, asking them to send food, clothes, jewelry and other valuables. These letters were carefully monitored to ensure that the truth about Thereseienstadt was not revealed; as a result, the letters often have a strange sunny tone. Writers sometimes tried to communicate in code. When packages arrived in response to the letters, everything was confiscated by the SS officers who ran the camp.

—A.H.

My dears,

Theresienstadt, July 13, 1944

Hope that my last postcard is in your hands and assume you are doing very well. Carsy and I are, thank God, healthy too. Many, many thanks for your packages. You would not believe how much pleasure these always bring me. I haven't heard yet from my family. Keep in touch and contact me again soon, many thanks and best greetings to you from your Thekla Haehnlein

Chris explains

To: E-mail readers everywhere
From: chris willis <chrisw@neu.com>
Subject: neu.communiqués vol. II
Cc:
Bcc:
X-Attachments:

Hi all,

There was a time not too long ago when I'd be bombarded daily by dozens of misdirected e-mails. Since Neumeier Design owns neu.com, I'd get all sorts of wayward messages intended for recipients @ neu.edu, neu.net, neu.org, etc.

The following collection includes some treasures I found amongst the trash over the years. Some names have been blacked out to protect the innocent, guilty, and potentially embarrassed. Other than that, the e-mails are presented just as I received them, in their original uncut versions.

Personal thoughts and feelings are routinely sent off across this impersonal medium—with every confidence they'll reach their intended destination safe and sound. This is a collection of a few wrong turns that made it to my screen.

I think it makes for some darn interesting reading, so enjoy.

Chris

drawings drawn by Jeffrey Brown

theholyconsumption.com

this photo FOUND by Nat Antman, NYC

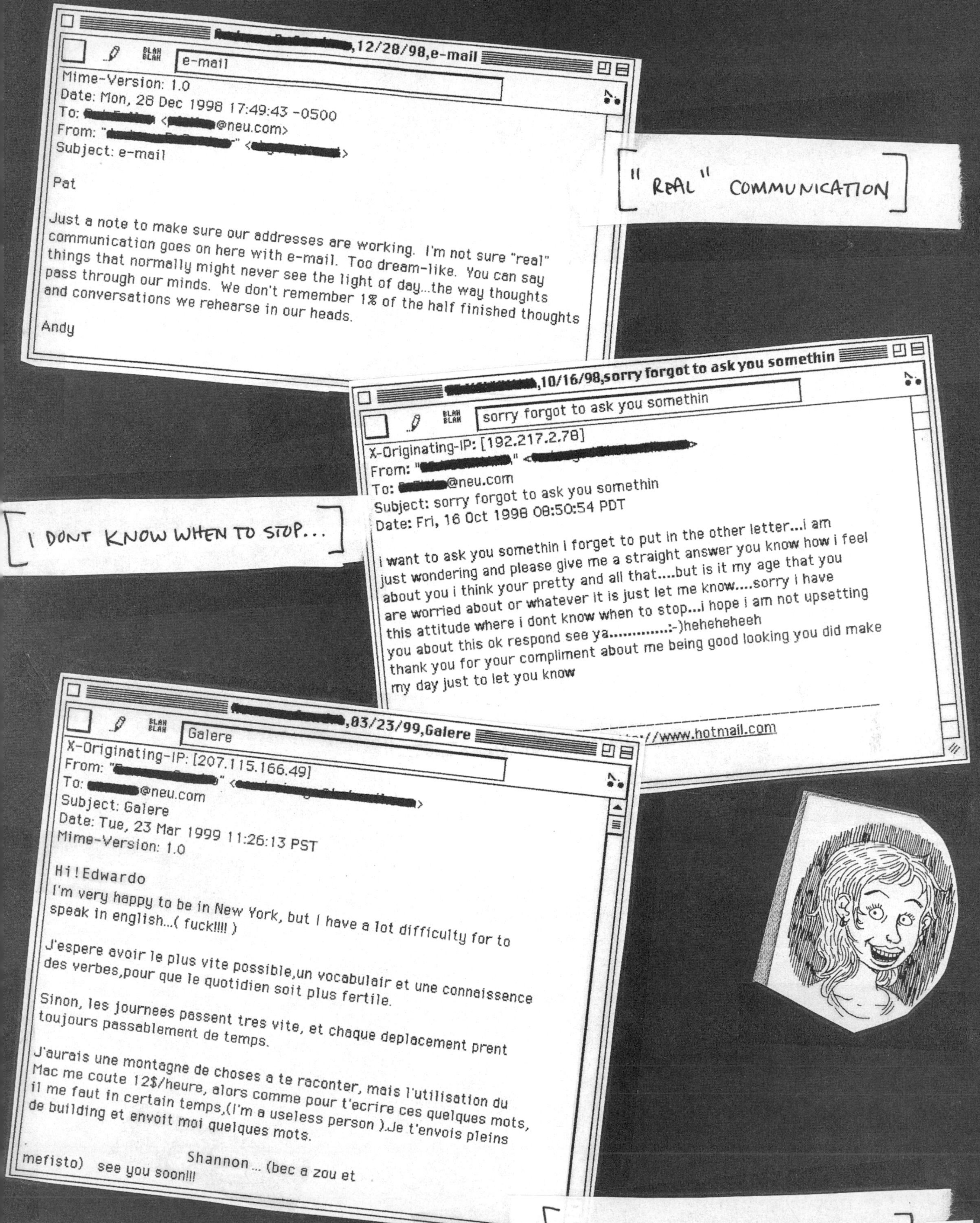
,12/28/98,e-mail

e-mail

Mime-Version: 1.0
Date: Mon, 28 Dec 1998 17:49:43 -0500
To: <@neu.com>
From: "" <>
Subject: e-mail

Pat

Just a note to make sure our addresses are working. I'm not sure "real" communication goes on here with e-mail. Too dream-like. You can say things that normally might never see the light of day...the way thoughts pass through our minds. We don't remember 1% of the half finished thoughts and conversations we rehearse in our heads.

Andy

[ "REAL" COMMUNICATION ]

,10/16/98,sorry forgot to ask you somethin

sorry forgot to ask you somethin

X-Originating-IP: [192.217.2.78]
From: "," <>
To: @neu.com
Subject: sorry forgot to ask you somethin
Date: Fri, 16 Oct 1998 08:50:54 PDT

i want to ask you somethin i forget to put in the other letter...i am just wondering and please give me a straight answer you know how i feel about you i think your pretty and all that....but is it my age that you are worried about or whatever it is just let me know....sorry i have this attitude where i dont know when to stop...i hope i am not upsetting you about this ok respond see ya............:-)heheheheeh thank you for your compliment about me being good looking you did make my day just to let you know

://www.hotmail.com

[ I DONT KNOW WHEN TO STOP... ]

,03/23/99,Galere

Galere

X-Originating-IP: [207.115.166.49]
From: "" <>
To: @neu.com
Subject: Galere
Date: Tue, 23 Mar 1999 11:26:13 PST
Mime-Version: 1.0

Hi!Edwardo
I'm very happy to be in New York, but I have a lot difficulty for to speak in english...( fuck!!!! )

J'espere avoir le plus vite possible,un vocabulair et une connaissence des verbes,pour que le quotidien soit plus fertile.

Sinon, les journees passent tres vite, et chaque deplacement prent toujours passablement de temps.

J'aurais une montagne de choses a te raconter, mais l'utilisation du Mac me coute 12$/heure, alors comme pour t'ecrire ces quelques mots, il me faut in certain temps,(I'm a useless person ).Je t'envois pleins de building et envoit moi quelques mots.

Shannon ... (bec a zou et mefisto) see you soon!!!

[ ENGLISH AS A SECOND LANGUAGE ]

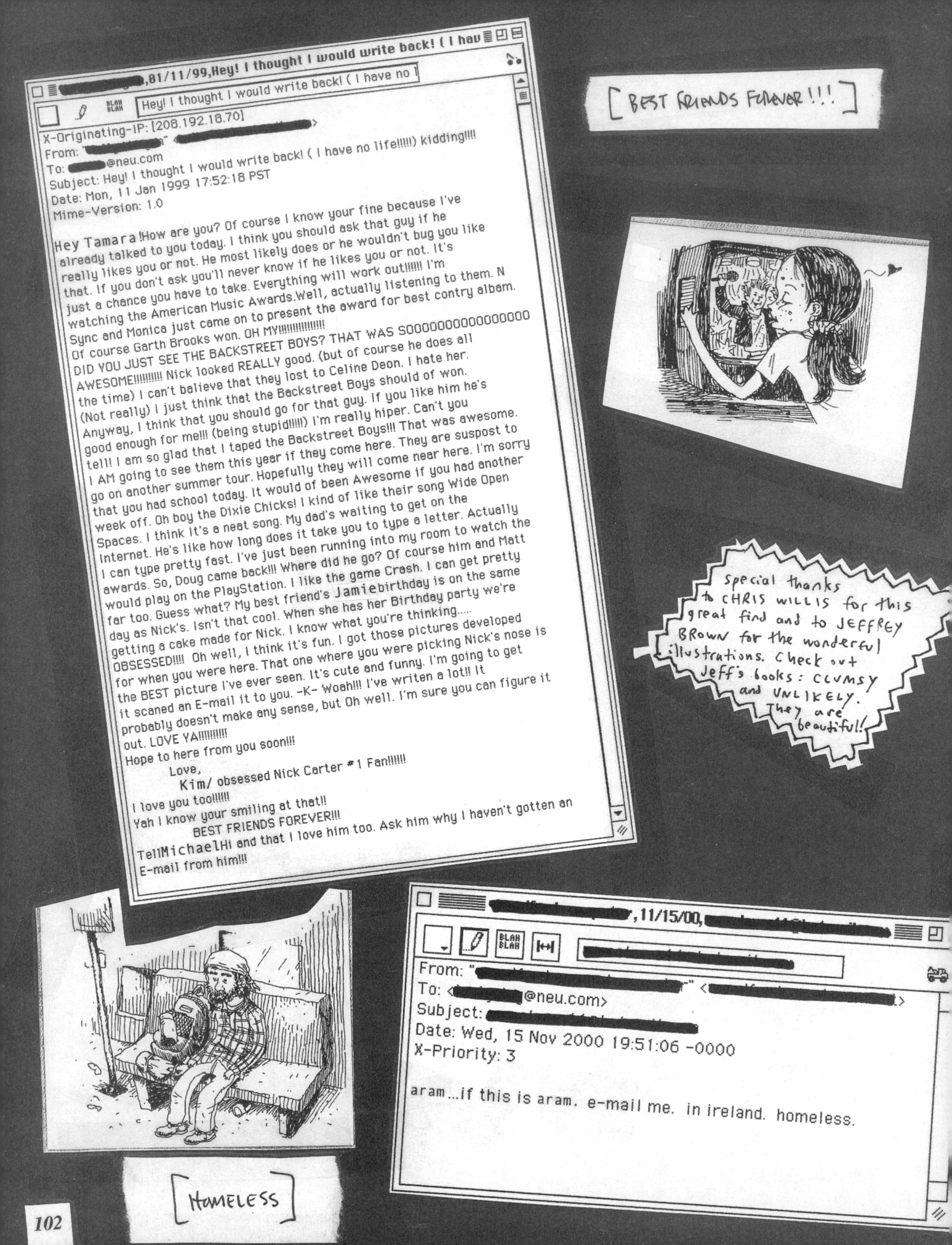

,01/11/99,Hey! I thought I would write back! ( I hav

Hey! I thought I would write back! ( I have no l

X-Originating-IP: [208.192.18.70]
From: "" <>
To: @neu.com
Subject: Hey! I thought I would write back! ( I have no life!!!!!) kidding!!!!
Date: Mon, 11 Jan 1999 17:52:18 PST
Mime-Version: 1.0

Hey Tamara!How are you? Of course I know your fine because I've
already talked to you today. I think you should ask that guy if he
really likes you or not. He most likely does or he wouldn't bug you like
that. If you don't ask you'll never know if he likes you or not. It's
just a chance you have to take. Everything will work out!!!!!! I'm
watching the American Music Awards.Well, actually listening to them. N
Sync and Monica just came on to present the award for best contry albam.
Of course Garth Brooks won. OH MY!!!!!!!!!!!!!!!!
DID YOU JUST SEE THE BACKSTREET BOYS? THAT WAS SOOOOOOOOOOOOOOOO
AWESOME!!!!!!!!!! Nick looked REALLY good. (but of course he does all
the time) I can't believe that they lost to Celine Deon. I hate her.
(Not really) I just think that the Backstreet Boys should of won.
Anyway, I think that you should go for that guy. If you like him he's
good enough for me!!! (being stupid!!!!!) I'm really hiper. Can't you
tell! I am so glad that I taped the Backstreet Boys!!! That was awesome.
I AM going to see them this year if they come here. They are suspost to
go on another summer tour. Hopefully they will come near here. I'm sorry
that you had school today. It would of been Awesome if you had another
week off. Oh boy the Dixie Chicks! I kind of like their song Wide Open
Spaces. I think It's a neat song. My dad's waiting to get on the
Internet. He's like how long does it take you to type a letter. Actually
I can type pretty fast. I've just been running into my room to watch the
awards. So, Doug came back!!! Where did he go? Of course him and Matt
would play on the PlayStation. I like the game Crash. I can get pretty
far too. Guess what? My best friend's Jamiebirthday is on the same
day as Nick's. Isn't that cool. When she has her Birthday party we're
getting a cake made for Nick. I know what you're thinking.....
OBSESSED!!!! Oh well, I think it's fun. I got those pictures developed
for when you were here. That one where you were picking Nick's nose is
the BEST picture I've ever seen. It's cute and funny. I'm going to get
it scaned an E-mail it to you. -K- Woah!!! I've writen a lot!! It
probably doesn't make any sense, but Oh well. I'm sure you can figure it
out. LOVE YA!!!!!!!!!!
Hope to here from you soon!!!
Love,
Kim/ obsessed Nick Carter #1 Fan!!!!!!
I love you too!!!!!!
Yah I know your smiling at that!!
BEST FRIENDS FOREVER!!!
TellMichaelHi and that I love him too. Ask him why I haven't gotten an
E-mail from him!!!

[BEST FRIENDS FOREVER!!!]

Special thanks to CHRIS WILLIS for this great find and to JEFFREY BROWN for the wonderful illustrations. Check out Jeff's books: CLUMSY and UNLIKELY. They are beautiful!!

,11/15/00,

From: ""
To: <@neu.com>" <>
Subject:
Date: Wed, 15 Nov 2000 19:51:06 -0000
X-Priority: 3

aram ...if this is aram. e-mail me. in ireland. homeless.

[HOMELESS]

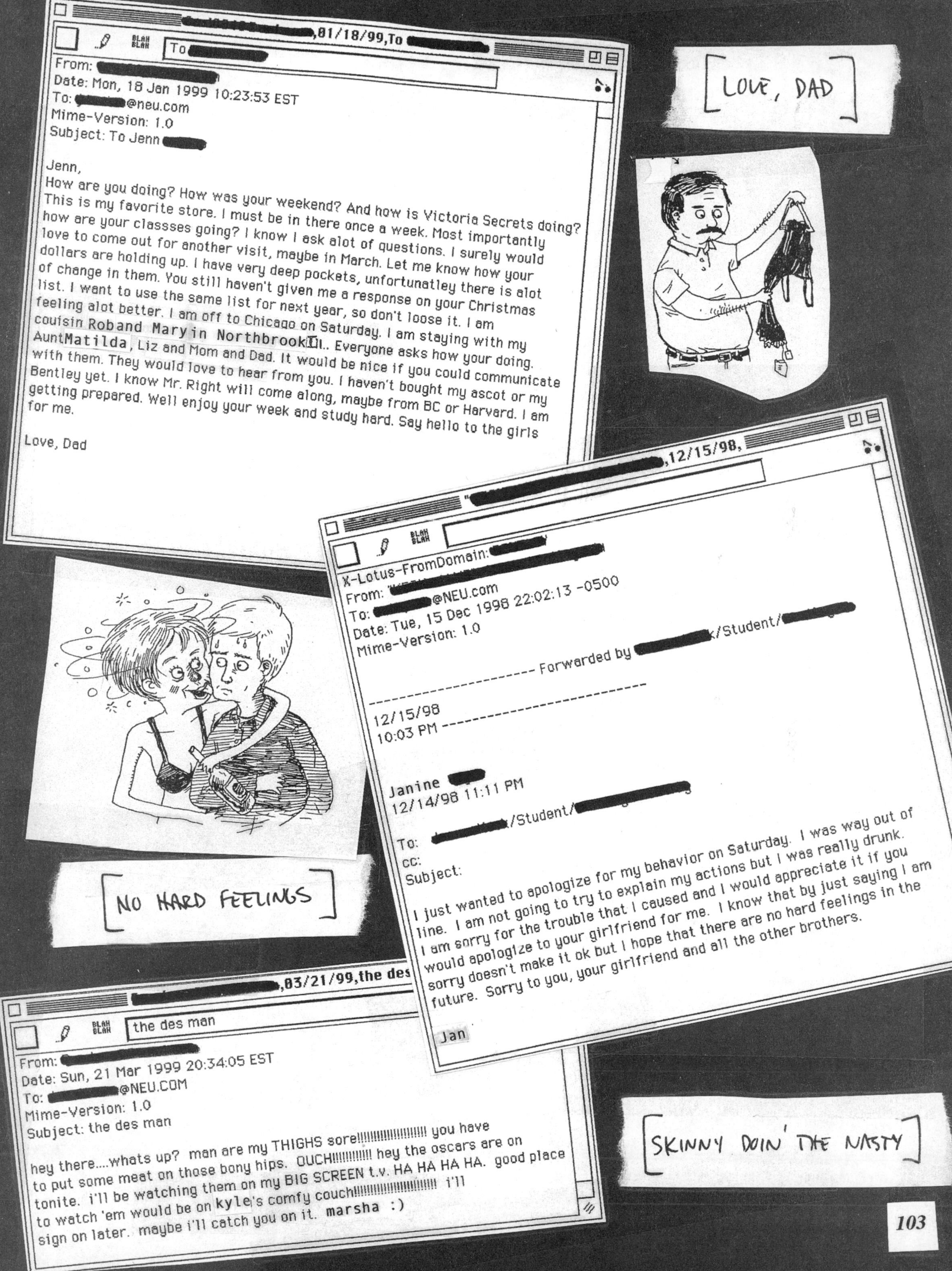

,01/18/99,To

To

From:
Date: Mon, 18 Jan 1999 10:23:53 EST
To: @neu.com
Mime-Version: 1.0
Subject: To Jenn

Jenn,
How are you doing? How was your weekend? And how is Victoria Secrets doing? This is my favorite store. I must be in there once a week. Most importantly how are your classses going? I know I ask alot of questions. I surely would love to come out for another visit, maybe in March. Let me know how your dollars are holding up. I have very deep pockets, unfortunatley there is alot of change in them. You still haven't given me a response on your Christmas list. I want to use the same list for next year, so don't loose it. I am feeling alot better. I am off to Chicago on Saturday. I am staying with my couisin Rob and Mary in Northbrook, Il.. Everyone asks how your doing. Aunt Matilda, Liz and Mom and Dad. It would be nice if you could communicate with them. They would love to hear from you. I haven't bought my ascot or my Bentley yet. I know Mr. Right will come along, maybe from BC or Harvard. I am getting prepared. Well enjoy your week and study hard. Say hello to the girls for me.

Love, Dad



,12/15/98,

X-Lotus-FromDomain:
From: @NEU.com
To: /Student/
Date: Tue, 15 Dec 1998 22:02:13 -0500
Mime-Version: 1.0

---------------------- Forwarded by /Student/
------------------------------------------

12/15/98
10:03 PM ---------------------------

Janine
12/14/98 11:11 PM

/Student/

To: /Student/
cc:
Subject:

I just wanted to apologize for my behavior on Saturday. I was way out of line. I am not going to try to explain my actions but I was really drunk. I am sorry for the trouble that I caused and I would appreciate it if you would apologize to your girlfriend for me. I know that by just saying I am sorry doesn't make it ok but I hope that there are no hard feelings in the future. Sorry to you, your girlfriend and all the other brothers.

Jan



,03/21/99,the des

the des man

From:
Date: Sun, 21 Mar 1999 20:34:05 EST
To: @NEU.COM
Mime-Version: 1.0
Subject: the des man

hey there....whats up? man are my THIGHS sore!!!!!!!!!!!!!!!!!!!! you have to put some meat on those bony hips. OUCH!!!!!!!!!!!! hey the oscars are on tonite. i'll be watching them on my BIG SCREEN t.v. HA HA HA HA. good place to watch 'em would be on kyle's comfy couch!!!!!!!!!!!!!!!!!!!!!!!! i'll sign on later. maybe i'll catch you on it. marsha :)

[JUST LISTEN TO ME]

,11/11/98,you better

you better

X-Originating-IP: [207.229.134.161]
From: "
To: " <
@neu.com
Subject: you better
MIME-Version: 1.0
Date: Wed, 11 Nov 1998 11:32:00 PST

Hey Babe,
I hate to repeat this to you (actually I don't mind bothering you) but it is extremely important that you follow through with your studies. What Cam's brother may have forgotten to tell you is that when you decide you are going to do something, you do it. Of course you may get a degree and good grades (which are somewhat important) BUT not nearly as important as how it makes you feel to get something done. Forget about the grades, forget that the teacher may think you're stupid or something. Forget about ALL the pressure people like your family or your friends are giving you about your future. Just listen to me. All these people obviously care about you and want you to succeed and its all nice and dandy that they are trying to tell you they care about you BUT what REALLY matters is that you figure out that YOU WANT THIS FOR YOURSELF. Forget about what people think of you. It is a very BIG step towards growing up, and a really GREAT one. I know you have already learned to not give a damn in some ways (cycling with vomit all over you on LSD) (FREAKING a girl all over the place at a club with all of those people watching) (dancing in front of that Indian Family to Indian beats-hell I don't even have that many guts) Anyhow this is about you telling yourself: I'm signing up for this class, and I am going to do the best that I can in it. If you follow through and stop making excuses for yourself, you will develop a feeling of respect for yourself. It will make you feel good. What anyone else thinks is besides the point. Sure people want the best for you but this is YOUR life brad. If anyone accomplishes anything great, it usually means you put what you want for yourself as the number one thing in your day, one day at a time, and start putting everyone else (including all your friends and family) on NUMBER TWO.. If you think you need to call people all the time so that you don't lose them as friends, what you have is LOW SELF ESTEEM. If you lose friends because all of a sudden you decide that your goals and your art is more important than they are-GUESS WHAT? then they are no good and defective friends anyway, probably people suffering with that desease of low self esteem.

Must go now. please think about these things, because I know you have the ability to really kick some ass out there.

,10/14/98,confidential

confidential

Date: Wed, 14 Oct 1998 23:52:24 +0000
From: <
>
Reply-To:
MIME-Version: 1.0
To: @neu.com
Subject: confidential

Mara..I thank you for your calls..
I went to talk to my mom. and she is so great..
I went to talk to my mom. and she is so great..
.tonite and I came home and,to be honest..cried ..most of the nite..you cannot know..how demoralizing this is..and some of the things people say..so hurtful..
it is a living nightmare..and the financial thing is horrible

..its almost too much to bare..I am up ,now..crying in my room..trying to figure out why this happened..
feeling terribly alome..
and when will it end? who knows..
I just want to crawl in a hole..everything is not the way it is supposed to be..

[CONFIDENTIAL]

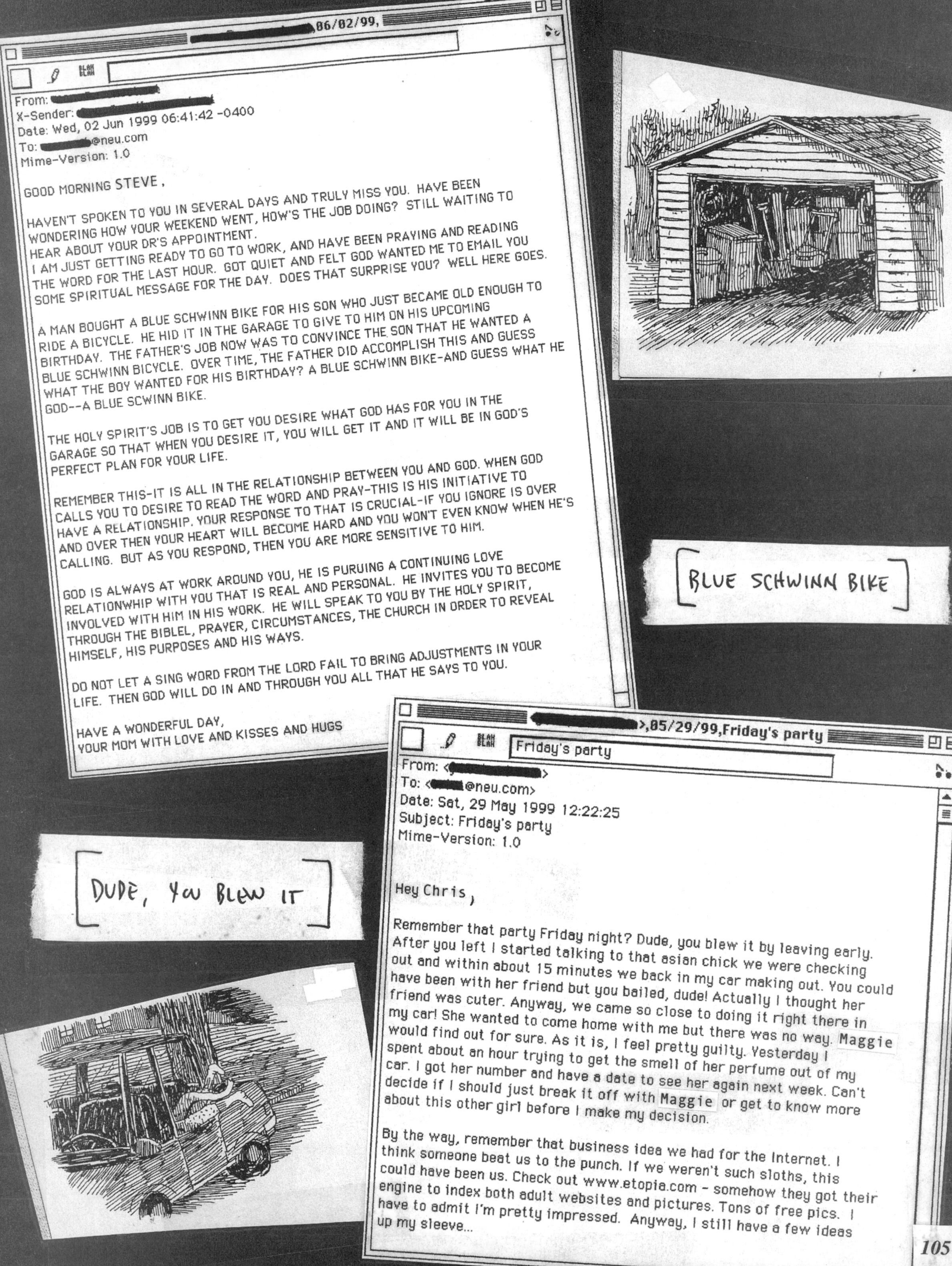

,06/02/99,

From:
X-Sender:
Date: Wed, 02 Jun 1999 06:41:42 -0400
To: @neu.com
Mime-Version: 1.0

GOOD MORNING STEVE,

HAVEN'T SPOKEN TO YOU IN SEVERAL DAYS AND TRULY MISS YOU. HAVE BEEN WONDERING HOW YOUR WEEKEND WENT, HOW'S THE JOB DOING? STILL WAITING TO HEAR ABOUT YOUR DR'S APPOINTMENT.
I AM JUST GETTING READY TO GO TO WORK, AND HAVE BEEN PRAYING AND READING THE WORD FOR THE LAST HOUR. GOT QUIET AND FELT GOD WANTED ME TO EMAIL YOU SOME SPIRITUAL MESSAGE FOR THE DAY. DOES THAT SURPRISE YOU? WELL HERE GOES.

A MAN BOUGHT A BLUE SCHWINN BIKE FOR HIS SON WHO JUST BECAME OLD ENOUGH TO RIDE A BICYCLE. HE HID IT IN THE GARAGE TO GIVE TO HIM ON HIS UPCOMING BIRTHDAY. THE FATHER'S JOB NOW WAS TO CONVINCE THE SON THAT HE WANTED A BLUE SCHWINN BICYCLE. OVER TIME, THE FATHER DID ACCOMPLISH THIS AND GUESS WHAT THE BOY WANTED FOR HIS BIRTHDAY? A BLUE SCHWINN BIKE-AND GUESS WHAT HE GOD--A BLUE SCWINN BIKE.

THE HOLY SPIRIT'S JOB IS TO GET YOU DESIRE WHAT GOD HAS FOR YOU IN THE GARAGE SO THAT WHEN YOU DESIRE IT, YOU WILL GET IT AND IT WILL BE IN GOD'S PERFECT PLAN FOR YOUR LIFE.

REMEMBER THIS-IT IS ALL IN THE RELATIONSHIP BETWEEN YOU AND GOD. WHEN GOD CALLS YOU TO DESIRE TO READ THE WORD AND PRAY-THIS IS HIS INITIATIVE TO HAVE A RELATIONSHIP. YOUR RESPONSE TO THAT IS CRUCIAL-IF YOU IGNORE IS OVER AND OVER THEN YOUR HEART WILL BECOME HARD AND YOU WON'T EVEN KNOW WHEN HE'S CALLING. BUT AS YOU RESPOND, THEN YOU ARE MORE SENSITIVE TO HIM.

GOD IS ALWAYS AT WORK AROUND YOU, HE IS PURUING A CONTINUING LOVE RELATIONWHIP WITH YOU THAT IS REAL AND PERSONAL. HE INVITES YOU TO BECOME INVOLVED WITH HIM IN HIS WORK. HE WILL SPEAK TO YOU BY THE HOLY SPIRIT, THROUGH THE BIBLEL, PRAYER, CIRCUMSTANCES, THE CHURCH IN ORDER TO REVEAL HIMSELF, HIS PURPOSES AND HIS WAYS.

DO NOT LET A SING WORD FROM THE LORD FAIL TO BRING ADJUSTMENTS IN YOUR LIFE. THEN GOD WILL DO IN AND THROUGH YOU ALL THAT HE SAYS TO YOU.

HAVE A WONDERFUL DAY,
YOUR MOM WITH LOVE AND KISSES AND HUGS





>,05/29/99,Friday's party

Friday's party

From: <>
To: < @neu.com>
Date: Sat, 29 May 1999 12:22:25
Subject: Friday's party
Mime-Version: 1.0

Hey Chris,

Remember that party Friday night? Dude, you blew it by leaving early. After you left I started talking to that asian chick we were checking out and within about 15 minutes we back in my car making out. You could have been with her friend but you bailed, dude! Actually I thought her friend was cuter. Anyway, we came so close to doing it right there in my car! She wanted to come home with me but there was no way. Maggie would find out for sure. As it is, I feel pretty guilty. Yesterday I spent about an hour trying to get the smell of her perfume out of my car. I got her number and have a date to see her again next week. Can't decide if I should just break it off with Maggie or get to know more about this other girl before I make my decision.

By the way, remember that business idea we had for the Internet. I think someone beat us to the punch. If we weren't such sloths, this could have been us. Check out www.etopia.com - somehow they got their engine to index both adult websites and pictures. Tons of free pics. I have to admit I'm pretty impressed. Anyway, I still have a few ideas up my sleeve...

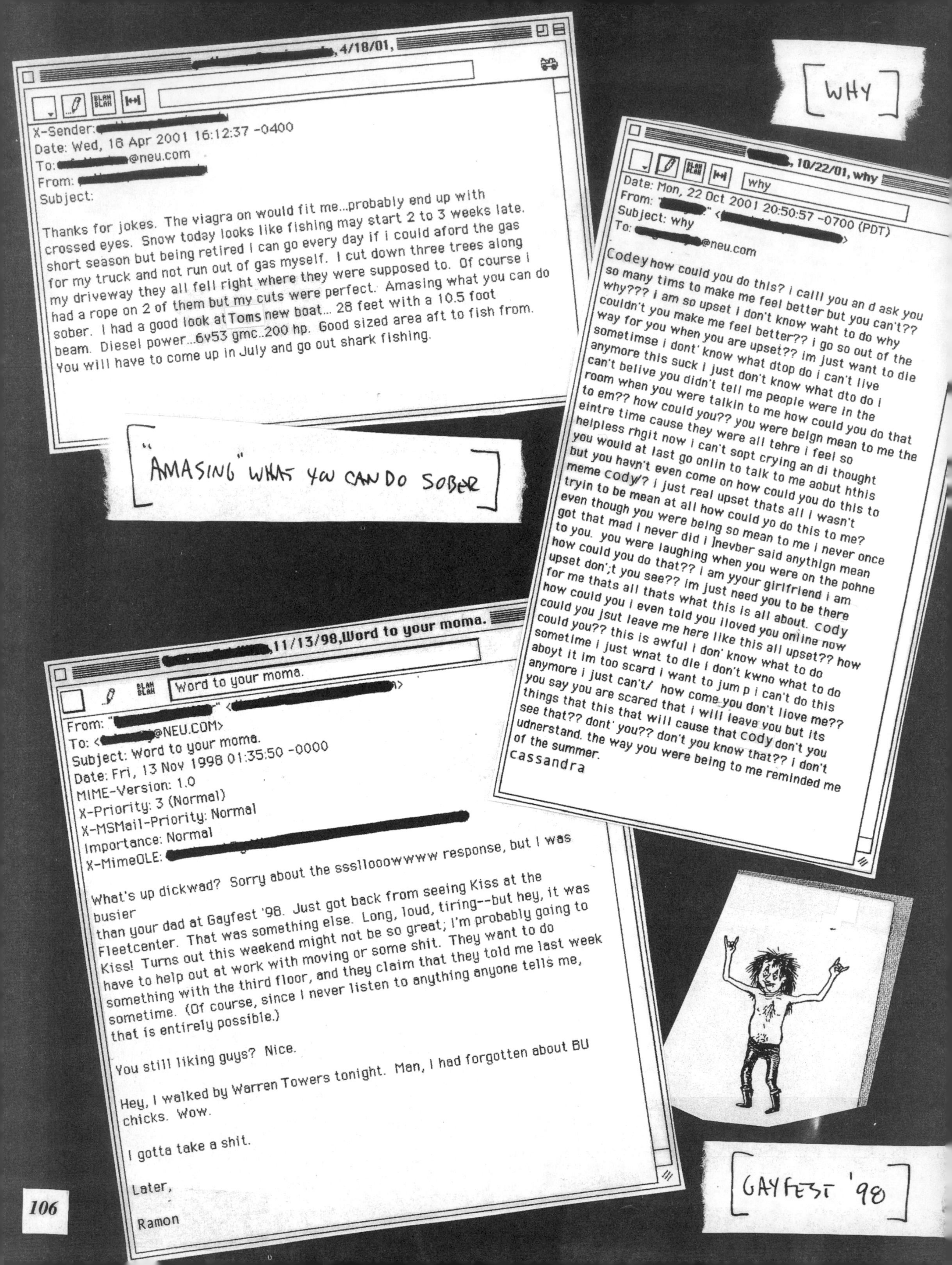

, 4/18/01,

X-Sender:
Date: Wed, 18 Apr 2001 16:12:37 -0400
To: @neu.com
From:
Subject:

Thanks for jokes. The viagra on would fit me...probably end up with crossed eyes. Snow today looks like fishing may start 2 to 3 weeks late. short season but being retired I can go every day if i could aford the gas for my truck and not run out of gas myself. I cut down three trees along my driveway they all fell right where they were supposed to. Of course i had a rope on 2 of them but my cuts were perfect. Amasing what you can do sober. I had a good look at Toms new boat... 28 feet with a 10.5 foot beam. Diesel power...6v53 gmc..200 hp. Good sized area aft to fish from. You will have to come up in July and go out shark fishing.



, 10/22/01, why

why

Date: Mon, 22 Oct 2001 20:50:57 -0700 (PDT)
From: " " <
Subject: why
To: @neu.com

Codey how could you do this? i calll you an d ask you so many tims to make me feel better but you can't?? why??? i am so upset i don't know waht to do why couldn't you make me feel better?? i go so out of the way for you when you are upset?? im just want to die sometimse i dont' know what dtop do i can't live anymore this suck i just don't know what dto do i can't belive you didn't tell me people were in the room when you were talkin to me how could you do that to em?? how could you?? you were beign mean to me the eintre time cause they were all tehre i feel so helpless rhgit now i can't sopt crying an di thought you would at last go onlin to talk to me aobut hthis but you havn't even come on how could you do this to meme cody/? i just real upset thats all i wasn't tryin to be mean at all how could yo do this to me? even though you were being so mean to me i never once got that mad i never did i ]nevber said anythign mean to you. you were laughing when you were on the pohne how could you do that?? i am yyour girlfriend i am upset don';t you see?? im just need you to be there for me thats all thats what this is all about. cody how could you i even told you iloved you online now could you jsut leave me here like this all upset?? how could you?? this is awful i don' know what to do sometime i just wnat to die i don't kwno what to do aboyt it im too scard i want to jum p i can't do this anymore i just can't/ how come you don't llove me?? you say you are scared that i will leave you but its things that this that will cause that cody don't you see that?? dont' you?? don't you know that?? i don't udnerstand. the way you were being to me reminded me of the summer.
cassandra

, 11/13/98, Word to your moma.

Word to your moma.

From: " " <
To: < @NEU.COM>
Subject: Word to your moma.
Date: Fri, 13 Nov 1998 01:35:50 -0000
MIME-Version: 1.0
X-Priority: 3 (Normal)
X-MSMail-Priority: Normal
Importance: Normal
X-MimeOLE:

What's up dickwad? Sorry about the sssllooowwww response, but I was busier than your dad at Gayfest '98. Just got back from seeing Kiss at the Fleetcenter. That was something else. Long, loud, tiring--but hey, it was Kiss! Turns out this weekend might not be so great; I'm probably going to have to help out at work with moving or some shit. They want to do something with the third floor, and they claim that they told me last week sometime. (Of course, since I never listen to anything anyone tells me, that is entirely possible.)

You still liking guys? Nice.

Hey, I walked by Warren Towers tonight. Man, I had forgotten about BU chicks. Wow.

I gotta take a shit.

Later,

Ramon

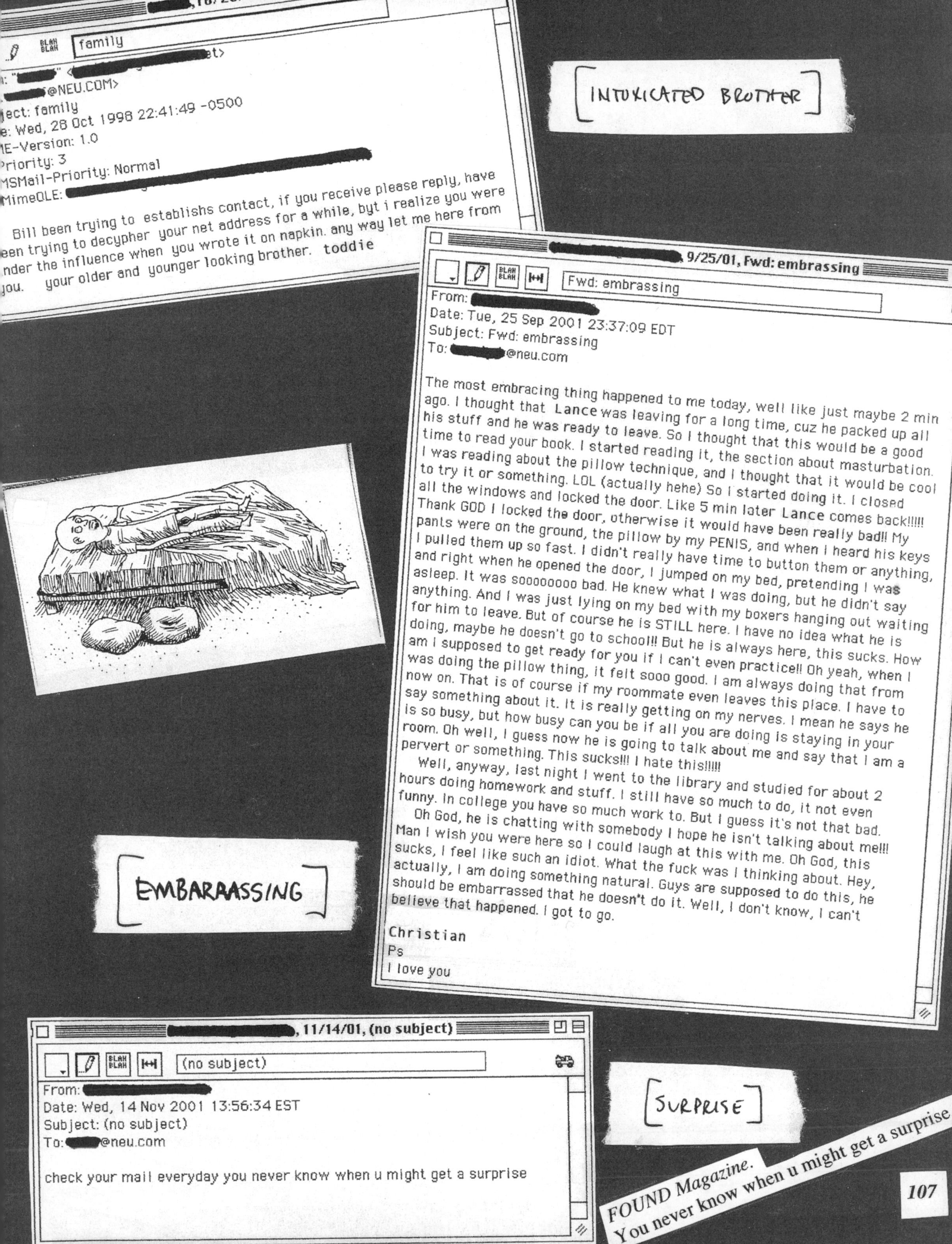

family

ject: family
e: Wed, 28 Oct 1998 22:41:49 -0500
IE-Version: 1.0
Priority: 3
MSMail-Priority: Normal
MimeOLE:

Bill been trying to establishs contact, if you receive please reply, have een trying to decypher your net address for a while, byt i realize you were nder the influence when you wrote it on napkin. any way let me here from you. your older and younger looking brother. toddie

[INTOXICATED BROTHER]

9/25/01, Fwd: embrassing

Fwd: embrassing

From:
Date: Tue, 25 Sep 2001 23:37:09 EDT
Subject: Fwd: embrassing
To: @neu.com

The most embracing thing happened to me today, well like just maybe 2 min ago. I thought that Lance was leaving for a long time, cuz he packed up all his stuff and he was ready to leave. So I thought that this would be a good time to read your book. I started reading it, the section about masturbation. I was reading about the pillow technique, and I thought that it would be cool to try it or something. LOL (actually hehe) So I started doing it. I closed all the windows and locked the door. Like 5 min later Lance comes back!!!!! Thank GOD I locked the door, otherwise it would have been really bad!! My pants were on the ground, the pillow by my PENIS, and when I heard his keys I pulled them up so fast. I didn't really have time to button them or anything, and right when he opened the door, I jumped on my bed, pretending I was asleep. It was soooooooo bad. He knew what I was doing, but he didn't say anything. And I was just lying on my bed with my boxers hanging out waiting for him to leave. But of course he is STILL here. I have no idea what he is doing, maybe he doesn't go to school!! But he is always here, this sucks. How am I supposed to get ready for you if I can't even practice!! Oh yeah, when I was doing the pillow thing, it felt sooo good. I am always doing that from now on. That is of course if my roommate even leaves this place. I have to say something about it. It is really getting on my nerves. I mean he says he is so busy, but how busy can you be if all you are doing is staying in your room. Oh well, I guess now he is going to talk about me and say that I am a pervert or something. This sucks!!! I hate this!!!!!

Well, anyway, last night I went to the library and studied for about 2 hours doing homework and stuff. I still have so much to do, it not even funny. In college you have so much work to. But I guess it's not that bad.

Oh God, he is chatting with somebody I hope he isn't talking about me!!! Man I wish you were here so I could laugh at this with me. Oh God, this sucks, I feel like such an idiot. What the fuck was I thinking about. Hey, actually, I am doing something natural. Guys are supposed to do this, he should be embarrassed that he doesn't do it. Well, I don't know, I can't believe that happened. I got to go.

Christian
Ps
I love you

[EMBARAASSING]

, 11/14/01, (no subject)

(no subject)

From:
Date: Wed, 14 Nov 2001 13:56:34 EST
Subject: (no subject)
To: @neu.com

check your mail everyday you never know when u might get a surprise

[SURPRISE]

FOUND *Magazine.*
You never know when u might get a surprise.

Cecilia Moss
English 111
3/1/03

Sex for Pay, the Reasons We Should

Who wouldn't like to fuck a whore? Picking up a woman on the street is easy, equally as easy as picking up a disease from that same woman. Prostitution is a growing evil in many American cities. What's worse is the fact that these women, often because it is a last resort, are not only beat-up by costumers and pimps, but also by the justice system. If prostitution were to be legalized it would put this underground activity of the streets under control, where it could be regulated and taxed.

If prostitution were to be legalized it could be taxed. Therefore the money could be put into good use, as well as tracked. So that the women, and men involved could not use the money for drugs or other illegal habits, or hobbies. Taxation of prostitution results in increased taxes collected by cities, counties and states. By taxation, prostitutes enjoy the benefits of unemployment insurance, disability insurance and social security; therefore giving prostitutes the choice of quitting their career in prostitution. Because prostitution is illegal it often forces the women to work for a "pimp". These pimps exploit their "ho's" and often take at least up to 50% of earnings. And I know, because I was a skeezy-ass whore in my youth. If legalized exploitation of these women, often including abuse, both physical and mental, would be eliminated. Cities would profit by legalizing and taxing prostitution, which[1] will result in a reduction of criminal prosecution costs. "Average arrest, court, and jail costs amount to nearly $2000 per arrest. Cities spend an average of $7.5 million on prostitution control every year. Ranging from

---

Moss Page 1

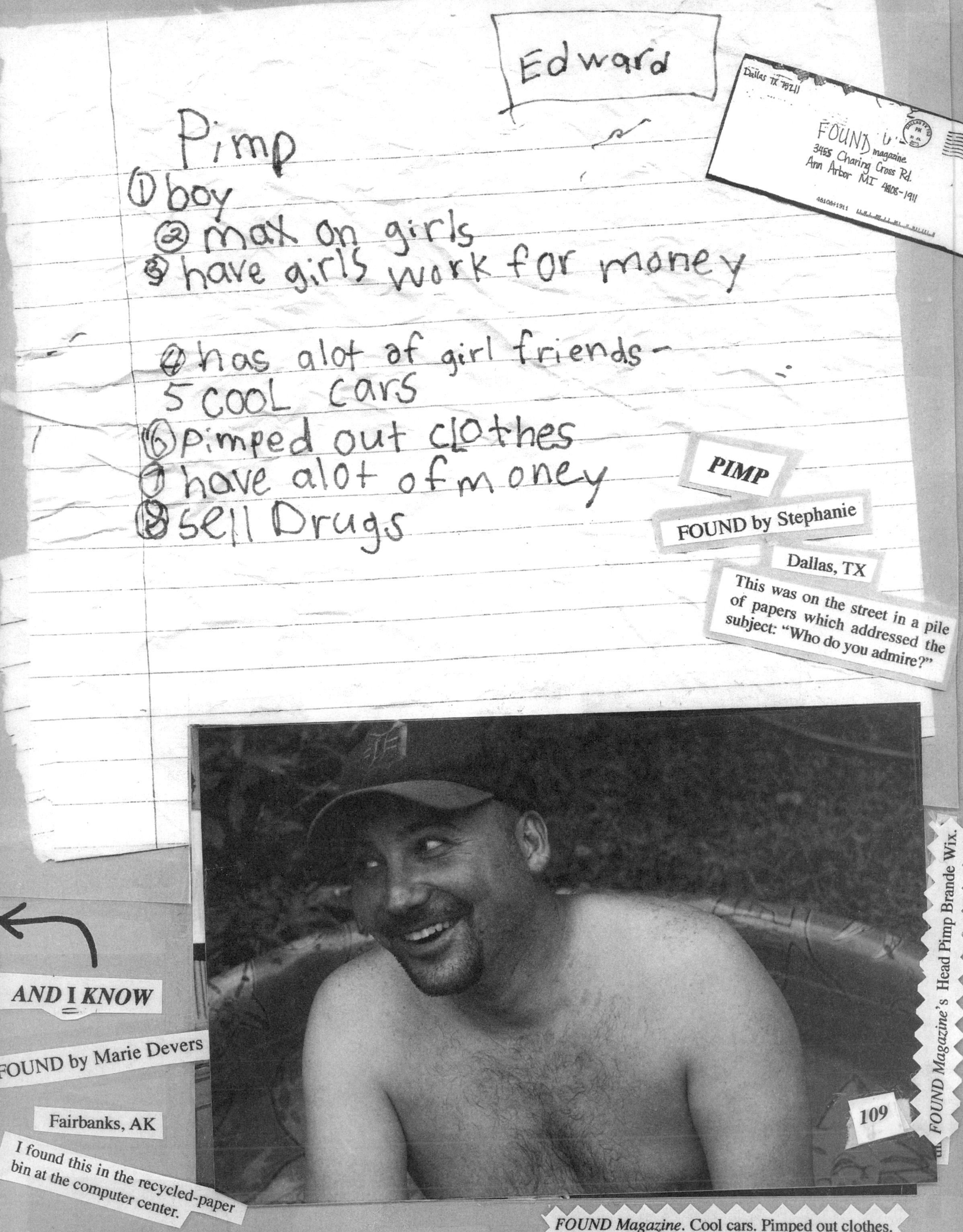
Edward
Pimp
① boy
② max on girls
③ have girls work for money
④ has alot of girl friends-
5 COOL cars
⑥ pimped out clothes
⑦ have alot of money
⑧ sell Drugs
Dallas TX 75211
FOUND magazine
3455 Charing Cross Rd.
Ann Arbor MI 48108-1911

**PIMP**

FOUND by Stephanie

Dallas, TX

This was on the street in a pile of papers which addressed the subject: "Who do you admire?"

***AND I KNOW***

FOUND by Marie Devers

Fairbanks, AK

I found this in the recycled-paper bin at the computer center.

*FOUND Magazine*'s Head Pimp Brande Wix.

*FOUND Magazine*. Cool cars. Pimped out clothes.

COLORADO PLATES

FOUND by Charla Engle

Fayetteville, AR

Hello. This note is going to seem very strange, and I have serious reservations about even writing it, but the circumstances are unusual, so I'll take a chance. I was on a walk tonight and I noticed that your car has Colorado plates. I met a girl several weeks ago (maybe 3), who was from Colorado, but I haven't run into her since. By chance, are you Julie who went to Creighton and is a pre-vet student @ the University? If so, I nervously introduced myself to you in the computer lab on the last day of summer session. You seemed like a very down to earth person and I hoped that we might meet again. I completely chickened out instead of giving you my phone number or asking you out, so I'm going out on a limb here by leaving a note. Trust me when I say that this is extremely out of character for me. I hope I haven't made you uncomfortable in anyway. You made an impression on me and I'd kick myself for ~~not~~ passing up a second opportunity to give you my #. Please don't take this as some kind of a crazy stalker note. Maybe I'll hear from you, though I'd be very surprised given how weird this seems. Take care.

—Alex 486-7579

P.S. If you're not Julie, then you should send this to Found Magazine b/c it will be accepted!

hey, check it out—it's the very first note that anyone has ever found and sent in to us which actually mentions FOUND Magazine!!



FOUND MAGAZINE - Pete: We met at Fergie's, 6/29, the FOUND Magazine reading. You came up to talk to Davy and I showed you my find: a sympathy card for Sergio with a Spanish phrase in it. You're cute, and I should have talked to you more and asked for your number. Interested?

↖ from the Philadelphia City-Paper classifieds

While I was busy getting drunk in celebration of landing a new job, young Alex was busy wondering if my Denver-based Volvo belonged to the one who got away.

On July 14, I found this note attached to the front windshield of my car in the main square of Fayetteville, Arkansas. Alex seems pretty sure you guys will like it, so, after a couple months of deliberating/forgetting to send it, I'm finally passing it along.

—C.E.

# WARNING

The iguana is loose on the porch. Before entering, make damn sure that she is not going to bolt out the door when you open it; Also, be sure to close screen door til it latches shut!!!!

Thank you

MAKE DAMN SURE

FOUND by Dan Kallman

Northfield, MN

illustration by Paul Koob

screenplay
DAD Builds
Houses, they always
Burn to the ground.
always lived in a
Burning house.
DAD is having some kind
of Japanese influence.
the west builds
monuments forever
EAST build wooden
huts that Burn
down every 100 years.
IN THE END IT TURNS
out that — he
was lighting them!!
WHY AM I
ALWAYS
BROKE?!
FUCK
LIFE
NEWCASTLE BROWN ALE
Back in its native North East of England, Newcastle Brown Ale is affectionately referred to as "The Dog". Nobody is quite sure as to how this nickname originated, but on most evenings in Newcastle you can hear the men leaving their houses for the local pub, shouting back to their wives in their local Geordie dialect: "I'm just gan doon the road to tak the dog for a walk!"
NJ, NH, PA, RI NO REFUND, MI 10¢ REFUND
NY, DE, MA, VT, CT, ME 5¢ DEPOSIT OK+ IA.
CA REDEMPTION VALUE
OREGON 5¢ REFUND
0 88345 10051 7
505811
GOVERNMENT WARNING: (1) ACCORDING TO THE SURGEON GENERAL, WOMEN SHOULD NOT DRINK ALCOHOLIC BEVERAGES DURING PREGNANCY BECAUSE OF THE RISK OF BIRTH DEFECTS. (2) CONSUMPTION OF ALCOHOLIC BEVERAGES IMPAIRS YOUR ABILITY TO DRIVE A CAR OR OPERATE MACHINERY, AND MAY CAUSE HEALTH PROBLEMS.
I WANNA GET FREAKY WIT YOU AND A LOBSTER.
OHHH YO SO GROSS.

***THE TWIST*** FOUND by Debbie Steinberg, Ann Arbor, MI

***INSUFFICIENT FUNDS*** FOUND by Tom Fitzgerald, Nevada City, CA

***THREESOME*** FOUND by Adam Sherlock Corson, Indianapolis, IN

Found this little sketch at a bar called the Alley Cat, drawn on the back of a Newcastle Brown Ale label, a fitting canvas for the work of this Saturday night artist.

—A.S.C.

this photo FOUND by Katie and Nina, St. Louis, MO

Hey Anthony

Hope this gets to you in time to get a new laptop before you have to give up penelope:

Thanks

Gruppo Cordenons

***GIVING UP PENELOPE***
FOUND by Brooke Catalena, Austin, TX

I ♡ Eddie's Jean's don't you?

***EANS*** FOUND by Annie,
Glenbrook South HS, Glenview, IL

Wendy ♡

GUM!

***GUM*** FOUND by Annie, Glenview, IL

# REWARD !!

(8-1-01) HAVE YOU SEEN THIS THIRD LUNG WELL SOMEONE **STOLE IT!!!!** WE ARE OFFERING A **REWARD** FOR THE RETURN OR LEAD TO WHOM HAS MY **PROPERTY** MAYBE YOU SEEN SOMEONE CARING A WHITE TARP IN THE MIDDLE OF THE NIGHT?

**IF YOU HAVE IT, I WILL FIND YOU!!!!! Trust me**

***YELLOW AND RED COVER, THIRD LUNG WITH 3 HOSES ATACHED***

**ANY INFO PLEASE CALL I HAVE MONEY FOR YOU**

**(954) or or**

***THIRD LUNG*** FOUND by Matthew Ericson, Hollywood, FL

***BEFORE*** FOUND by Genevieve Eustis, Brooklyn, NY

# SEPTEMBER 11TH FINDS

I was at
when I see an
I was so surprised,
frome a window i
but you could see t
explosion you could
how loud it was.
people standing arou
little ants. Moving ver
saw firefig
trying to threw
took a lot of time
It all looked fake
a while they got it
that was left was
of fire everywhere

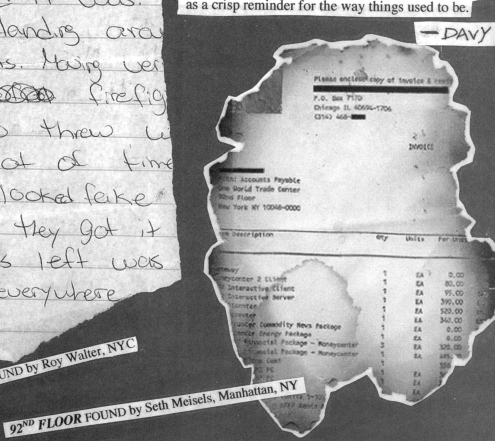

**IT ALL LOOKED FAKE** FOUND by Roy Walter, NYC

One of the strangest and most amazing things about the fall of the World Trade Centers is the fact that so much paper survived the devastation. Concrete and steel was vaporized, while bits of singed notes and letters and financial reports (like the one below) drifted down into the streets and even people's backyards as far as fifteen miles away.

Meanwhile, a torn scrap from a kid's journal (left) found near a lower Manhattan school, recounted the horror of that morning. And a snapshot (above) found in an alley months after September 11th, served as a crisp reminder for the way things used to be.

—DAVY

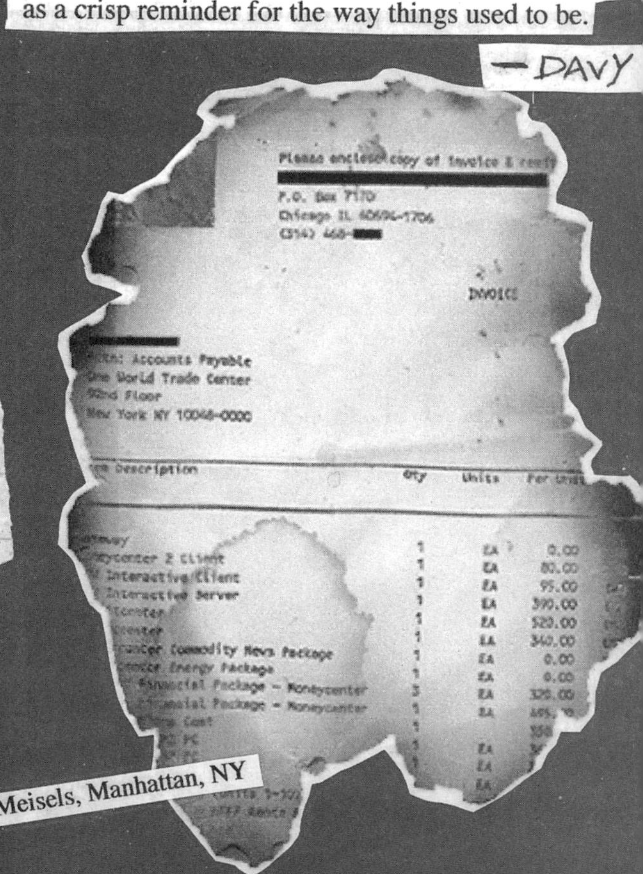

Please enclose copy of invoice &
P.O. Box 7170
Chicago IL 60696-1706
(314) 468-

INVOICE

Attn: Accounts Payable
One World Trade Center
92nd Floor
New York NY 10048-0000

| Description | Qty | Units | Per Unit |
| --- | --- | --- | --- |
| Gateway | | | |
| Moneycenter 2 Client | 1 | EA | 0.00 |
| Interactive Client | 1 | EA | 80.00 |
| Interactive Server | 1 | EA | 95.00 |
| | 1 | EA | 390.00 |
| | 1 | EA | 520.00 |
| Commodity News Package | 1 | EA | 340.00 |
| Energy Package | 1 | EA | 0.00 |
| Financial Package - Moneycenter | 1 | EA | 0.00 |
| Financial Package - Moneycenter | 3 | EA | 320.00 |
| Cost | 1 | EA | 695. |

**92ND FLOOR** FOUND by Seth Meisels, Manhattan, NY

PREMONITION

FOUND

by Davy Rothbart

# MISSING

## One World Trade Center, 100th Floor

**Height:** 5' 8"
**Weight:** 185 lbs.
**Hair:** Brown w/ grey beard
**Eyes:** Blue
**Age:** 53

## Roger Mark Rasweiler

**(a.k.a., R. Mark Rasweiler or Mark Rasweiler)**

**Any information, please call**

**908- *or* 908-**

***or* 908-**

A few days after the September 11th attack, I walked down through Lower Manhattan toward the site where the World Trade Centers had stood. I guess I wanted to see things for myself to help get my mind around what had happened. Six blocks away I paused and spent a few minutes sorting through a damp pile of papers which had survived the collapse and had come to rest in a tiny fenced-in triangular lot of weeds and brush.

Most of the stuff was unremarkable—office memos and stock quotes, page after page filled with numbers that meant nothing to me. I found a torn half of a handwritten note that said, "—is the way if you ask me!" I also found a map of Branson, Missouri. Then, at the bottom of the pile, I was stunned and spooked to discover this MISSING flyer.

I'd seen plenty of flyers with faces of the missing; they're posted up all over the city. But for a long dazed and dreamlike moment, it seemed to me that this one—buried among other paper debris from the towers—must have sailed from the towers as well, which meant it had been printed before the morning of the 11th. The idea that someone had *known*, had made this flyer before it would have made sense to anyone, boggled and terrified me. A second later I came to my senses—obviously someone had dropped it there in the last couple of days; maybe they'd even posted it on the fence and the rain and wind had brought it down. Still, though, that initial shock, that strange, eerie pocket of unreality, stays with me. —DAVY

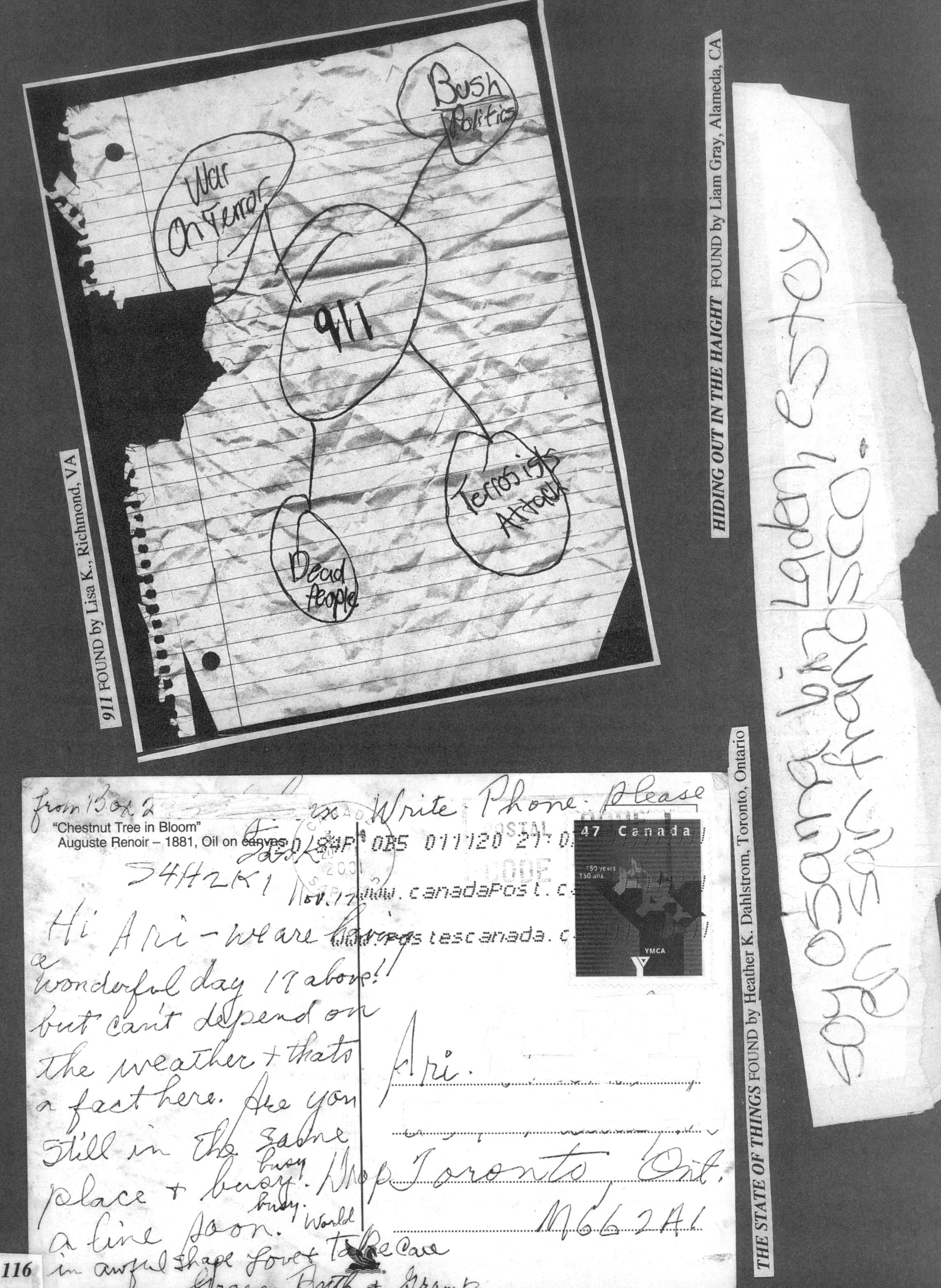

*911* FOUND by Lisa K., Richmond, VA


*HIDING OUT IN THE HAIGHT* FOUND by Liam Gray, Alameda, CA

from Box 2
Write Phone: please
"Chestnut Tree in Bloom"
Auguste Renoir – 1881, Oil on canvas
S4H2K1 Nov. 17
www.canadapost.ca
www.postescanada.ca
47 Canada
150 years
150 ans
YMCA

Hi Ari – we are having a wonderful day 17 above!! but can't depend on the weather + that's a fact here. Are you still in the same busy place + busy. Drop a line soon. World in awful shape Love + take Care
Gram. Ruth + Gramp.

Ari.
Toronto Ont.
M6G 2A1

*THE STATE OF THINGS* FOUND by Heather K. Dahlstrom, Toronto, Ontario

Mr. : A. S. HAMAL
BAGHDAD,
P.O. BOX : 48108
IRAQ

*Dear Sir:*

It's my pleasure to correspond your air line, and quite interested in your region, as my work which that in a connection with this type of air line and my hobbying of collecting catalogs and all things there fore. I sent you the depth of respectability because you are prove your ability in raising the quality and kindness in your plane, so I'd like to get some details about your air line for me and for my close friend such as ..
((Catalogs, posters, and photo picture )) or any thing just for a keepsake from you.

Thanking you in advance and remain with kindest regard.

My friend's a dress :
Mr : Etienne F.
Fahoud Mahanti Al-Eva
P.O. BOX: 35' IRAQ .

Yours
**Mr. : A. S. HAMAL**

**THE LINK BETWEEN SADDAM AND OSAMA**
FOUND by Heather McCabe

One guy went to register like he was suppos~~e~~d to comp~~letely~~ disappeared.

where?

You have to register at gov't + buildings and no one knows where this guy and several other guys who registered are implying our gov't did something with them, kill them, torture, whose knows

***THE DISAPPEARED***
FOUND by Joe Martinez, Santa Barbara, CA

this drawing FOUND by Michael Gray, L.A., CA, one week after Sept. 11th

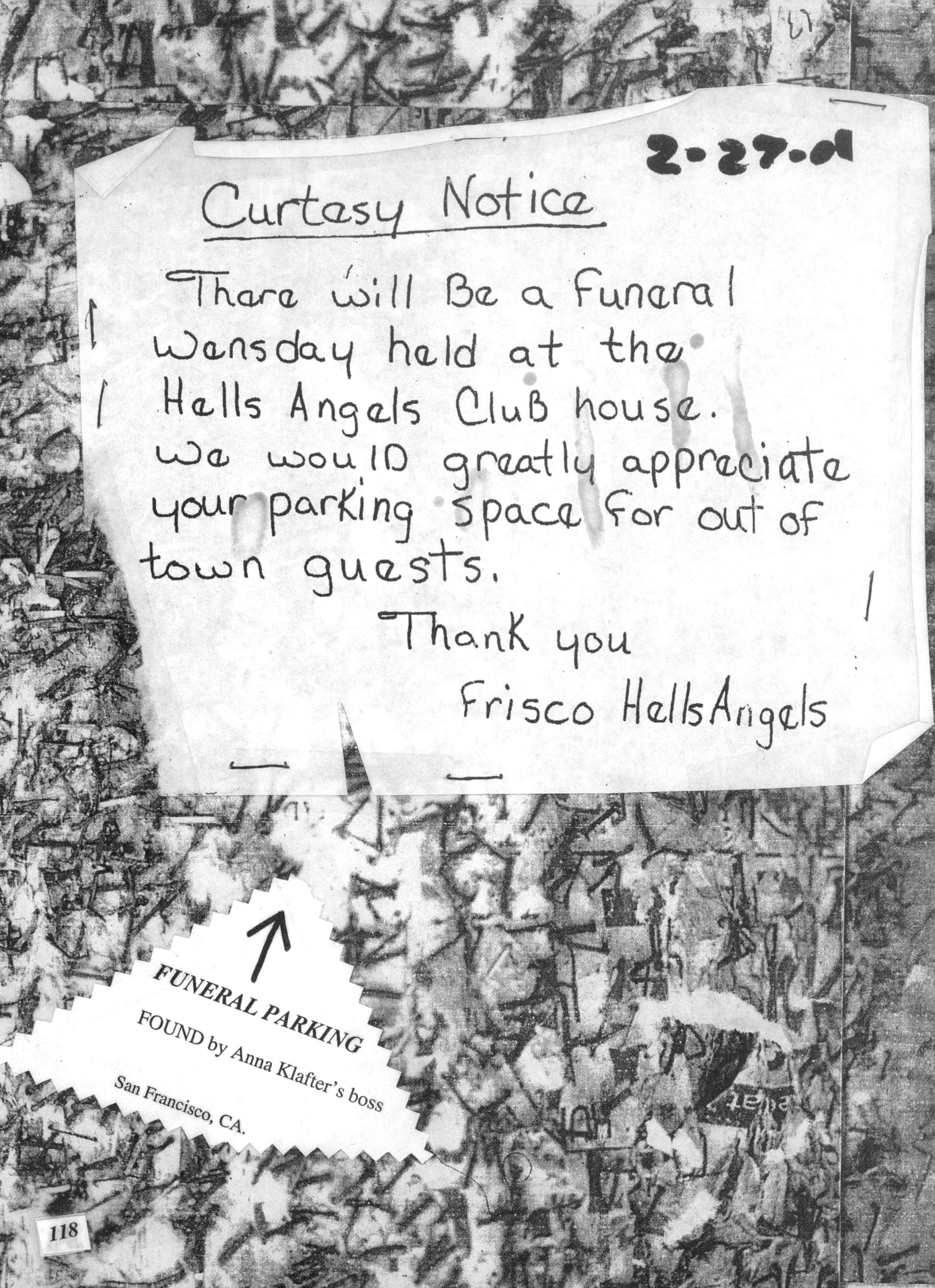
2-27-01
Curtasy Notice
There will Be a funeral
Wensday held at the
Hells Angels CluB house.
We woulD greatly appreciate
your parking space for out of
town guests.
Thank you
Frisco HellsAngels

FUNERAL PARKING

FOUND by Anna Klafter's boss

San Francisco, CA.

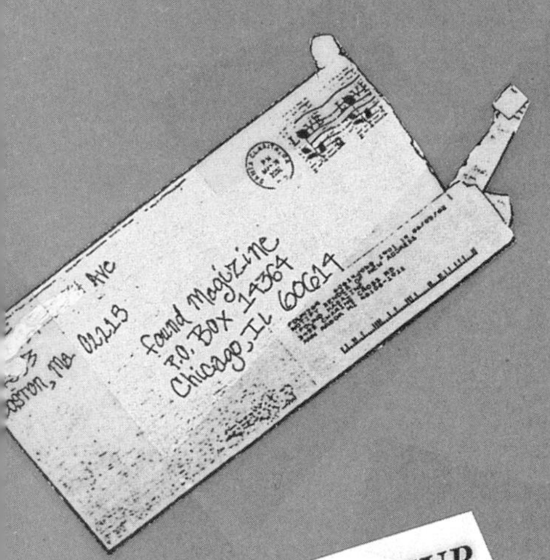


# BARF BAG BREAKUP

FOUND by Sarah Zurier

People will write on just about anything. FOUND at LAX airport.

—S.Z.

TO FACE YOUR FEARS, I'm HERE BUT I CAN'T SHOW YOU HOW.

WHEN I LOOK INTO YOUR EYES YOUR SOUL TOUCHES ME. It's LIKE A DRUG.

WE CAN BE FRIENDS BUT RIGHT NOW YOU SHOULD TAKE CARE OF THINGS (FIND OUT FOR YOURSELF

I'm sorry to have to say this in an email, but I'd rather not have this conversation over the phone.

I think this is it for us. It has been for awhile. You don't even know how much of a tremendous loss this is for me. INSIDE OF YOUR WALLS IS SOMEONE I RESPECT MORE THAN ANYONE ELSE IN THE WORLD. YOU DON'T EVEN KNOW ~~HOW MUCH IS INSIDE YOU~~ WHAT YOUR CAPABLE OF. WHO YOUR TRYING TO HIDE IS VERY MUCH THE PERSON I'D LIKE TO BE.

I HOPE IT WILL BE EASIER

## GUESS I NEED TO

FOUND by Cormac Symington

San Francisco, CA

KENDRA DOES NOT MEAN ONE BIT OF ANYTHING TO ME, NOT ONE GOD DAMN THING! YOU ARE THE LOVE OF MY LIFE, & SHE IS SO OUT OF MY REALM OF THINKING THAT I DIDNT THINK TO GO THROUGH ALL OF POSSESIONS & RID MYSELF

(front)

I OFTEN THINK OF US MAKING LOVE, I MISS YOUR TOUCH. I YEARN FOR YOU. YOUR HANDS ARE SO MARVELOUS AND YOUR KISS IS EXPLOSIVE. YOUR GENTLENESS. I WANT TO FEEL YOU. WHEN WE MAKE LOVE ITS LIKE MY PHYSICAL BODY IS THERE WITH YOU, BUT MY SPIRIT IS IN A WONDERFUL PLACE.

**A WONDERFUL PLACE** FOUND by Justin Rhody, Columbus, OH

## *BEACH LEAK*

FOUND by Charles Negendank

Knoxville, TN

Found in the U. of Tennessee photo lab, Art & Architecture Building, Floor 4. It looks like the guy is peeing, but it's kinda pretty.

—C.N.

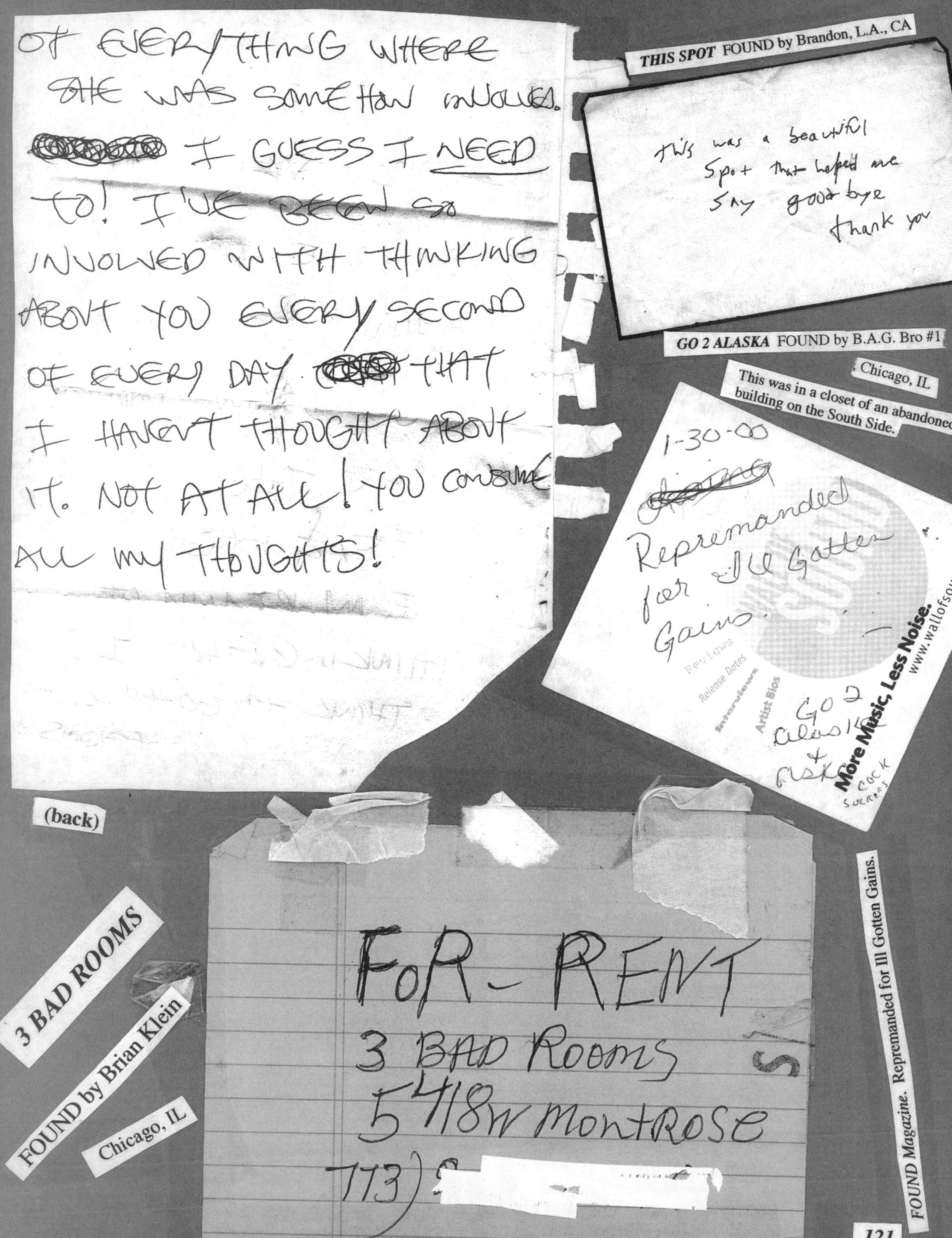
OF EVERYTHING WHERE
SHE WAS SOMEHOW INVOLVED.
I GUESS I NEED
TO! I'VE BEEN SO
INVOLVED WITH THINKING
ABOUT YOU EVERY SECOND
OF EVERY DAY THAT
I HAVEN'T THOUGHT ABOUT
IT. NOT AT ALL! YOU CONSUME
ALL MY THOUGHTS!
(back)
THIS SPOT FOUND by Brandon, L.A., CA
This was a beautiful
Spot that helped me
Say good bye
thank you
GO 2 ALASKA FOUND by B.A.G. Bro #1, Chicago, IL
This was in a closet of an abandoned building on the South Side.
1-30-00
Repremanded
for Ill Gotten
Gains.
Reviews
Release Dates
Interviews
Artist Bios
GO 2
alaska
+
fiske
COCK
SUCKERS
More Music, Less Noise.
www.wallofsound.com
3 BAD ROOMS
FOUND by Brian Klein
Chicago, IL
FOR - RENT
3 BAD ROOMS
5418 W MONTROSE
773)

FOUND *Magazine.* Repremanded for Ill Gotten Gains.

*AJ,*

*We have your binder. You will never see it again unless you leave a sum of $3.50 directly under the clock to the left of the door at precisely 1:15. Please do not inform any teacher of this transaction. If you mess this up you WILL regret it.*

*If you do not comply than you will never see it again.*

**BLACKMAIL**

FOUND by Jennifer Jones

Milwaukee, WI.

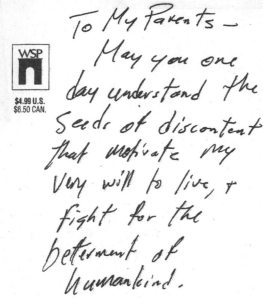

To My Parents—
May you one day understand the seeds of discontent that motivate my very will to live, & fight for the betterment of humankind.
Love,
Jon
1998

$4.99 U.S.
$6.50 CAN.

JN

# A SPECTER IS HAUNTING EUROPE— THE SPECTER OF COMMUNISM!

**Thus Marx and Engels introduce their program for social change.**

More than any other political or economic work written within the last hundred years, *The Communist Manifesto* has influenced and reshaped the course of history, not only erupting in such cataclysmic events as the Russian Revolution, but also lurking beneath the subversive antagonism toward democracy apparent in the Cold War and the hostility of many developing nations.

**About the Editor**

Francis B. Randall, Ph.D., has taught at both Amherst College and Columbia University and is currently on the faculty of Sarah Lawrence College. He has edited Thomas Hobbes's *Leviathan* and Bernard Pares's *Russia Between Reform and Revolution: Fundamentals of Russian History and Character*, and is the author of several critical articles on Communism and on Russian writers of the nineteenth century.

## OUR SON, THE COMMUNIST

FOUND by Paul Nama

Portland, OR

*I* bought this copy of *The Communist Manifesto* at a used bookstore. I imagine its previous owner as a young man who did not get along well with his parents. He gave them the book as an honest attempt at philosophical reconciliation, and his parents cried because their son had not only gone astray but was a Commie to boot. They did not read one word and sold the book at their earliest opportunity. The mint condition of the book—and its unbroken spine—supports this theory.

—P.N.

bed watching your naked body; one of them was gay and his stare was innocent, but the other stared with tainted glory. Middle of the night now, maybe one or two. It was a Thursday, the first day in August. Two packs of Beer and deceite brought on this un-godly act. You are gay girl, you are gay. Failing to consider your girlfriends dismay. what exactly were you thinking? You insist that it was due to the ruling of your self-hatred. as heterosexual boy lay in our bed, next to you, his drunken, sex hands caressed your exposed thigh. He smiled as you glidded joy though his hair and on his head. He climed on top of your half naked body Putting his lips all over yours. Then you lay on top of him, with your hand on his stomach and kiss him everywhere, with a smile and a grine. Yet in your lustful like, you still swear you hated it, you hated him. SURE! In our bed, in my house you fucked beall over. Upon my return, to say my goodbyes, you beg your love, you promi your truths. Hurt and weery, I keep you in your pure. Jaded and distrought I am forced to work through the curse. And yes, you should know my love, at times I have thought my decision to stay a great mistake. Night after night, Naked, sleeping with you in the very same Bed. Four months have passed and in it numerous struggles, all that indirectly refer back to him, that, i Yes we have struggled together, and in thoughs pains we have come to love eachother deeper. So now Friend, with this newly aquierec connection; with such deep love what could you possibly do to sho me such softness? What tender gifts do you bring? A Flow a kiss, maybe a ring. No.... I don't think so. Four months Later, after the rebuild of these broken temple walls, after th lost trust has been retrieved, after you've asked me to be your queen. You go to the Lovely boy, the same Lucky boy and you Fuck him. You get in his car, knowingly having it planned to allow his penitration. You sit in his house, on his couch, you slide the condom onto his hard cock, and you squeez your pussy into his hardness. You Fucked him. Surely I am so pleased with such a nice gift from my loving girlfriend. And after your done, you so kindly pick up the phone and ca me, drunk out of your mind, at 3:00 in the morning. Saddened to be awakened in mid-night to your absence, I fall back asleep Two hours Later I am I opened again to your naked body crawling into my bed. You dirty Bitch, you just fucked a man and now your crawling into Fuck your patner with th contaminatd remains of your Flesh. You cry, you say you hate yourself, you beg my love once again. I retreat, you've ravished me

Monday, December 16, 2002

**THE FIRST DAY IN AUGUST**

FOUND by J Provine

Sacramento, CA

1118 Jefferson, St.
Savannah, Ga.
April,18,1928

Dear Sweatheart,

Mildred, will you please tell me whether you love me or not. As you know I am graduating this year. Our principal asked me to go away and study to be a Priest. I told him that Iwould asked my daddy. I did asked him and he said that I could go if I wanted to. Mildred I have always loved you and I always will. If you really love me I will not go, because if I tell the principal yes, Ican not see you for ten years. So please Mildred, tell me "yes " or "no ". TELL ME NOTHING BUT THE TRUTH?

Your loving sweetheart

James

P. S. DON'T FORGET NOTHING BUT THE TRUTH.

FOUND by Jeff Brown
Savannah, GA

FOUND by Rebecca Green
Arkadelphia, AR

羅拔臣

HEY Found!
I found this spooky note in the pants that I got at the thrift store.
Spooky yes? Bust the Action
Brent

January 29, 2000

Dear Family @ 1100 Thornapple Lane,

Thank you so much for your input regarding the "why is the man dead with a sword in his back in the snow?" conversation between myself and my 4 year old son… it was a true joy, I assure you.

I would like to help with your "families" necessary counseling. Your children or your neighbors children must need it for obvious reasons but you as the parents might want to take me up on my offer due to allowing it to stay in your yard for days on end. This offer is genuine, so please allow me to help with the counseling for this real to life sickness (please let me know the names of the neighbor children so I can get you a group discount). I have left my number and return address at the bottom feel free to contact me at your convenience.

As a return favor for my offer of help I would ask that you let me know where your or these children go to school so that my boys are assured of never being around them.

Thank you in advance for your time. Best of luck in your future.

Ted

WHY IS THE MAN DEAD WITH A SWORD IN HIS BACK IN THE SNOW?

FOUND by Brent McAllister

Edmond, OK.

# BED WITH A HISTORY

FOUND (and illustrated) by Lev

San Francisco, CA

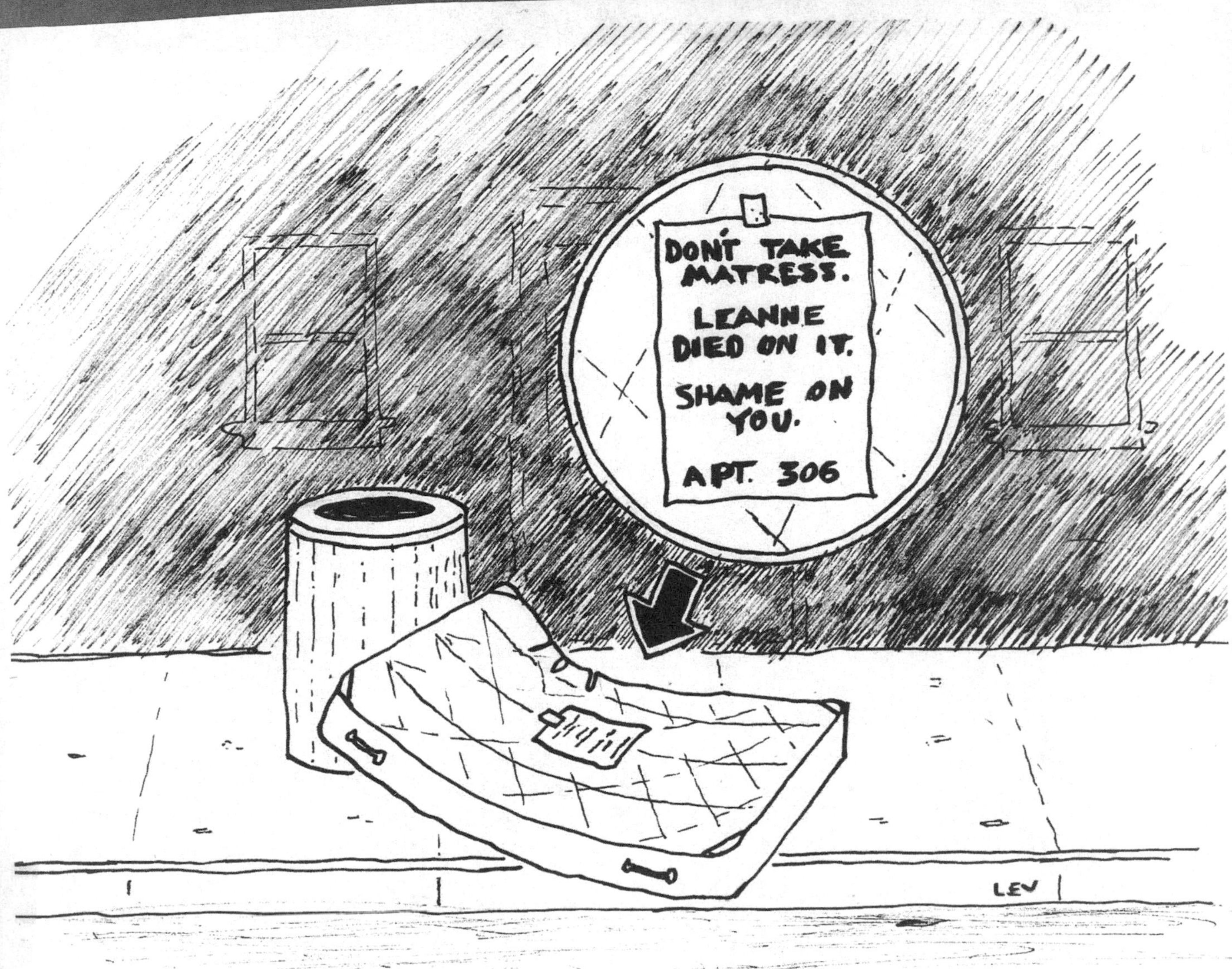


I was biking home last September, and I saw a mattress lying in front of an apartment building with this note attached to it.

—LEV

# THE ELEPHANT BECAME ANGRY

FOUND by Wendy Dorr

Brooklyn Heights, NY

at Kinko's on Court Street

On July 10, 1995, my family, friends and associates attended a circus performance held at Forest Park, Woodhaven New York.

The circus performance was just about over. They were bringing out the elephants. My godsister (Sherri ) and I went to stand on top of the barriers, (barriers were approximately 12" - 16" wide and approx. 12" - 16" deep, which made up the performance ring) to take pictures of the elephants as they come out.

The elephants came on around the ring about 200 degree angle before making a complete 360 degree circle, as to where the elephants are now facing myself. The third elephant bumped into the second, the second into the first, and the first into the trainer. The trainer then took his switch and hit the first elephant across the ear. The elephant kneeled down to the ground (only his front legs and face) and then came up with the loudest roar I've ever heard in my life. It appeared to me that the elephant became angry. All of a sudden the elephant went berserk. He began to run wildly out of control. He then started running towards the seats where we all were sitting. (Mind you I am not sitting in my seat, I am still standing on top of the (barriers). I immediately yelled Oh my God the kids. I started in the direction towards the kids but had to stop dead in my tracks because the elephant was still going in that direction. The elephant kicked the barriers causing it to fly into one of the girls who was trying to run with her baby, causing her to fall to the ground. At this time no one was sitting in there seats. They were all trying to run to the back of the tent. They had to run otherwise the elephant would have trampled them.

I thank God to this day that I got up from my seat to take pictures. The elephant would have definitely trampled me because I was suffering from a back injury, in which I could barely walk more or less run.

I witnessed the barrier hitting a lady who was running with her approx. 6-8 month old baby, and people stepping on her back while she laid on the ground with her baby underneath her. Meanwhile the elephant was still charging in that direction.

I witnessed my Godmother (Odelia ) trying to run with her cane to the back of the tent as fast as she could. My daughter saw that her grandmother was having difficultly, she stopped to help her. I heard her yell hurry up grandma, as she grabbed her grandma's hand. All of a sudden my godmother fell. Everyone was running, pushing and shoving to make it to the back of the tent. It was the only place for them to go. The elephant was still headed in their direction.

The trainers were trying desperately to calm the elephant or to stop it from running wildly, but was unsuccessful.

The seats where we were sitting approximately 1-12 rows were now

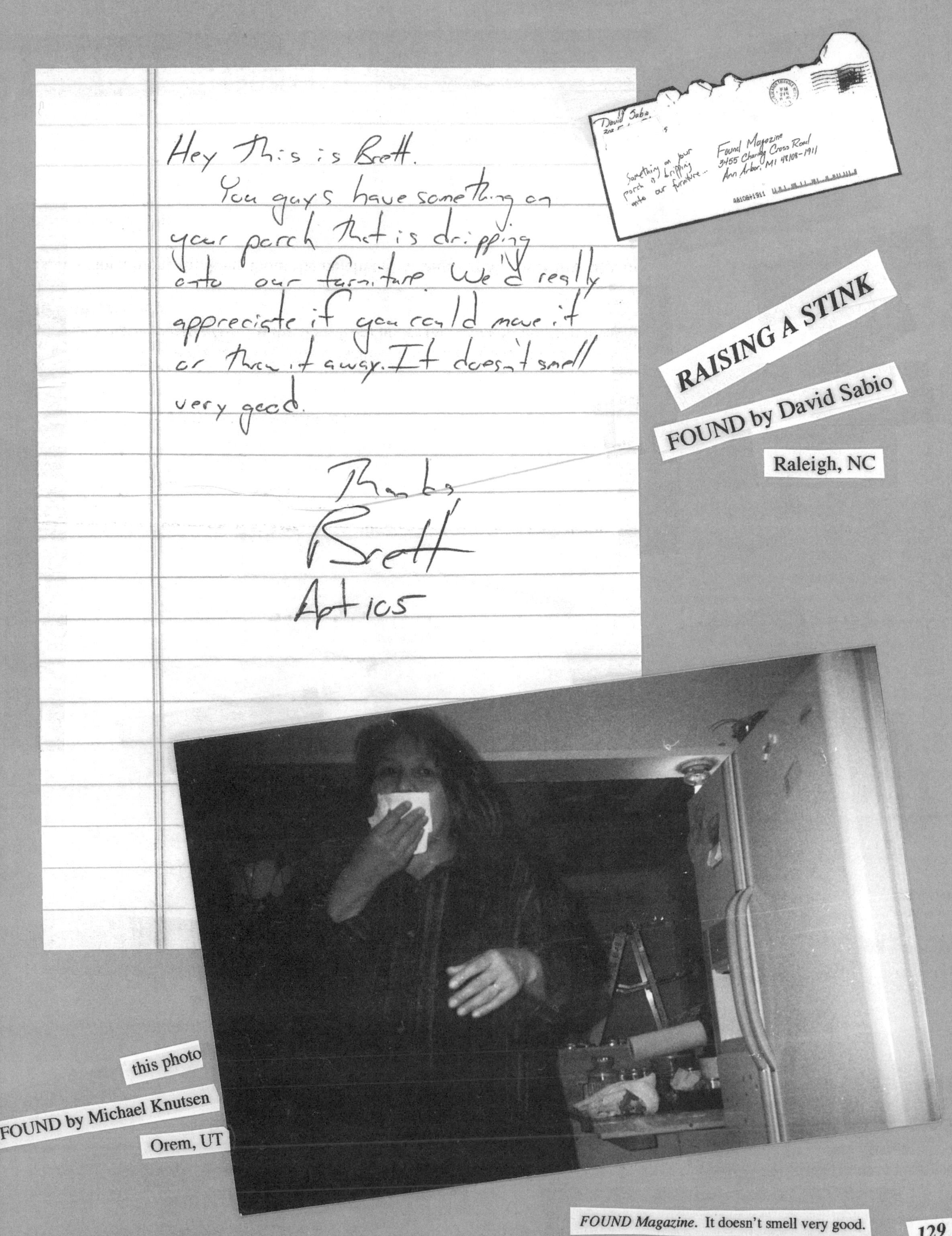
Hey This is Brett.
You guys have something on your porch that is dripping onto our furniture. We'd really appreciate if you could move it or throw it away. It doesn't smell very good.

Thanks
Brett
Apt 105



RAISING A STINK

FOUND by David Sabio

Raleigh, NC

this photo

FOUND by Michael Knutsen

Orem, UT

LOST BLANKIE

* Lost Wed. Evening 6·18·03
* yellow 1 side/white 1 side
* soft cotton knit
* John Lennon animal DRAWINGS
* About 3 feet square
* Lost on West side near Slauson School + West Park

CALL

FOUND by Cat Lardas, Ann Arbor, MI

also FOUND by Claudette Stern!

HAVE YOU SEEN MY LITTLE GIRLS BEST FRIEND?

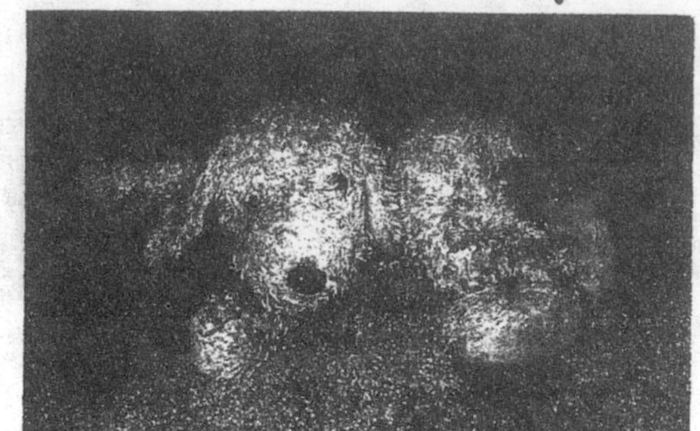

HE IS BEIGE + VERY WORN

IF YOU HAVE ANY INFORMATION PLEASE CALL US AT.

510

FOUND by Joanna Vaughn, Oakland, CA

# LOST FLYERS

I NEED A MIRACLE!

HUGE REWARD

On July 4th, AT 7:30 P.M. I accidentally left a shopping bag filled with my babies (my favorite dolls) on christopher + Bleecker st.

I really miss them, they are like children to me.

please call (212)

OR (201)

CONTACT

christopher st. N.Y.

I am desperate to see them again please help!

REWARD: $150.00

On Friday July, 4th, I lost a bag of dolls. Someone found them and returned all the dolls to me except for 1 doll that he gave to someone at the STONEWALL BAR. The doll was a chucky doll.

If anyone has this doll I will pay $150.00 for his return.

Please call (212)

Thank you so much!

I miss the little guy.

FOUND by Jon, New York, NY

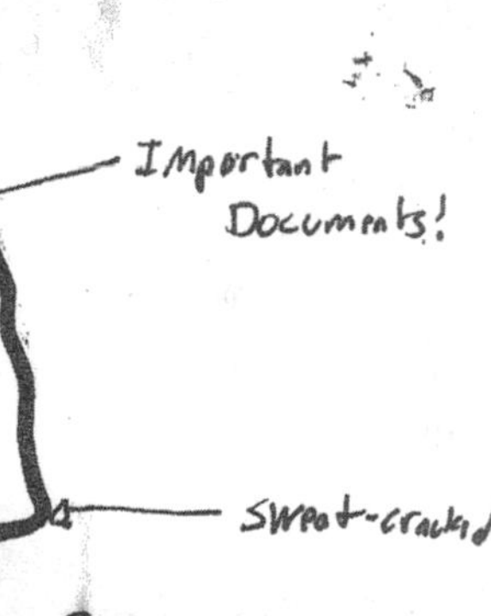

CAll:
412

# LOST

WED. MARCH 12.

Approx. 2:45 p.m.

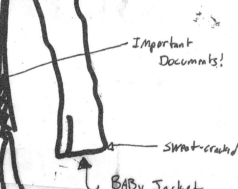

Quilted!

SCRAtches!
ABRASIONS!
FUNNY Smells!
AMERICAN MADE!
1 OWNER!

Dougher's teething MARKS!

Ripped INNER sleeve!

Black!

Important Documents!

Sweat-cracked

BABy Jacket Stuffed in sleeve!

REWARD: 100$ CASH + CASE OF good Beer OR 2 cases of O.K. Beer + Deepest Respect

Seaquence of Events: I set it on top of the car when I put My Baby Daughter into her car Seat. SHe had been cranky + Fussy + crying since 6.a.m, until something finally tickled her fancy and she Laughed her wonderful Baby laugh and I forgot about being broke. I forgot about my anxity over being a New parent. I forgot about imminent WAR. I forgot My Jackit. Then I drove away. The prize possesion that Made Me Happy caused me to forget the prize possesion that MADE ME HAPPY. I know what FINDERS/KEEPERS means, AND I Realize the Jacket and its contents CAN Be Replaced as they are only MATERIAL Goods, but, MAN, I sure would LIKE that JACKET BACK

412-

FOUND by Scott Robishaw, Pittsburgh, PA

Good news—most things that are lost are eventually FOUND. The jacket was recovered, as was the lost blankie and stuffed animal. Meanwhile, the Chucky doll still has not made it home.

~DAVY

# The NBA

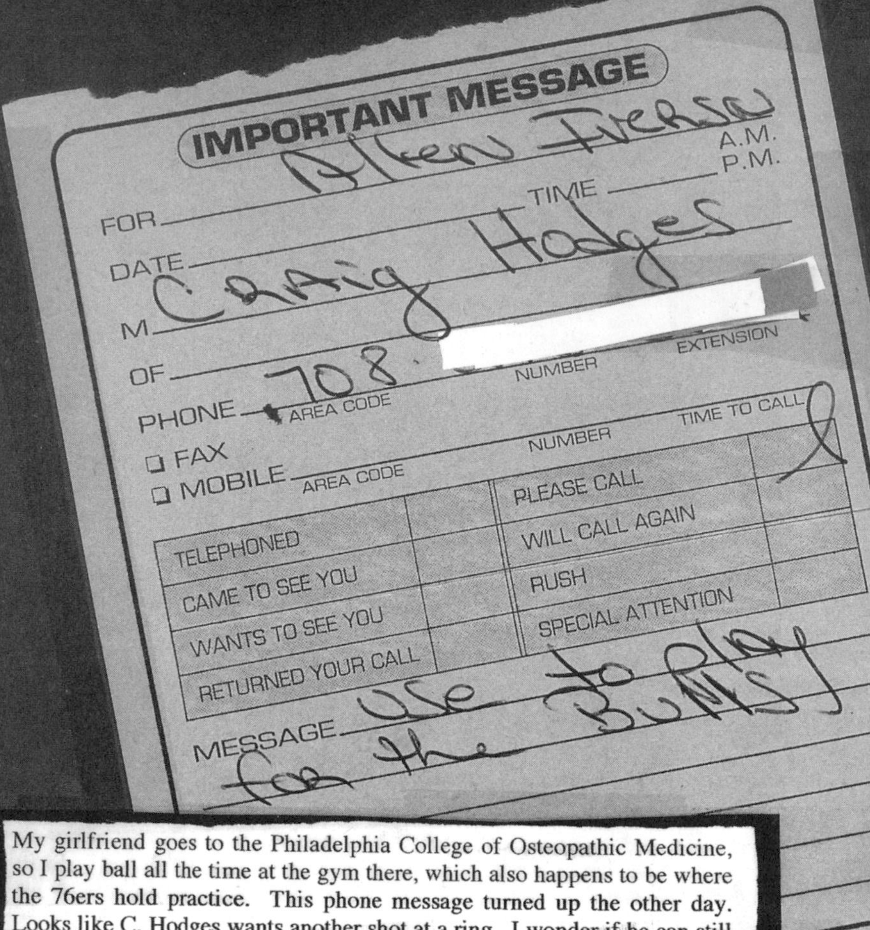
IMPORTANT MESSAGE

FOR Alken Iverson

DATE TIME A.M. P.M.

M Craig Hodges

OF

PHONE 708 AREA CODE NUMBER EXTENSION

FAX / MOBILE AREA CODE NUMBER TIME TO CALL

| TELEPHONED | | PLEASE CALL | ✓ |
|---|---|---|---|
| CAME TO SEE YOU | | WILL CALL AGAIN | |
| WANTS TO SEE YOU | | RUSH | |
| RETURNED YOUR CALL | | SPECIAL ATTENTION | |

MESSAGE Use to play for the Bulls

SIGNED

TOPS. FORM 3002P MADE IN U.S.A.

## PLEASE CALL

FOUND by Mike DiBella

Philadelphia, PA

MFD
264,
Philadelphia, PA.
19144

FOUND S.R.

Davy Rothbart
FOUND MAG.
3455 Charing Cross Rd.
Ann Arbor, MI. 48109-1911

My girlfriend goes to the Philadelphia College of Osteopathic Medicine, so I play ball all the time at the gym there, which also happens to be where the 76ers hold practice. This phone message turned up the other day. Looks like C. Hodges wants another shot at a ring. I wonder if he can still bang those threes.

—M.F.D.

# KOBE BRYANT

Most people think that Kobe was wrong for not going to college and going strait to the pros . They thought that Kobe was not mature enough to handle the older men on the NBA LA Lakers team and to adjust his speed to their plays. some people think that he would not be able to handle his money. I think that Kobe is A great ball player and I think he did the right thing by going strait to the pros. I think he plays just like me.

## JUST LIKE ME

FOUND by Joseph Derer  I found this outside a gas station while walking to work.

Ann Arbor, MI.

## Free Style

By Jason B. (age 11)

I swat balls like Yao,
Make the crowd go wow!
Four fouls
Don't have a cow,
Time for me to take a bow,
Cause your team's in trouble now

I step up like T-mac,
Watch your back
Play D like the Glove
Show me some love
Explosive like Kobe,
You're gonna know me.

Assist like Jason, and I'm only a kid.
My team supports me like in a war,
Where you have to protect the fort.
I rock the rim, I own the court.

## *ONLY A KIDD*

FOUND by Todd Martin
& Beth Isaacson
Washington, D.C.

this picture FOUND by David Smallwood, Arlington, VA

## EXISTENTIAL BALLER

FOUND by Dave & Rose
Ann Arbor, MI

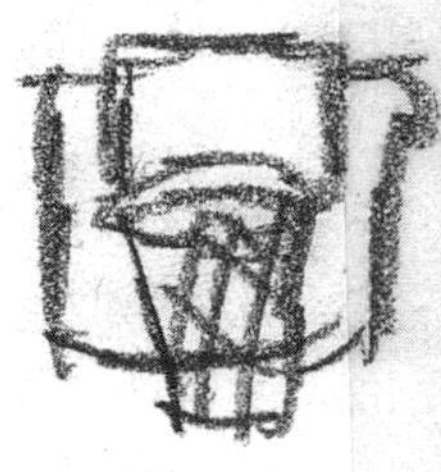

What am I suppose to do?

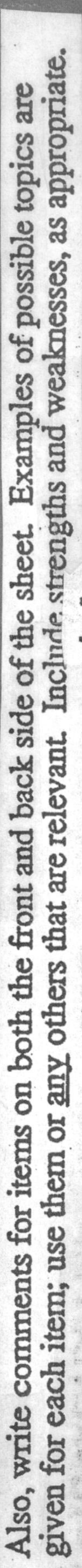
Also, write comments for items on both the front and back side of the sheet. Examples of possible topics are given for each item; use them or any others that are relevant. Include strengths and weaknesses, as appropriate.

3 = adequate

0 | 1) **COURSE**
*Comments* (e.g., content, structure, approach, educational value)

I CAN NOT REMEMBER ANYTHING ABOUT THE CONTENT OF A SPECIFIC ~~OF THE~~ CLASS ~~APPROACH~~ ANY MORE THAN I COULD ~~[illegible]~~ RECALL THE MOST BORING MOMENTS OF MY LIFE. THE EDUCATIONAL VALUE WAS SO PHENOMENALLY LOW THAT MY FRUSTRATION GREW INTO HATRED FOR HER, AND THEN IT BECAME MORE WIDESPREAD, AFFECTING MY FAMILY AND FRIENDS AND POSSIBLY PEOPLE I HAVE NEVER MET BEFORE, UNTIL I FINALLY REACHED THE POINT WHERE I HATED MYSELF FOR ~~[illegible]~~ BEING THERE.

(e.g., content, structure, approach, educational value)

structure ?? which one?
no educational value
we learned nothing
one-sided introduction to NYC. - Only Beth's view
the guest lectures were sometimes interesting - only interesting thing

# **TEACHER-COURSE EVALUATION**

FALL 19

8) **ADJECTIVE** What adjective best describes this course? HORRIFYING

0 | 3) **INTELLECTUAL STIMULATION** (e.g., amount and type of thinking you did)
*Comments*

~~[illegible]~~ "Bullshit" is the only word I can think of, excuse my French. Ellen didn't try to stimulate, and the material didn't stimulate me. When it came time to write papers, I made bullshit up because I didn't care one way or the other.

5 | 3) **INTELLECTUAL STIMULATION**
*Comments* (e.g., amount and type of thinking you did)

WHEN HER TWENTY-FIVE POUND CAT CLAWED ME IN THE GENITALS.

6) **EVALUATION METHODS** (e.g., the educational value of tests, papers, homework)

The papers were obviously intended as thought exercises, and they succeeded passing well as such, but what they had to do with any of the other papers, readings, presentations, or discussions is quite beyond me. In fact, what any paper, reading, presentation, or discussion had to do with any other paper, reading, presentation, or discussion, or the ostensible program topics, is an issue which has yet to be clarified.

...ON **METHODS** (e.g., the educational value of tests, papers, homework)

RATHER MEAN SPIRITED EVALUATION OF OUR PAPERS, BUT I CAN'T BLAME HER FOR ANYTHING EXCEPT FOR THE IDIOTIC TOPICS SHE REQUIRED US ~~[illegible]~~ TO WRITE ABOUT.

2 = fair

6) **EVALUATION METHODS** (e.g., the educational value of tests, papers, homework)

I have no idea how I'm being evaluated.

7) **CLASSROOM DYNAMICS** Circle term for type of course: **lecture / seminar / lab / other =** ______
(e.g., given this type of course, assess student participation, interest level, discussions, peer review)
There basically was no dynamic. Students not showing up, coming excessively late, and sleeping, that was the dynamic.

9) **ADDITIONAL COMMENTS**
a note about the cats: the litterbox was the bathroom. It contained, well, cat shit, one of the most repulsive substances known to the human race. If the instructor hadn't wanted us in the bathroom, she could have selected a less unpleasant method of signalling it.

**4 = good**

7) **CLASSROOM DYNAMICS** Circle term for type of course: **lecture / seminar / lab / other =** ______
(e.g., given this type of course, assess student participation, interest level, discussions, peer review)
At times, it seemed that if someone were to begin speaking in tongues, we all would have nodded and pretended that it was an insightful comment, just because someone had actually SAID something.

***BLOOD AND TEARS***

FOUND by Jesse B.

Durham, NC.

**5 = excellent**

...**MENTS**
IF I COULD WRITE THIS IN BLOOD AND TEARS I WOULD.

7) **CLASSROOM DYNAMICS** Circle term for type of course: **lecture / seminar / lab / other =** ______
(e.g., given this type of course, assess student participation, interest level, discussions, peer review)
TWO DAYS A WEEK I FOUGHT OFF CAT HAIR, LISTENED TO HER UNINSPIRED, ANIMATED BABBLE ABOUT ART THEORY, AND IF I WAS LUCKY I COULD CHEW ON A STALE BAGEL THAT I PAID OVER TWENTY THOUSAND DOLLARS FOR.

[ 2 ] 3) **INTELLECTUAL STIMULATION**
*Comments* (e.g., amount and type of thinking you did)
Some, came out of irritation forceful confrontation with the subject.

[ 2 ] 3) **INTELLECTUAL STIMULATION**
*Comments* (e.g., amount and type of thinking you did)
Ummm... I frequently contemplated my watch during class. Sometimes I would speculate as to what Ben Daniels or Dave Kurtz looked like, since they never came to class.

**1 = poor**

Please enter a number from 1-5 in the box next to each item on this page, using this scale:

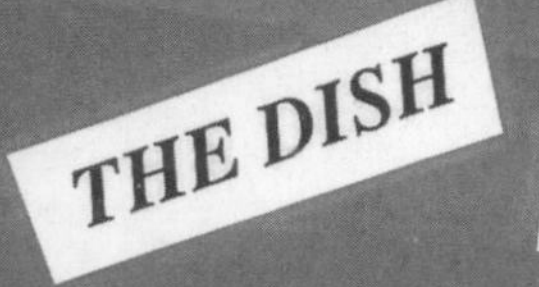


FOUND by Big Em

Chicago, IL.

Inbox for @yahoo.com — Yahoo! - My Yahoo! Options - Sign Out - Help

powered by hp — Mail Addresses Calendar Notepad

Reply | Reply All | Forward | inline text — Prev | N

Delete | - Choose Folder - | Move — Mark as

Download A

Flag This Message — Printable View - F

| Block Address | Add to Address Book

```
Message-----
From:
[mailto:                    g]
Sent: Wednesday, May 15, 2002 10:05 AM
To:                    '           ';
'       @hotmail.com';
'          @hotmail.com'; '          @hotm
'          @hotmail.com'; '          @ho
'          @hotmail.com'; '          u
          ';
          u'; '          ica
          @hotmail.com';
'          .com';
'          .com'; '          .com
'          @hotmail.com';
          @hotmail.com'; '          @hotmail.
          .com';
```

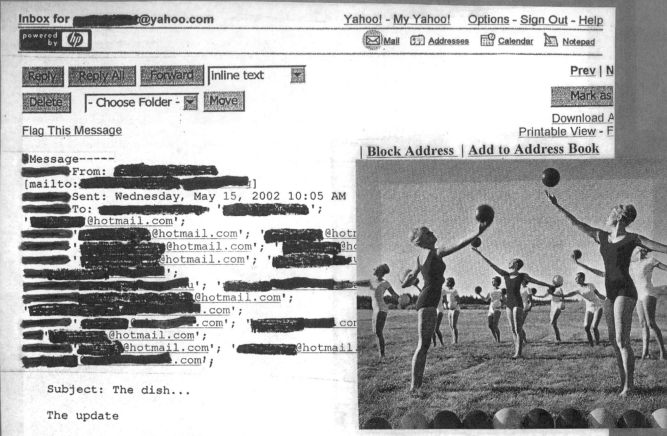

Subject: The dish...

The update

Well...Mr. Colin ██████ showed up at my door at about 8:15ish. Sporting a pair of cute jeans, a button up and a black jacket. For his outfit I would give him about a B. As for looks, he was cute but on the shorter side and his hair was a little too long. Far from a mullet but longer than I would prefer but let's not dwell on that because he can kinda get away with it. So for looks, I would probably give him another B. Car- BMW, like I stated before. A great car, he'll have to get and A for that. He gets and A+ for his manners and politeness. Marcie, he opened the car door everytime! Super polite. Overall general appearance will cap at a B+.

AS for the place we went to, another "A". The Tasting Room is an excellent date place. I was never the wine connoisseur but I'm gradually thinking I could become one. We had 4 glasses each of different white wines and a cheese flight, which was the perfect food mecca to go with the wine. Place is awesome, I recommend all of you guys to attend this place for a night out with your man/woman. We also headed over to this place called the Black Duck. Another great place! The date place itself gets an overall "A".

By the way Girls, this summer we must hang out on Randolph, so many awesome places!

I can go into great detail of what we talked about and such but, that would make for an extremely long email.

The date ended with me getting intoxicated but not like crazy intoxicated, but I was drunk. No hangovers. I'm assuming he was fairly intoxicated but since he was driving, I didn't want to know, so I never asked.

found magazine
3455 charing cross road
ann arbor, mi 48108-1911
www.foundmagazine.com

SEND

Yahoo! Mail

By the way, as for myself, I get an overall A+ for how damn cute I looked. I sported a pair of fun longer Capri pants from Guess in a darker khaki color with my white shirt from Hanger 18, that has my lower back showing with my new cute fitted black jacket with empire sleeves from Armani. I was a BABE. He didn't stand a chance. My worries of not being cute were so swept under the rug with the outfit I pulled off last night.

Before jumping to any conclusions, YES, I stayed the night, only because I semi passed out on his couch and he was polite to ask if I wanted to head home and I just said he could take me home in the morning, NOTHING happened. Honestly only a kiss derived from this date and it didn't even happen at his place. I believe it might have been executed at the Black Duck but I'm not so sure on the exact time and location. But can I add, GREAT kisser. The date kiss gets an "A". Really, I haven't had that great of a kiss since, well we won't go there but it has been a long time. I might have to go with the fact that I might have mastered the skill of French kissing, no joke. As long as I have potential to work with, I can execute a pretty intense kiss.

Lara- you would have loved Colin's attitude. Actually I think all of would have appreciated how he called me out on my stupid logic of thinking.

Somehow, it came up on how random it was for us to meet and shit and how when he said the very first time we talked for me to give him a call and my response was, "Really, I'll let you know now, I won't call you, so I suggest you write my number down and give me a call". Hence the wait of a week or so for his first initial call was due to my shallowness or whatever you would like to call my way of playing the field. Doesn't really matter, he still called and I didn't.

So, question is, where do I stand on the whole outlook of Mr. Colin and the date... The car, the money, the job, the cute apartment, the boat- which by the way only seats 6 people, so I really don't consider that really amazing, his mannerism and his great kiss will probably lock in another date but...I can tell you now unless he cuts his hair and sends me gifts, it won't lead me to seek anything more than my 1st 30 year old FRIEND (Oh by the way, I think he's only 28, but still, I'm rounding up). Plus, the summer is just around the corner and guys are EVERYWHERE, I need to keep the options open and my schedule free to lock in some other great summer flings...

Well, I hope you've enjoyed the day in the life of Miss Jackie [illegible] and please feel free to comment on my date, my outfit, the kiss, or whatever else. If you need any more major details of the date please contact me in one of the following ways: phone, email, personal visit or text messaging.

Oh, I might be heading to a Cubs game with him next week. We'll see.

Oh by the way ladies- His cute friend Brian, is single and also a day trader. Which by the way, being a day trader is pretty money, literally in a sense but he gets to throw on lounge wear for work and is home no later than Noon. Are you kidding me? Where was being a day trader on career day in Elementary school?





FOUND Magazine. "A+!"

**PLEASE ADMIT JOSH**

FOUND by Janelle Parsons and Kymmb Brierly

San Luis Obispo, CA

Please admit
Josh

10:55

5/21

I passed this find on to my cousin Josh and he has since used it, along with a photo ID—and a fair bit of bravery and boldness—to gain entrance into Manhattan's ritziest clubs, major league baseball games, county fairs, private parties, zoos, hotel pools, and the Hungarian Museum of Commerce and Catering in Budapest. What velvet-rope bouncer would dare to override the authority of [signature]?

—DAVY

this photo FOUND by Kimberley Koopmans,

Fort Erie, Ontario

on the back it says 'JUGOSLAVIA'

Rules of Engagement
in order to use DF
you must know-
Shout Halt 2 twice
No warning shot
Protect the innocent
unless the situation involves
property vital to National
Security.
Shoot to wound

this photo FOUND by Lisa Bee, Milwaukee, WI

T-8 Hand and Arm Signals
Combat Formations -
Test tomarrow
Lost Fucking Job by
Missing two Questions

**DEADLY FORCE**

FOUND by Hannah Gedeon

Bowling Green, OH

**THE NEW DEAL**

FOUND by Kelli Sousanne

Alvord, IA

7/12/00

6:17 p.m.

I Tamara montes will take care of all the paying of the bills and housewhole needs, And in this agreement my Husband Ken montes will have a set Allowance of $75.00 per month.

7/12/00 Tamara Montes (BOSS)

7/12/00 Ken Mont (My loving Husband).

TWO STRIKES

FOUND

by Nate Cordero

Sacramento, CA

Contract

This what Sarah needs to go Outside for this Shift 10/12/02

(1) Sarah needs to be

(A) polite/NOT RUDE

(B) NOT SWEARING

(C) ~~Quiet/NO YELLING~~

(D) NOT BANGING, THROWING PEOPLE OR THINGS

(2) The NURSES WILL DECIDE if you have accomplished This

(3) You will have 3 Strikes that will COUNT you OUT

A B C D

||

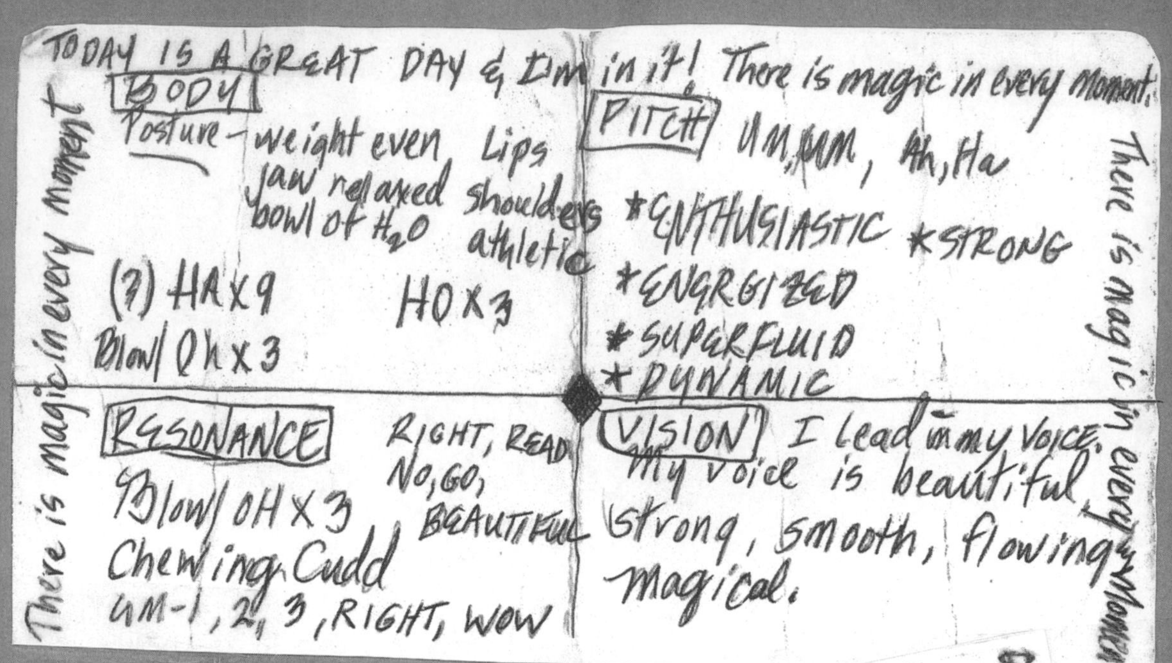

TODAY IS A GREAT DAY & I'm in it! There is magic in every moment.

BODY
Posture — weight even
jaw relaxed
bowl of $H_2O$
Lips
shoulders
athletic

(?) HA x 9
Blow/Oh x 3
HO x 3

PITCH
Um, Mm, Ah, Ha
*ENTHUSIASTIC *STRONG
*ENGRGIZED
*SUPERFLUID
*DYNAMIC

RESONANCE
Blow/OH x 3
Chewing Cudd
um-1, 2, 3, RIGHT, WOW
RIGHT, READ
No, GO,
BEAUTIFUL

VISION
I lead in my voice.
My voice is beautiful,
strong, smooth, flowing,
magical.

There is magic in every moment
There is magic in every moment

## DAILY AFFIRMATIONS #1

FOUND by Amy Kasten

Denver, CO

Courage, Dignity & Grace

I AM A CHAMPION

I feel so good promoting health and the service I share
I see the good in others adds to my wealth
I notice my nervous mess with love
& compassion
I stick with my foundation to maintain
integrity & wholeness
I count to 10 in stressful situations & breathe
with humor
I talk with ease & joy
I do my best with impeccable words, without
assumptions, without taking others stuff personally

GOLDEN RETRIEVER WAG YOUR TAIL!

Golden retriever Wag your tail!

## DAILY AFFIRMATIONS #2

FOUND by Terri Fisher

Ann Arbor, MI

you fuck up you always fuck up your a fucker just like all the other fuckers you call fucker you are a fuck up you always try but you always fuck up try harder it just takes longer just to make the fuck up time more suspenseful you always fuk up you always fuckl up what have you done good what havn't you fucked up nothing you fuck up everything you are a fuck up i love you i can't get rid of you but what do you do with a fuck up nothing because they always fuck up because you are a fuck up you always are a fuck up because you are a fuck up fuckup being a fuck up and fuck up.

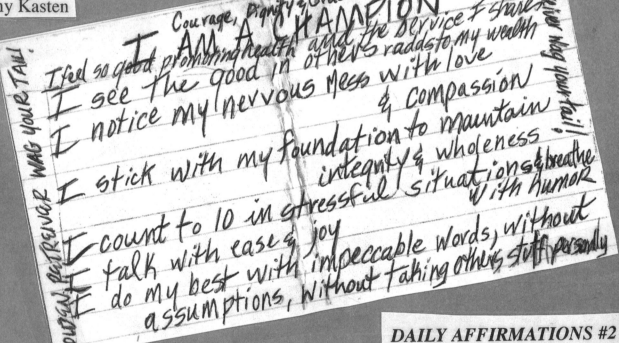

## INSTRUCTIONS WHILE I'M AWAY #1

FOUND by Chris Rush

Tucson, AZ

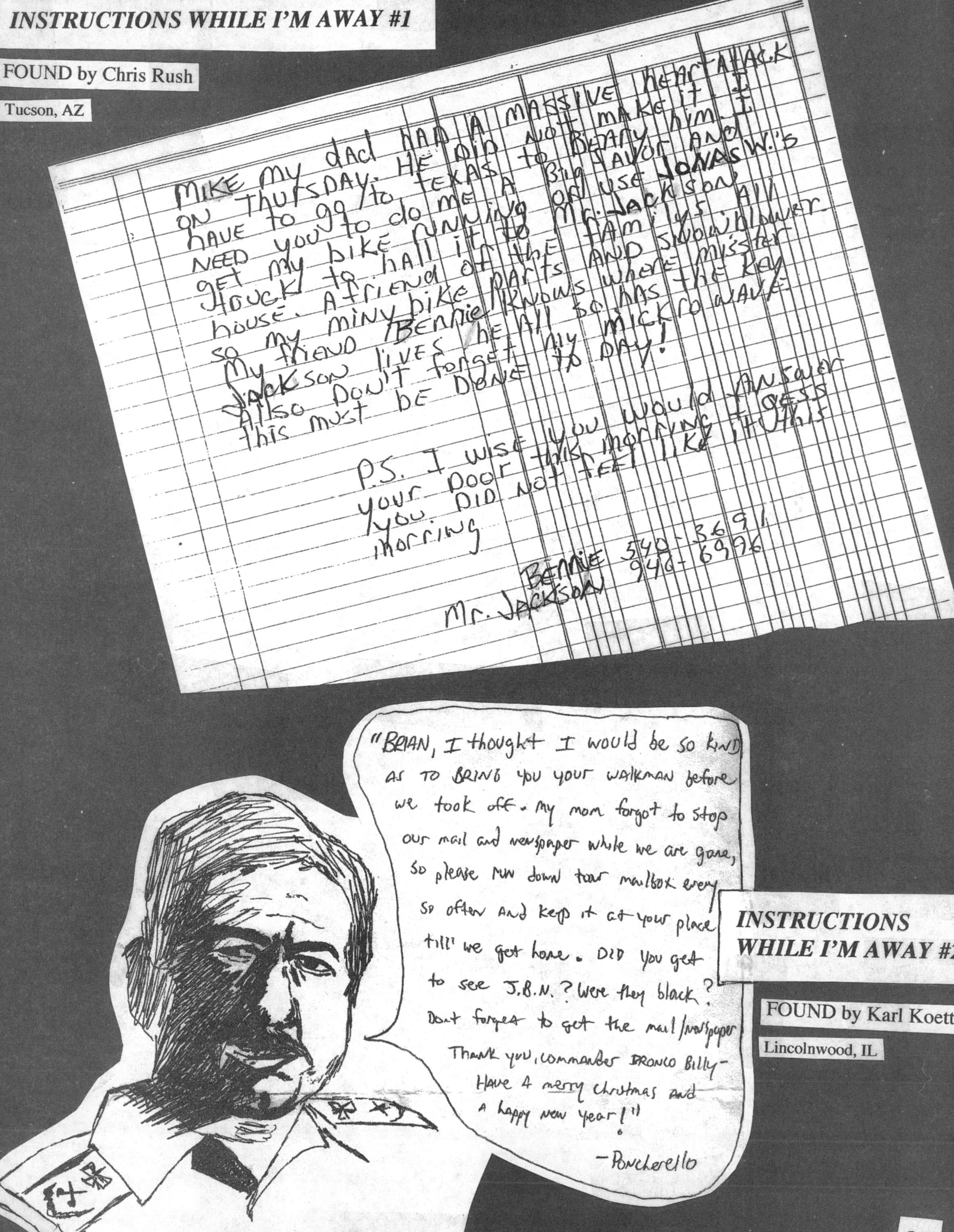
MIKE my dad HAD A MASSIVE heart attack on THURSDAY. HE DID NOT make it. I have to go to Texas to Berry him. I NEED you to do me A Big favor and get my bike running or use JONAS W.'s trouck to hall it to Mr. Jackson. All house. A friend of the family's snowblower so my miny bike parts AND mister My friend Bennie knows where the key Jackson lives. he All so has my Mick ro wave. Also DON'T forget my mick ro WAVE this must BE DONE to DAY!

P.S. I wise you would Answer your Door this morning I gess you DID not feel like it this morring

BENNIE 540-3691
Mr. JACKSON 946-6976

"BRIAN, I thought I would be so kind as to BRING you your walkman before we took off. My mom forgot to stop our mail and newspaper while we are gone, so please run down to our mailbox every so often and keep it at your place till' we get home. DID you get to see J.B.N.? Were they black? Dont forget to get the mail/newspaper Thank you, commander BRONCO Billy- Have A merry christmas and a happy new year!"

-Poncherello

## INSTRUCTIONS WHILE I'M AWAY #2

FOUND by Karl Koett

Lincolnwood, IL

4/23/03

William [illegible]
[illegible]

you stupid Jackass that why
I never let your ass
borrow anything
cuz you wont give it back

*Fuck You Ho Stupid
thats why you don't
let me borrow
anything I take it Bitch
for myself

*Fucking*
Bitch!

Fuck you bitch
you mothafucker
you aint nothing bot a bitch,
well you need 2 give me my
pen back

broke down
Bitch

* Your mamma bitch
you 2 face bitch skank
ho slut tramp, trailer white
mexican trash you are a descrace
to mexico.
whos the Bitch now?

**MY PEN**

FOUND by Miriam

Appleton, WI

(from



This note seems to be two girls writing back and forth to each other in class. For maximum enjoyment, try reading out loud back and forth with a friend!

—DAVY

I wouldnt be talking you back you aint worth anything, you bitch, trash, whore, hoe Like you said you are a 2 face bitch you think you're the shit, but you aint nothing lameass times get a fucking hair cut and while you are there get you face fixed cuz you scared the poor little kidz

Bitch

At least I aint the one whose going to fail this year and go to summer school AGAIN! and got fucked on top of the drier what are you trying 2 say bitch will see about that

BITCH

you aint that smart you self aint nobody Perfect o.k anywayz, Bitch when I went to Sommer school waz in 6 grade, I dont ever wonna talk 2 you again ever in my Life, Don talk 2 me Stupid bitch "Fuck you"

mothafucker

Are you mad god I was just playing well see ya later

pussy bitch

BITCH! fuck you

Bitch

Dont play with cuz when you play with me you play with fire

(back)



FOUND Magazine. Ain't nobody perfect, OK?

CAESARS INN
P.O. BOX 2202 STATELINE, NEVADA 89449
PHONE (702) 588-3544

DEAR AL & LAM –

THANK YOU FOR YOUR GENEROSITY AND PATIENCE. THOUGH FINANCIAL INSTABILITY HAS MADE THINGS WORSE IT IS NOT, IN THE END, WHY I HAVE ENDED MY PAINFILLED EXISTENCE.

I HAVE NAMED JEREMIAH MY EXECUTOR AND HAVE ASKED LOURDES' SISTER TO CONTINUE MY SSI CLAIM. BOTH HAVE INSTRUCTIONS TO PAY OFF MY FINANCIAL DEBITURES* TO YOU (I OWE YOU MORE THAN MONEY.) I'M SORRY TO LEAVE THE PLACE SO BAD OFF. BUT, I LEAVE THE LOFT, YOU OUGHT TO CHARGE MORE* ($595.00 AT LEAST) FOR THIS PLACE, IT'S QUIETEST, LIGHTEST – PEOPLE ARE SURPRISED TO FIND OUT WHAT I PAY.

(JUNE IS MY LAST MONTH)

AL KEYS
LAM PIERSON

*BY THE GODDESS BLESSED BE ☮ ♡. KK

PHOTOGRAPHY BY JOHN NULTY

KV2260 U.S.A.

***MY LAST MONTH*** FOUND by Carlos B., San Francisco, CA

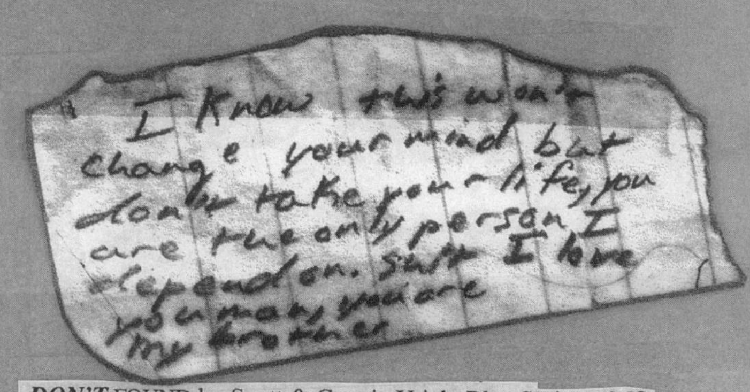
I know this won't change your mind but don't take your life, you are the only person I depend on. Still I love you mom, you are my brother.

***DON'T*** FOUND by Scott & Connie Urich, Blue Springs, MO

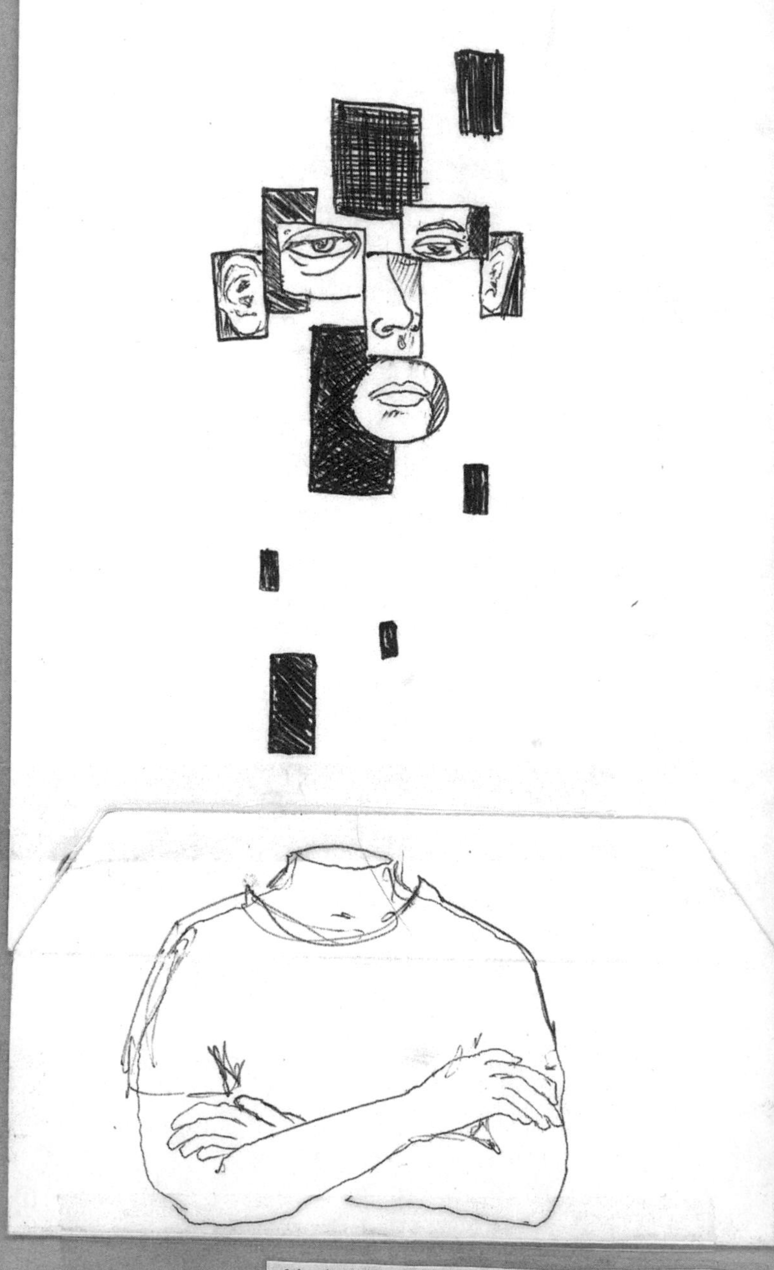

this drawing FOUND by Kovar Lee, Lincoln, NE

this drawing FOUND by Debbie Steinberg, Ann Arbor, MI

to whoam ever it may concern my last wishes are as fallows n/ sole ~~[illegible]~~ heirs aRe Deb Wain and Mollie Neb to Deb W. gose whats at my home and Mollie my car 86 Daytona my last pay check to Mollie also.

Love all

[illegible]

**LAST PAYCHECK** FOUND by

The cat looked around with curiosity at the tall drums of fish food, pills, dips and chips and at the body floating face down from the shallow end to the deep.

246

**SHALLOW END** FOUND by Nora Lidgus, Grand Rapids, MI

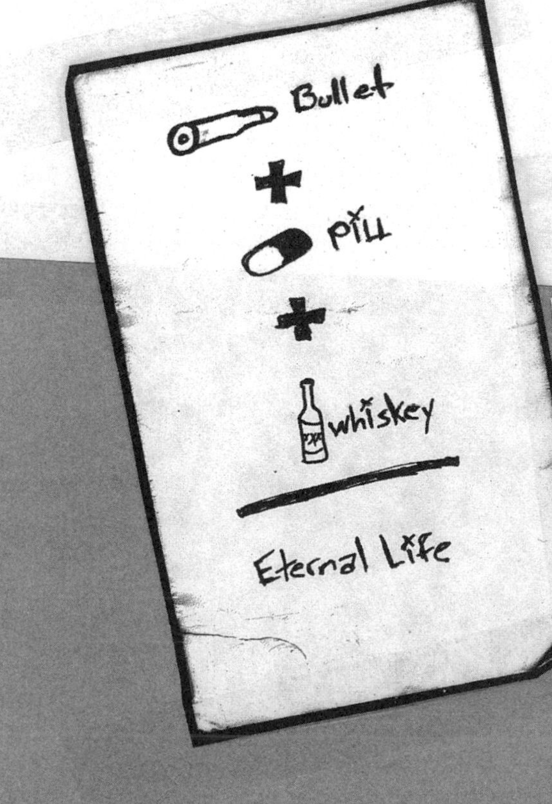


this equation FOUND by Kovar Lee, Lincoln, NE

# STEPHANIE'S FOLDER

FOUND by Alissa Fle

Boston, MA

Dear Stephanie,

I have missed meeting with you the past two days that we were supposed to meet for tutoring. I am wondering what is going on with you and if you are okay - I am actually worried about you. When I was 15 and 16, I remember that life could sometimes be so hard and I felt like no one in the world understood. I actually used to get pretty pissed off at all the adults in my life – they really annoyed me. We both know that the reason that you are having trouble in math is not really about math. You are very bright! The last time that we met you solved one of the problems that I couldn't even figure out how to do. It must be more about other things happening in your life. I called your house and your mom's boyfriend said that he would tell you that I called if you came home. Just so you know, I ran away a couple times when I was a teenager and I hated my mom and I was pissed at my dad for leaving our family. It's rough sometimes. But I see in you so much more than you let out to the world. You are very bright and kind and I know that you will be able to overcome whatever is bothering you in your life. It may not be easy, but I know that you have the power.

So, although the tutoring center told me that they could assign me a new student, I told them I wasn't giving up on you so easily. I really like you and I want to work with you. I'd like to offer you the opportunity to start off on a clean slate. If you would like, we can structure our meetings in anyway that you want. If you want to work on other subjects, we can. If you want to just talk we can. You just let me know what you need. I am here for you and I'm offering to help you with whatever you need from me. In case you are wondering why I even care, it's because I see myself in you. I went through a lot of really tough things in my teenage years and I was thankful for those few people who took the time to understand me. The ball is in your court and I won't be showing up for tutoring until I hear something from you. Please call me and let me know what you decide either way. I trust your judgement in your decision.

Home
Work

Take care,

Shawna

I found a girl's school folder on the bus; these were among the papers inside.
—A.F.

Butchie,
I miss you so much. How can I live like this. I don't know if I can go on knowing that you could be over there with some other girl. I know I might seem selfish, but I don't care. I mean I don't want you ~~to~~ sit there and constantly think about me, but I also can't stand the thought in my mind that your with someone else. Did you forget about me already. I think about you constantly. There is a boy down here that is trying to get with me, and I really like him too, but the thoughts of you hold me back. The pictures, the memories, the dreams.. How can anyone else compare to you? Your sweet, nice, funny, caring, and everything else I want. This other boy is always coming so close to kissing me, then I just turn away. It's

not your fault, it's ~~just~~ that I can't ~~stop~~ thinking about you.

Stephanie

She wept & wept all the thoughts of him running through her mind, until she just couldn't take it anymore.

# I MOST DO MY HOMEWORK

FOUND by Krista North

Minneapolis, MN

1. I most do my homework
2. I most do my homework
3. I most do my homework
4. I most do my homework
5. I most do my homework
6. I most do my homework
7. I most do my homework
8. I most do my homework
9. I most do my homework
10. I most do my homework
11. I most do my homework
12. I most do my homewo
13. I most do my homew
14. I most do my home w
15. I most do my home
16. I most do my home
17. I most do my homework
I most do my homework
I most do my homework
20. I most do my homework
21. I most do my homewor
22. I most do my home w
23. I most do my homew
24. I most do my home
25. I most do my home
26. I most do my homework
27. I most do my homewo
28. I most do my hom
29. I most do my h
30. I most do my ho
31. I most do my
32. I most do m
33. I most
34. I most do
35. I most do my
36. I most do my homework
I most do my homework
homework

this photo FOUND by Lisa Bee, Milwaukee, WI

***I SHALL NOT OBSTRUCT TRAFFIC WHILE LOADING OR UNLOADING***

FOUND by Sarah Lahalih and Julia

Chicago, IL

20 I Shall ...
loading ...
21 I Shall not Ob...
loading and unlo...
22 I Shall not obstruct ...
loading or unloading
23 I Shall not obstruct trafic while lo...
or unload
24 I Shall not Obstruct trafic while loading
or unloading
25 I Shall not obstruct trafic while loading
or unloading
26 I Shall not obstruct trafic while loading
or unloading
27 I Shall not obstruct trafic while loading
or unloading
28 I Shall not obstruct trafic while
loading or unloading
29 I Shall not obstruct trafic While
loading or unloading
30 I Shall not obs trafic while
loading or unloading

this photo FOUND by Lisa Bee, Milwaukee, WI

# THAT LITTLE GUY

FOUND by Adam Bork

Austin, TX

*FOUND* under my truck's windshield wiper. I wish I'd found the final pages, too…

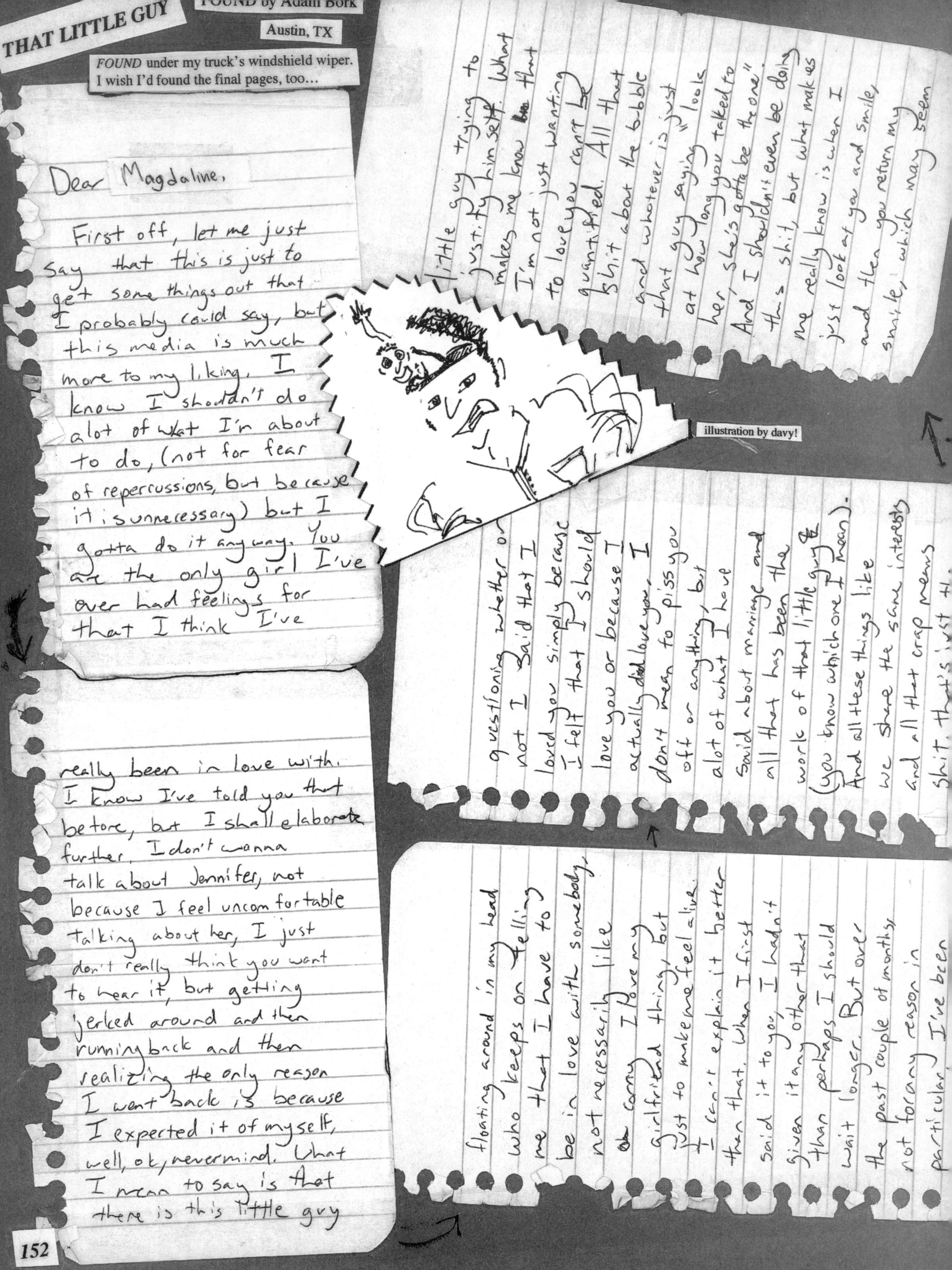

Dear Magdaline,

First off, let me just say that this is just to get some things out that I probably could say, but this media is much more to my liking. I know I shouldn't do alot of what I'm about to do, (not for fear of repercussions, but because it is unnecessary) but I gotta do it anyway. You are the only girl I've ever had feelings for that I think I've really been in love with. I know I've told you that before, but I shall elaborate further. I don't wanna talk about Jennifer, not because I feel uncomfortable talking about her, I just don't really think you want to hear it, but getting jerked around and then running back and then realizing the only reason I went back is because I expected it of myself, well, ok, nevermind. What I mean to say is that there is this little guy floating around in my head who keeps on telling me that I have to be in love with somebody, not necessarily like carry "I love my girlfriend" thing, but just to make me feel alive. I can't explain it better than that. When I first said it to you, I hadn't given it any other thought than perhaps I should wait longer. But over the past couple of months, not for any reason in particular, I've been questioning whether or not I said that I loved you simply because I felt that I should love you or because I actually love you. I don't mean to piss you off or anything, but alot of what I have said about marriage and all that has been the work of that little guy (you know which one I mean). And all these things like we share the same interests and all that crap means shit, that's just that little guy trying to justify himself. What makes me know that I'm not just wanting to love you can't be quantified. All that shit about the bubble and whatever is just that guy saying "look at how long you talked to her, she's gotta be the one." And I shouldn't even be doing this shit, but what makes me really know is when I just look at you and smile, and then you return my smile, which may seem

illustration by davy!

These ten musical gems came to me by way of Greg Warner in Phoenix. A few years back Greg's friend Nigel Morgan found an unmarked cassette-tape on the street in Ypsilanti, Michigan which contained a string of minute-long booty-rap anthems. Apparently some thugged-out white kids with a drum machine had put together a demo tape.

I've given these dudes the name Ypsilanti All-Starz and titled each of the songs. My favorites are "Yo' Shit Be Up in My Face," "Yo' Ass is So Fine" and "Wiggle on the Flo'."

What's remarkable to me is the earnestness with which these songs are performed. Some folks disagree with me but I don't think the Ypsilanti All-Starz are aware of their comic brilliance.

This tape circulated around south-east Michigan for two years, copied and recopied. Then Greg played it for someone who said, "I know these guys!" This person said it was not a satire; these guys were out to make it big. They were fully confident they'd sell a million records. If it means anything to the Ypsilanti All-Starz, I'd buy one.

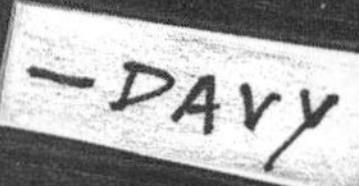

THE YPSILANTI ALL-STARZ

FOUND by Nigel Morgan

1. Wave Yo' Booty in the Air (Bounce)
2. Yo' Ass is So Fine
3. Ass-Whomp Bustin' Out of Yo' Back Pocket
4. Yo' Shit Be Up In My Face
5. Wiggle On the Flo'
6. Booty Time
7. Taste That Booty Flava'
8. Booty Shake (a capella)
9. Your Booty Don't Stop
10. (She Got a) Big Fat Booty
11. Wave Yo Booty in the Air (remix)
12. Yo' Ass is So Fine (heartfelt remix)
13. Ass-Whomp (re-dux)
14. Yo' Shit Be Up in My Face (abandoned)

**TO LISTEN TO THESE SONGS, GO TO FOUNDMAGAZINE.COM!!**

MONTH OF:________________

| | ITEM | TOTAL |
|---|---|---|
| NO | MACARENA. | |
| NO | GREASE STUFF | |
| NO | COUNTRY/WESTERN | ONLY 1 (IF REQUEST) |
| NO | NEW HUSTLE (NOT STEVIE WONDER). | |
| NO | Bob Seeger | |
| NO | Hanson | |
| NO | U2 | |
| NO | Group Dancing | → 2 polkas |
| NO | DROP THE BOMB | |
| NO | SUPERFREAK. | → Big Band |
| NO | 50's | |
| NO | GREENDAY. | |
| NO | LADY IN RED | |

No - Garter
- Bouquet

## *NO SUPERFREA*

FOUND by Eileen Sprou

Edmonton, Alberta

## *FIFTY IS NIFTY*

FOUND by Pete Cropley

Jamaica Plains, MA

# LYNDA BARRY

## COLLECTIONS

PART OF SCHOOL THIS YEAR IF YOU HAVE MISS RONSON IS YOU HAVE TO START COLLECTING SOMETHING LIKE IT'S YOUR HOBBY. MARLYS IS TRYING TO DECIDE WHAT.

ROCKS? TOO AVERAGE. CERTAIN ANIMAL THINGS LIKE PIG FIGURINES OR FROGS OR EVEN PLASTIC HORSES? ALSO TOO AVERAGE.

ONE IDEA SHE HAD WAS, IN MY OPINION, GENIUS: THINGS FOUND ON THE SIDEWALK. I AM A PERSON WHO IS ALWAYS LOOKING DOWN, FINDING THINGS OTHER PEOPLE DROPPED: PENS, COMBS, LETTERS THAT SAY, *"I love you so much, please don't leave me."*

YOU LIKE THAT IDEA? HAVE IT.
SERIOUS?
HECK, I GOT SO MANY IDEAS. HAVE IT.

ON MY WAY TO WINKY'S LIQUOR STORE TO GET A BOX FOR MY NEW COLLECTION, MY EYES WERE SO EXCITED. I FOUND: A BLUE BARETTE SHAPED LIKE A SCOTTIE DOG, TWO PERFECT CIGARETTES, A STIFF, RUN-OVER GLOVE GIVING THE PEACE SIGN, AND A COUPON-"BUY 3, GET ONE FREE"-FOR CHICKEN DELIGHT.

HOW YOU GONNA ORGANIZE IT?
WHAT DO YOU MEAN?
YOU KNOW, ALPHA-BETICAL, CRONO-LOGICAL, DEWEY DECIMAL.
OLDE SKULLPOPPER
12

MARLYS SAYS ORGANIZATION AND PRESENTATION ARE VERY IMPORTANT TO MISS RONSON, IF I WANT A DECENT GRADE ON MY COLLECTION. ALSO WHAT IF THE PEOPLE START CALLING ME "SCROUNGE"? SHE KEPT SAYING THINGS THAT MADE ME FEEL DOUBTFUL UNTIL I FIGURED OUT SHE JUST WANTED HER IDEA BACK.

NO.
WELL, CAN I AT LEAST HAVE ONE OF THE CIGS?

# the FOUND INTER-VIEW

**davy**: *do you remember when you first became interested in FOUND stuff and why?*

**lynda**: I was always pretty much of a scrounge. Part of it might have been bugs. I really really liked bugs and when you are look around at ants on the ground or potato bugs or caterpillars you sort of will run into trash and some of the trash will be interesting. At least in my neighborhood this was true. I remember finding brown paper bags with glue wads inside. The glue sniffer's corner. And a whole block of houses was empty up the street. We all went inside, dug through things. Opened drawers. Bums were there. People set corners on fire. Peed on things. Made out. Places like that totally magnetized me. I loved finding things there that would give me a weird chill. A hairbrush. A pile of letters. And there was a dump, an unofficial dump, actually it was a mile long stretch along a ravine down the hill where people threw things out, and I used to go poking around there, looking for tossed off weirdness. This is when I was really little, like around eight. I would walk down there by myself, digging around in the piles of garbage. Finding suspenders and stoves and photos of people. There was a store called Pay'n'Save near my house and I used to look around their garbage area, trying to find broken things they threw out. Nothing really good comes to mind, I just liked looking. It relieved a certain kind of itch I didn't know any other way to scratch.

**davy**: *what is your attraction to FOUND stuff? what does FOUND stuff mean to you?*

**lynda**: I guess because it gives me something to imagine into both while on the prowl and after I find something. I especially like found notes and I used to keep them all together but my organizing has since exploded. I love conversation notes between two people in class. Two kinds of hand-writing ripping on a teacher. Mainly I like the story that smokes up from certain found things. And I like the collections of things one can put together. I collected playing cards found on the street with the eventual hope of getting a whole deck. A weird sort of life long game of solitare. I still run into the cards all over my house. No organization! When I was in college I nailed rows and rows of nails on one wall and then went out and picked up anything that was U-shaped and hung it on the nail upside down. Everything from tiny little twist-ties in a U shape to an actual letter U that fell off a marquee. I loved being able to pick a shape and look for it. This was twenty five years ago so I can't remember much about it except by the end of the year the wall looked amazing and no one could believe I found all the U- shapes on the street.

*Scrounging had everything to do with why I married a certain someone.*

In high school I started to notice shoes in the road, a single shoe laying here or there and I would think about how the hell that happened. Who loses one shoe in the road and how? I used to stop my 1964 Valiant and go get the shoe and throw it in my trunk. I loved opening my trunk and seeing all of these shoes that had no mates. I probably did it to be a way-out hippie and impress boys. But usually boys have nothing to do with why I scrounge. Although scrounging had everything to do with why I married a certain someone. I'm married to the KING of scrounging. My husband has furnished our house from dumps and alley-ways. He is always coming home with some insane thing he found. Once he brought home a stuffed grizzly bear head. Someone had cut it off of their bear-skin rug and put it out on the street with the trash. We dig the found lifestyle. I've been with people who were horrified when I bent to pick something up or slammed on the brakes to dig though a pile of trash on the side of the street. "You don't know where that has been" is either a nightmare or a dream statement depending on the person picking up the thing.

I think mainly it's two things that makes me love trash. One is the imagined story that comes with it (like who cut that bear head off the rug? How long did they think about it before they did it? What did they use to do it? Did they think a grizzly bear skin would be less offensive minus the head? What did people say after they saw the rug without the head? ) The other is the feeling of rescuing some otherwise over- lookable thing from oblivion. That might be a way that I identify with trash. Understand trash. Empathize with trash. I will call it trash. "Found Object" is a nice term but it reminds me when I was in college and looked down on comics so much that I called what I did "Drawings with Words." Now I'm a cartoonist and a trash lady.

**davy**: *what are some of your favorite + most memorable things you've found?*

**lynda**: Well the first thing that always comes to mind is a tiny bowling bag purse that would have fit in my hand when I was about seven. It was perfect with a little zipper and it had five bucks in it. I found it in the woods, in this totally unexpected area that kids were using to race bikes around piles of dirt. I loved that bowling bag! It was green and white and made me feel huge. I remember finding porn all over the place. It's amazing how much porn is laying around certain neighborhoods. I never understood the migration of porn. How did it leave the indoors for the outdoors. How did it get under the lunchroom portable up at the school? I found a series of notes in a notebook a man and a woman had been writing each other over a year. She worked nights. He worked days. It ends with her writing LIES! LIES! LIES! all over the last pages. In a certain way my favorite or memorable thing is hard to identify because it's been a life of picking up trash. As I look around the room right now I can see that only the computer and stereo and other tech stuff are new. Mostly it's found or church rummage sale which is a paid-for kind of trash. About my favorite kind. My husband Kevin has a thing about push lawn mowers. He finds them set out for the trash man. We have eight of them in the basement, lined up like they were for sale. We do not have a mowable lawn. He has to struggle with himself to keep from picking up more.

*I never understood the migration of porn. How did it leave the indoors for the outdoors.*

He restores prairie. That's his job. He's a plant freak. So sometimes when a development is going in we go over to the planned site right before they start digging and find all the native plants and rescue them. This counts as found, I think, if you consider the rescue aspect of finding. Once I found a migrating song bird in the middle of down town Chicago, just standing in the street. He'd just come over lake Michigan and was pretty tired. I picked him up and put him in my purse because I'd just seen a show about bird smugglers so I knew birds could ride ok in a purse if they were in a small space. I took him home and he was feeling a lot better after some food and water. He was yellow and black. Kevin would have known what he was if he could have seen him but he was gone by the time Kevin got home. As I write this there is another found bird making a lot of noise. "Mr. Birdis" who is a sparrow with a dislocated wing we found in the back yard. We've had him for about a month. I dig Mr. Birdis!

One of the things I used to LOVE to do is take something really eye-catching that I didn't want any more and put it outside somewhere on display and see how long until it was "found." I used to love to take my penny jar and make tall stacks of pennies in funny places in alleys. The kind of places kids might look but adults would not. I loved walking and checking on the pennies. Seeing which of the stacks had been located.

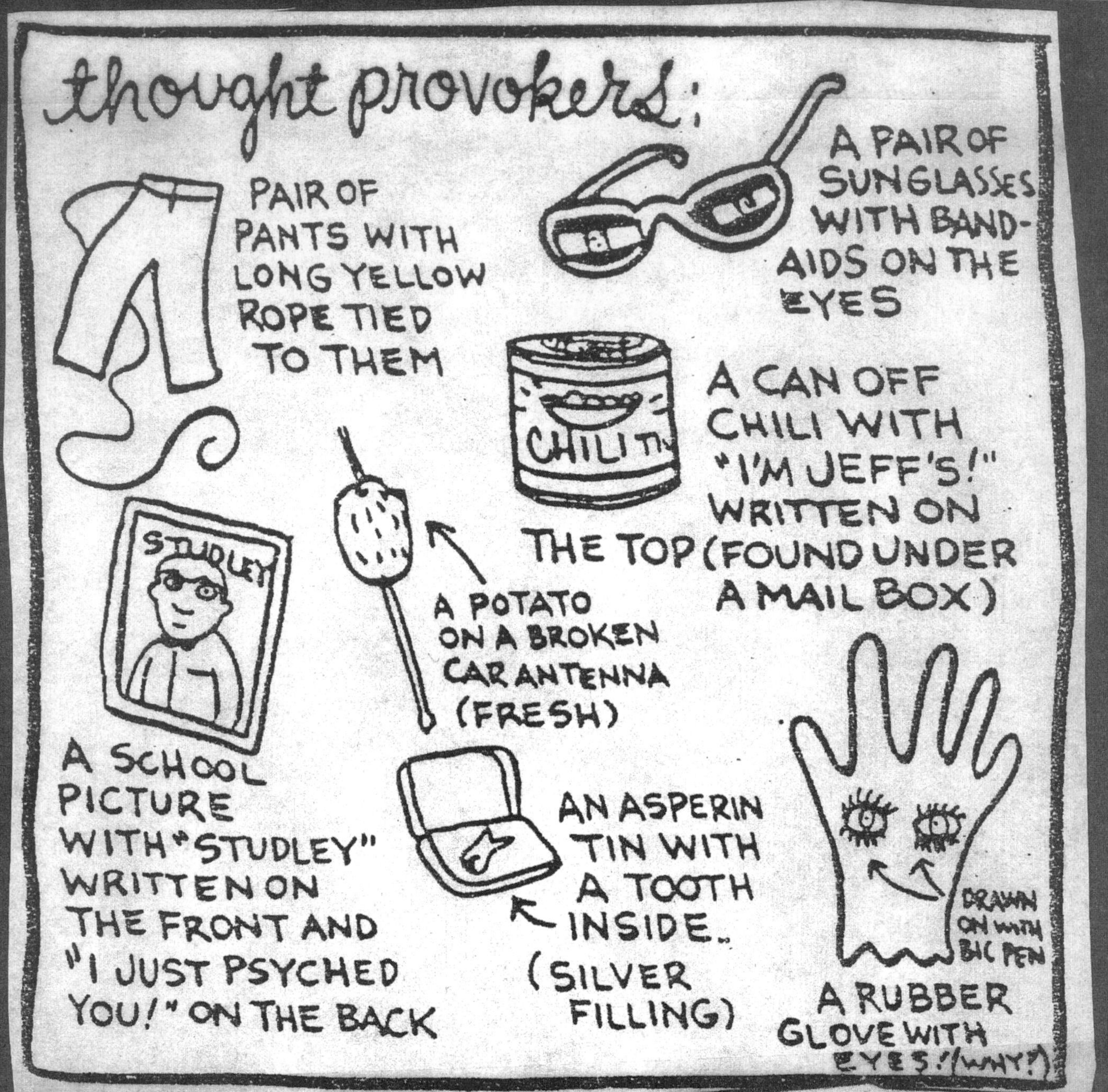


**davy:** *could you talk about those 2 specific comics you did which dealt with FOUND stuff (scroungina). How did you pick marlys' sad post-winter finds?*

**lynda:** Well the name Scroungina came from being friends with a guy named Scrounge. When he phones, he always says, "Hey, it's Scrounge." so I started saying "Hey, it's Scroungina" and that name turned into something in the strip the day I went for a walk and **noticed** all the left over stuff from the most recent thaw. In the midwest where the snow stays awhile and gets added to, there is this wild layering of trash that shows itself only once a year in true splendor. For some people spring is the cherry blossoms. For me it's all the hats, gloves, cans, and things that finally come out of the snow. When Kevin and I were first married his wedding ring flew off while he was sprinkling ashes on the icy walkway out front. A month and half later, he found the ring, right on the side of the walkway. We live on a well-walked street but no one saw it. Kevin's the kind of guy who looks down. My kind of guy.

*You have to be tender with other people's work.*

**davy:** *does something qualify as FOUND if you know who it belongs to? like last summer i was staying with my friend at another friends house in michigan who was gone. my friend got drunk and the next morning i found on the dining table all these pained rap lyrics he'd written at 4 in the morning. i mean, i knew it was him who'd wrote them, but still, it felt like a FOUND find because when i read the lyrics new things about him were revealed to me, things i dont think he would have shared with me in any other way. does this still count as FOUND? it might be dangerous if it does qualify because then it might condone snooping: "look, i know you caught me reading your journal, but i FOUND it in your sock drawer!"*

**lynda:** To me that doesn't count as found at all because you know who did it so the story that normally comes from a found thing, *the wondering* which in some weird way is a kind of wondering about ourselves, I don't think that would be there if I knew who wrote it. It would be *something*, but it would be something else. It reminds me of a conversation I heard on the train between two teenage girls. One had the other's cassette and she wanted it back. The one holding the cassette said "I'll give it back to you only if you can give me one good reason besides the fact that it's yours." Your friend's rap makes me think of that. You have to be tender with other people's work. Especially when they write it in the middle of the night and they might have been drunk when they did it. You wouldn't treasure their barf, right? In a way something like that is as private as barf. Why it becomes less private than barf if you DON'T know who did it, I'm not sure, but it's different when you don't know the origin. The things in our house we've gotten from the neighbors aren't as light or lively because I can always feel the "true story" in the object. I know Tammy got that vase from someone she hated, put it on the trash pile, I took it from the trash pile (asking first) but I can always feel Tammy there and that relationship so in a way the vase will never be free of that thing. I like it less than a vase that could come from anywhere and any situation. A good piece of trash has just enough information to make you wonder but not so much to make you stop.

**davy:** *well, thanks a lot, lynda. Send us some FOUND stuff!*

**lynda**: I will! It was fun thinking about this.

***FOUND Magazine.* Understand Trash.**

**THE HIDDEN SPOT**

FOUND by Lilly and Mary

Reno, NV

$150.00 REWARD!!

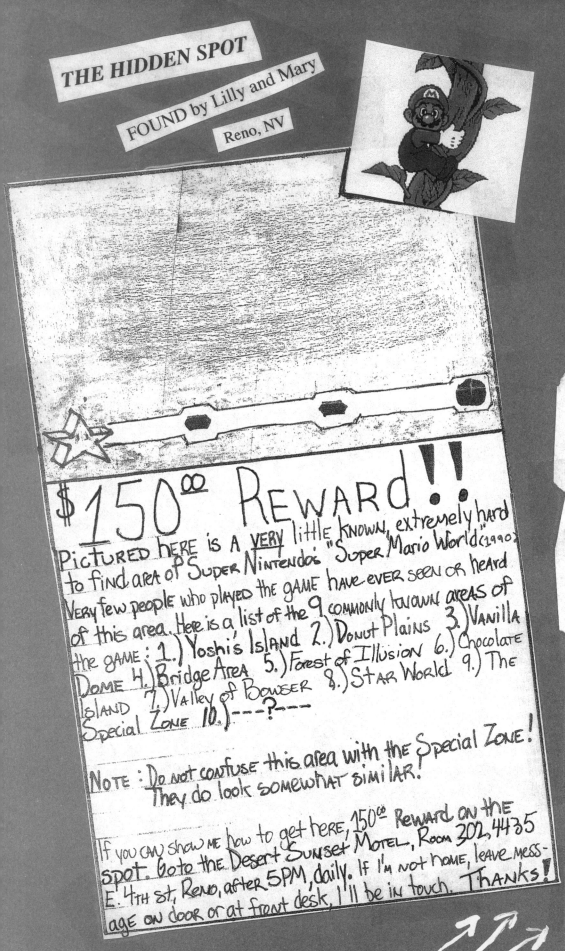

PICTURED HERE IS A VERY little KNOWN, extremely hard to find area of SUPER NINTENDO'S "SUPER Mario World" (1990) VERY few people who played the game have ever seen or heard of this area. Here is a list of the 9 commonly known areas of the game: 1.) Yoshi's Island 2.) Donut Plains 3.) Vanilla Dome 4.) Bridge Area 5.) Forest of Illusion 6.) Chocolate Island 7.) Valley of Bowser 8.) Star World 9.) The Special Zone 10.) ---?---

NOTE: Do not confuse this area with the Special Zone! They do look somewhat similar!

If you can show me how to get here, 150.00 Reward on the spot. Go to the Desert Sunset Motel, Room 302, 4435 E. 4th St, Reno, after 5PM, daily. If I'm not home, leave message on door or at front desk, I'll be in touch. Thanks!

**Have you seen this doll?**

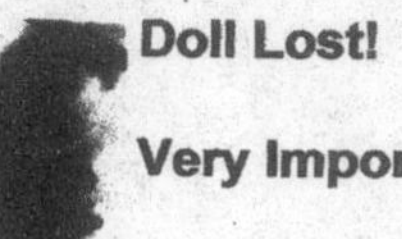

**Doll Lost!**

**Very Important!**

Her name is Lily, and she is an irreplaceable doll made with my mommy's hair. Unfortunately my mommy can't grow her hair again fast enough to have another doll made.

I have a lot of trouble sleeping at night without my Lily.

If you have found her, could you please call my mommy?

She was lost on Thursday, November 28 around 2:30pm somewhere around Montana & 9th St. She didn't have any clothes on. She is made of purple fabric, with stars and moons on it.

Please call (310) and ask for Karin or Vicente.

Thank you!

**LOST JACKET**

**BLUE/BLACK SOFT THIN LEATHER – ZIPPER FRONT – PRADA**

**LOST FRIDAY, JULY 25TH AT 6 PM FILM SOCIETY SCREENING OF SEA BISCUIT (LEFT IN END SEAT AGAINST RIGHT WALL TOWARDS REAR OF THEATER)**

**EXTREME SENTIMENTAL VALUE – SPECIAL GIFT FROM FATHER WHO IS RECENTLY DECEASED – I'M TOTALLY HEARTBROKEN – LOSING SLEEP**

**PLEASE RETURN (ANONYMOUSLY) TO WGA THEATER LOST AND FOUND – NO QUESTIONS ASKED – ANY INFORMATION CALL (213)**

**REWARD**

REWARD

Substantial reward offered for the return of or information leading to the return of a

Twin Bed

– cherry – 4-poster

It was on loan to a friend & was accidentally thrown out of

39 Porter Street

in May, 2003.

My father made it for me when I was little, & it is very precious to me.

Please call 302-

*NO CLOTHES ON* FOUND by Lauren Rimkus, Pacific Palisades, CA
*AT SEABISCUIT* FOUND by Anonymous, Beverly Hills, CA
*MISSING BED* FOUND by Jennifer Campbell, Boston, MA

# FITNESS PLAN

FOUND by Alan Thompson

Westminster, CO

303-289-4747
8310 North Washington
Denver, CO 80229
Fax: 303-288-1874

Fitness Plan (: ")

5-6 meals a day ← this is most important 2-are shakes

NO STARBUC'S -saves $ & calories

NO DRINKING ~ wine (1 glass w/meal :-)

5-10 warm up

30-50 lift

10-20 cool down w/stretching

8-10 glasses $H_2O$ - also important

SEX - LOTS of it (" )

2002

this drawing FOUND

by Mitch O'Connell

Chicago, IL

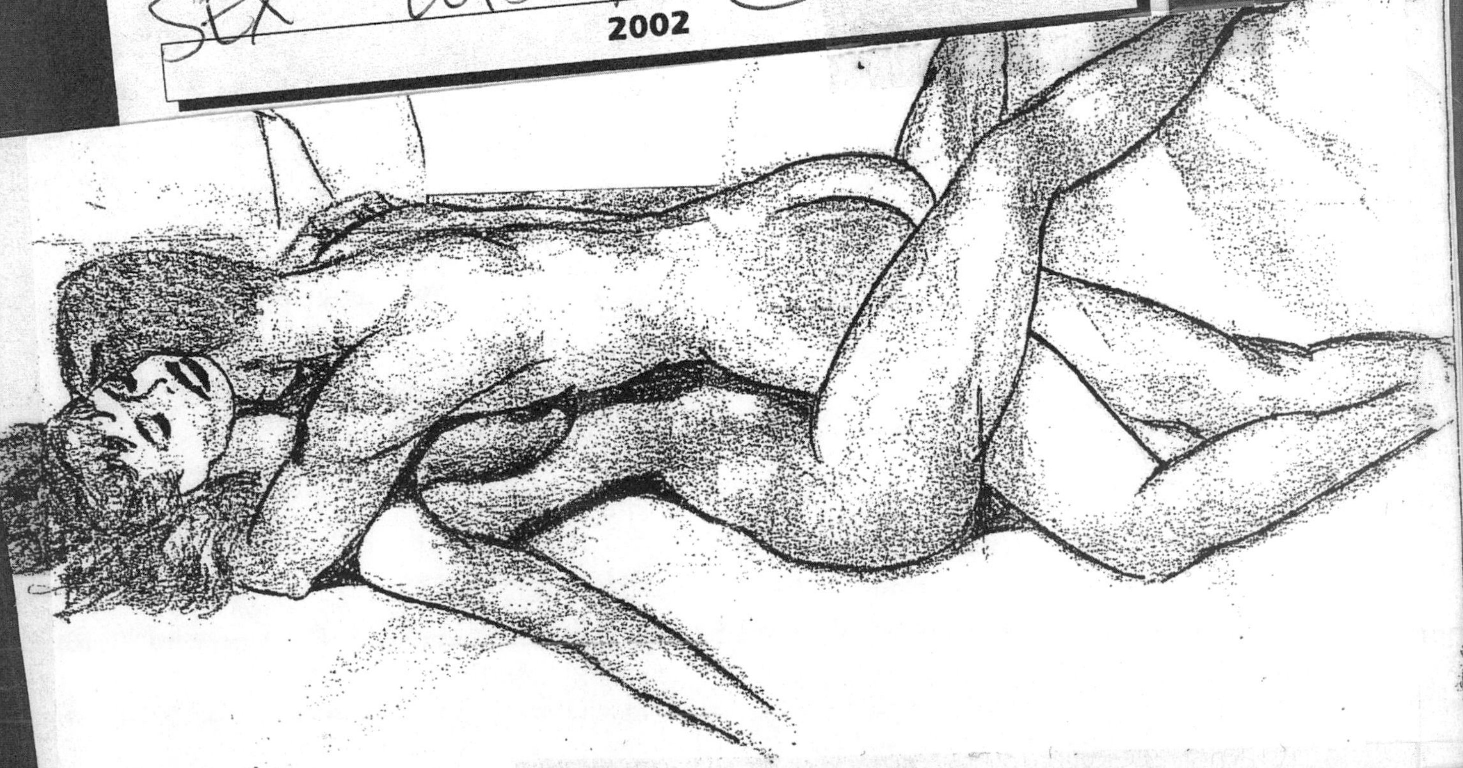

After all that has happend i am finally comming round to the idea that it is finnished

Helen leaving, being very cold, didn't want to come back, only came back because her mother told her i needed her as i was upset. leaving the next night then appologising on the morning saying we would go to counciling but she didn't know if it would work. Telling her friends she only came back because she was drunk and agreed to councilling to make it easyer for me to accept it was over leaving again to her friends saying she needed more time. Telling people it had been over 2 years ago when i have photos of her very happy in that time telling me she loved me everyday of our lives together. Telling me she didn't find me physically attractive then saying she met someone in town who thought she was hot are all these things ment to hurt me to the point i make the decision for her. The grasping at straws that i maybeable to get her back but deep down knowing im only delaying the enevitable how do i carry on from here to help me sleep, eat, and concentrat on my future. Realise my mistakes and work to change be an allround better person who is more positive, loveing, careing and thinks of other people more. I have good friends who all want to help me get through this as painlessly as possible i know there are millions of people out there who have gone through this (i was so cocksure i wouldn't be one of them) and are now happy with different partners. How do i coape when helen finds another partner. How do we split up what we have and still be friends afterwards, with all the hurt around i can see it being difficult. Do i try to support helen in her decision as she is hurting too or cut her off compleatly quickening the end if after 3 months and she has had her freedom and flings then changes her mind is it worth trying again or will it be completly broken am i again clutching at straws?

How did it get to go this far. what changes do i need to do so i don't repeat this mess up some time in the future i didn't think i was a bad person i know i need to change just for my own selfesteem it sad when you don't really like yourself but hopefully i will come out a better person

## *BURNT PALMS*

FOUND by Andrew Sears

Los Angeles, CA

I found this charred postcard near the corner of Santa Monica Blvd. and Vermont Avenue while wandering around after the L.A. riots. The building on the corner had burnt to the ground, the National Guard was defending the Sears nearby, and the rest of the world knew a little more about Los Angeles.

—A.S.

## HURRICANE HELEN

FOUND by Sandy W.

Paget, Bermuda

I found this self-reflective note among all the debris after Hurricane Fabian swept through Bermuda. It felt appropriate; a storm seems to have whirled through this guy's life as well.

—S.W.

## DAVIDIAN TOOTHBRUSH

FOUND by Joanna Santana

Waco, TX

After the whole Branch Davidian / David Koresh thing went down, I visited the compound; in the dried-up mud near the burnt wreckage I found this partly-melted toothbrush. 81 people died in the fire.

—J.S.

PLEASE DO NOT PUT CRAB ON MY CAR JUST CUT IT OUT !!!

NOTE ON MY WINDSHIELD

FOUND by Ed Faktorovitch

Los Angeles, CA.

RYAN SIAS

On November 28, 2001, I was wandering around the utterly empty outside pool area of the Excalibur Hotel in Las Vegas, NV. On a swoopy concrete ramp over the pool I found Item A, enclosed.

It's a piece of loose-leaf paper, torn loose from a three-ring binder. On it, in pencil, is a enciphered note.

Several months after finding the note, I showed it to some friends who are cryptography fans. We quickly determined that the note was enciphered with the "fence post" cypher.

While we weren't expecting secret weapon plans or an Al-Qeada communiqué, the contents of the note were still a bit unexpected:

ANDREW DOSN
KNOW THAT HE
IS THE BIGGEST
FAG FROM HELL
HA HA HA
- OOMPA

I hope you find the note and incident of use.

Best,

Stefan Jones

**BREAKING THE CODE**

FOUND by Stefan Jones

Las Vegas, NV

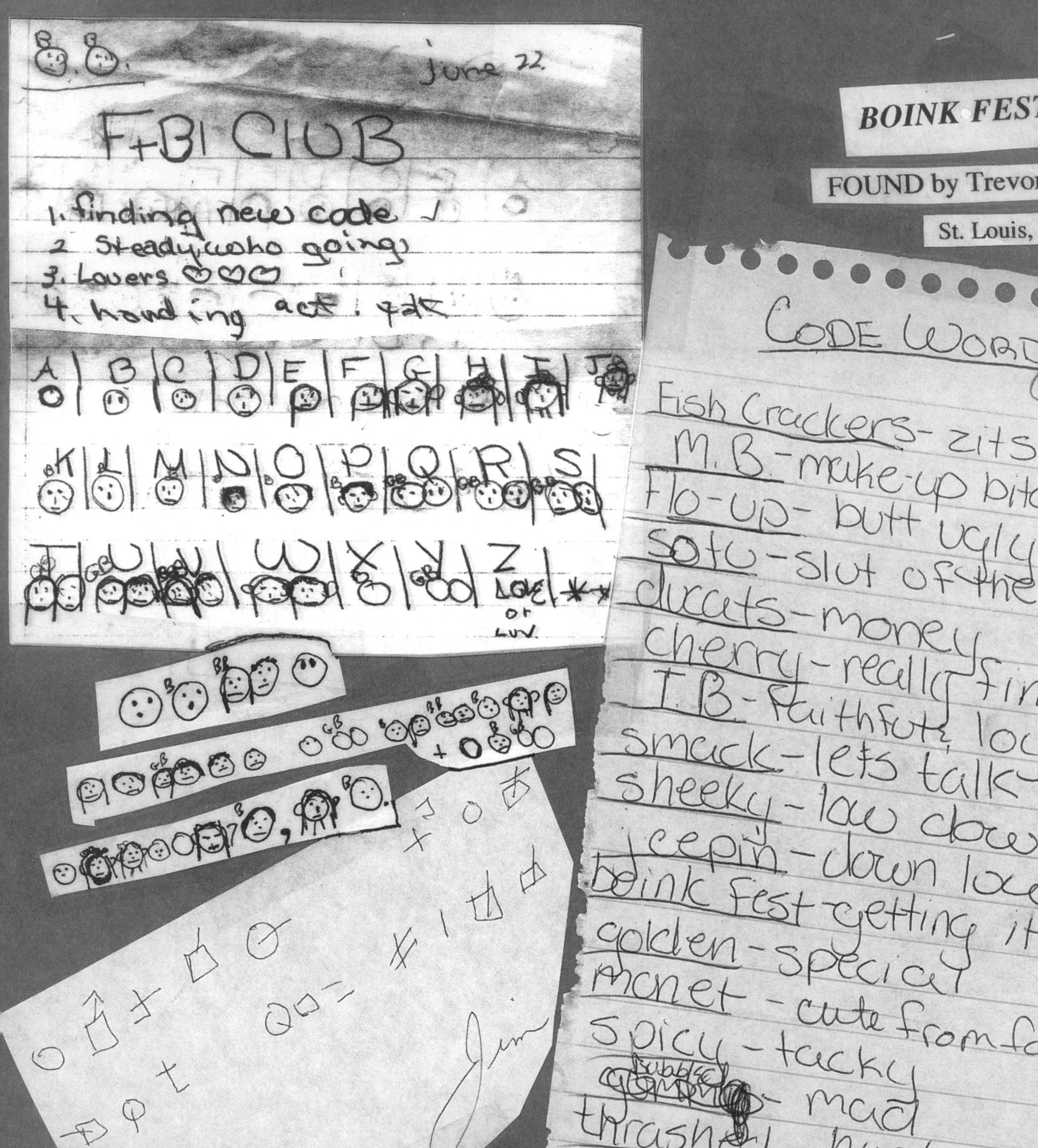


**BOINK FEST**

FOUND by Trevor Harris

St. Louis, MO

***I'D LIKE TO BUY A VOWEL***

FOUND by Tony Desmond

Chicago, IL

Travis,

I wanted to tell you Something in Code:

| | | | |
|---|---|---|---|
| A= • | F= ☺ | k= ♀ | P= 3 |
| B= \ | G= Z | L= ♡ | Q= 4 |
| C= ? | H= ⊤ | M= o | R= 6 |
| D= $ | I= — | N= △ | S= ≡ |
| E= ¢ | J= X | O= φ | T= 1.1 |
| U= " | V= □ | W= ◎ | X= 9 |
| | Y= 2 | Z= O | |

— □ ¢ 6 ¢ • ♡ ♡ 2 ♡ — ♀ ¢ $

2 φ " ~~☺ φ 6~~ • ♡ φ △ Z

1.1 — o ¢

— ◎ • ≡ • ☺ 6 • — $ 1.1 φ

1.1 ¢ ♡ ♡ 2 φ "

↑ this will explain everything!

write back or call me

holy

this drawing FOUND by Sarah Osment, Tucson, AZ

FOUND by John L. White

Hampden Academy, ME

this drawing FOUND by Danny and Nikki Jo, Pittsburgh, PA

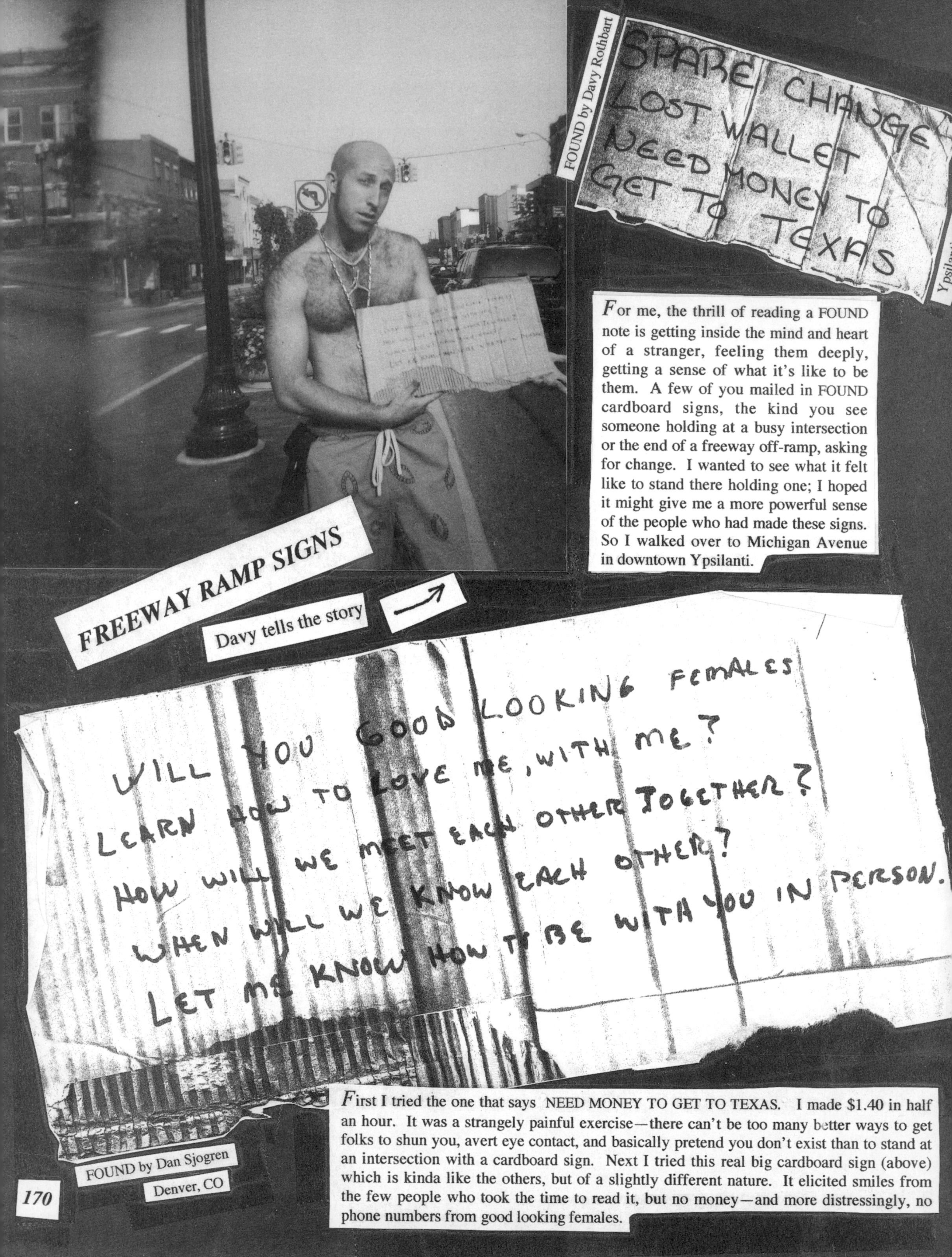


*F*or me, the thrill of reading a FOUND note is getting inside the mind and heart of a stranger, feeling them deeply, getting a sense of what it's like to be them. A few of you mailed in FOUND cardboard signs, the kind you see someone holding at a busy intersection or the end of a freeway off-ramp, asking for change. I wanted to see what it felt like to stand there holding one; I hoped it might give me a more powerful sense of the people who had made these signs. So I walked over to Michigan Avenue in downtown Ypsilanti.

# FREEWAY RAMP SIGNS

Davy tells the story

WILL YOU GOOD LOOKING FEMALES
LEARN HOW TO LOVE ME, WITH ME?
HOW WILL WE MEET EACH OTHER TOGETHER?
WHEN WILL WE KNOW EACH OTHER?
LET ME KNOW HOW TO BE WITH YOU IN PERSON.



FOUND by Dan Sjogren
Denver, CO

*F*irst I tried the one that says NEED MONEY TO GET TO TEXAS. I made $1.40 in half an hour. It was a strangely painful exercise—there can't be too many better ways to get folks to shun you, avert eye contact, and basically pretend you don't exist than to stand at an intersection with a cardboard sign. Next I tried this real big cardboard sign (above) which is kinda like the others, but of a slightly different nature. It elicited smiles from the few people who took the time to read it, but no money—and more distressingly, no phone numbers from good looking females.

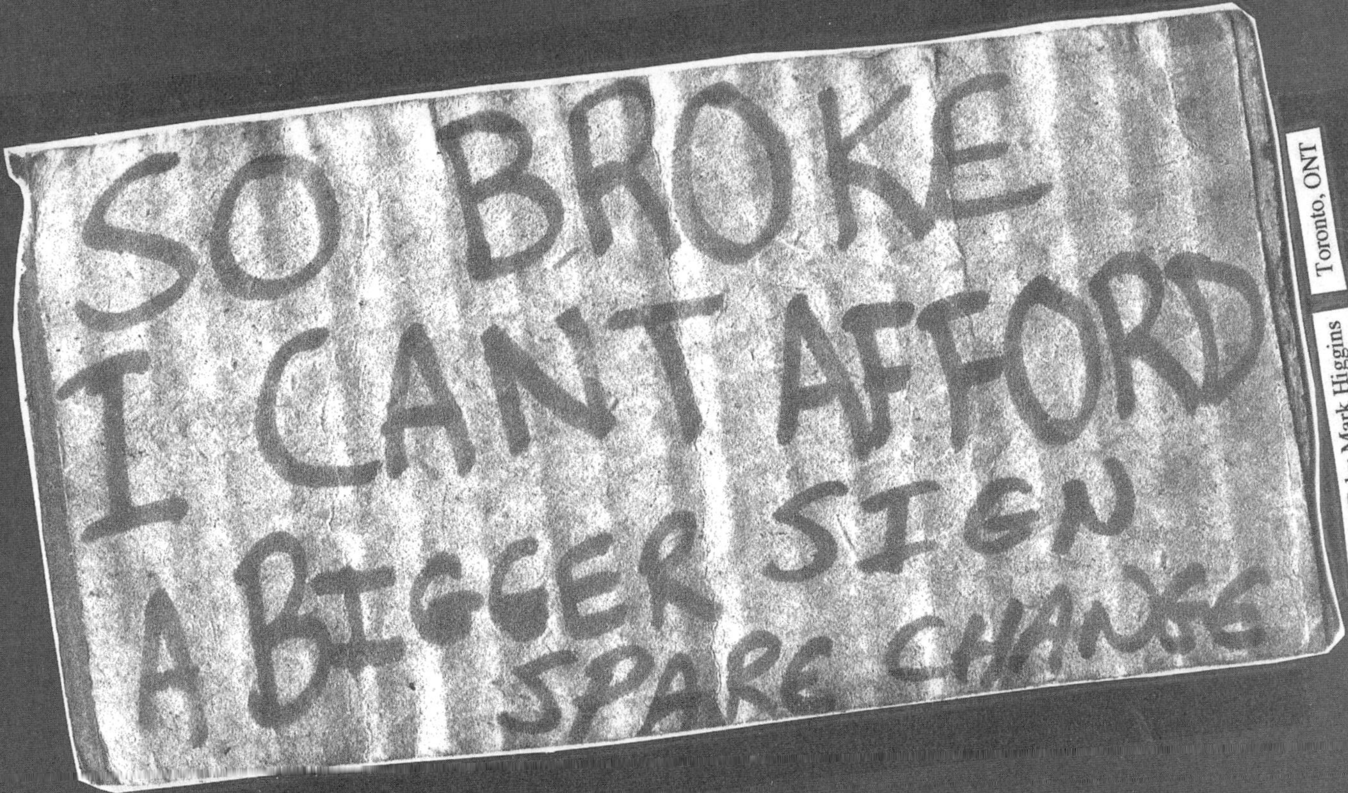

SO BROKE
I CANT AFFORD
A BIGGER SIGN
SPARE CHANGE

Toronto, ONT

FOUND by Mark Higgins

*T*he other signs on these pages have been shrunken way down but this one (above) is its actual size. Humor, apparently, is an effective panhandling device—I made almost five bucks in half an hour with this one.

photos by Dorothy Gotlib

*I* didn't make any money with this one (below), but I did get a phone number. Then I walked home. A couple weeks later, I gave all the money I'd made that day to a guy who was holding a cardboard sign in the same spot.

—DAVY

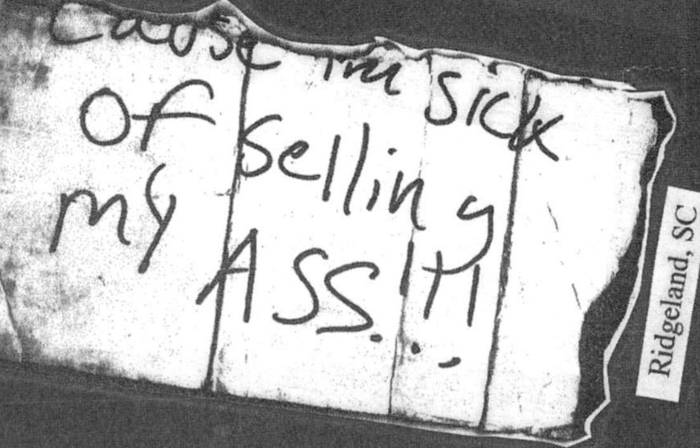


ND by Gulliver Gold

Ridgeland, SC

*FOUND Magazine.*

Let me know how to be with you in person.

Benjamin,

Hey baby, How are you doing. I just wanted to tell you I really appreciate you doing that for me, you do so much for me. Thank you for going out of your way At midnight for me. that's true love. You telling me that if I die or kill myself you will kill yourself. I LOVE you so much. You know what I LOVE buying you things that you want or need because you do so much for everyone and don't get a thankyou or people don't even consider how kind you are and I like to give you something to say I relize it and you deserve it. I like shopping for you and buying stuff because you're my baby and you always have to pay for school, computer, help your mom out etc. And deserve something for your hard work. That's why I think I have enough $ for Matrix call me at work telling me the times of the movie today and maybe we can catch a late show

P.S. 100 brownie points

Love ya without my heart
Shanti

mead



**$ FOR MATRIX**

FOUND by Emily Long

Chicago, IL

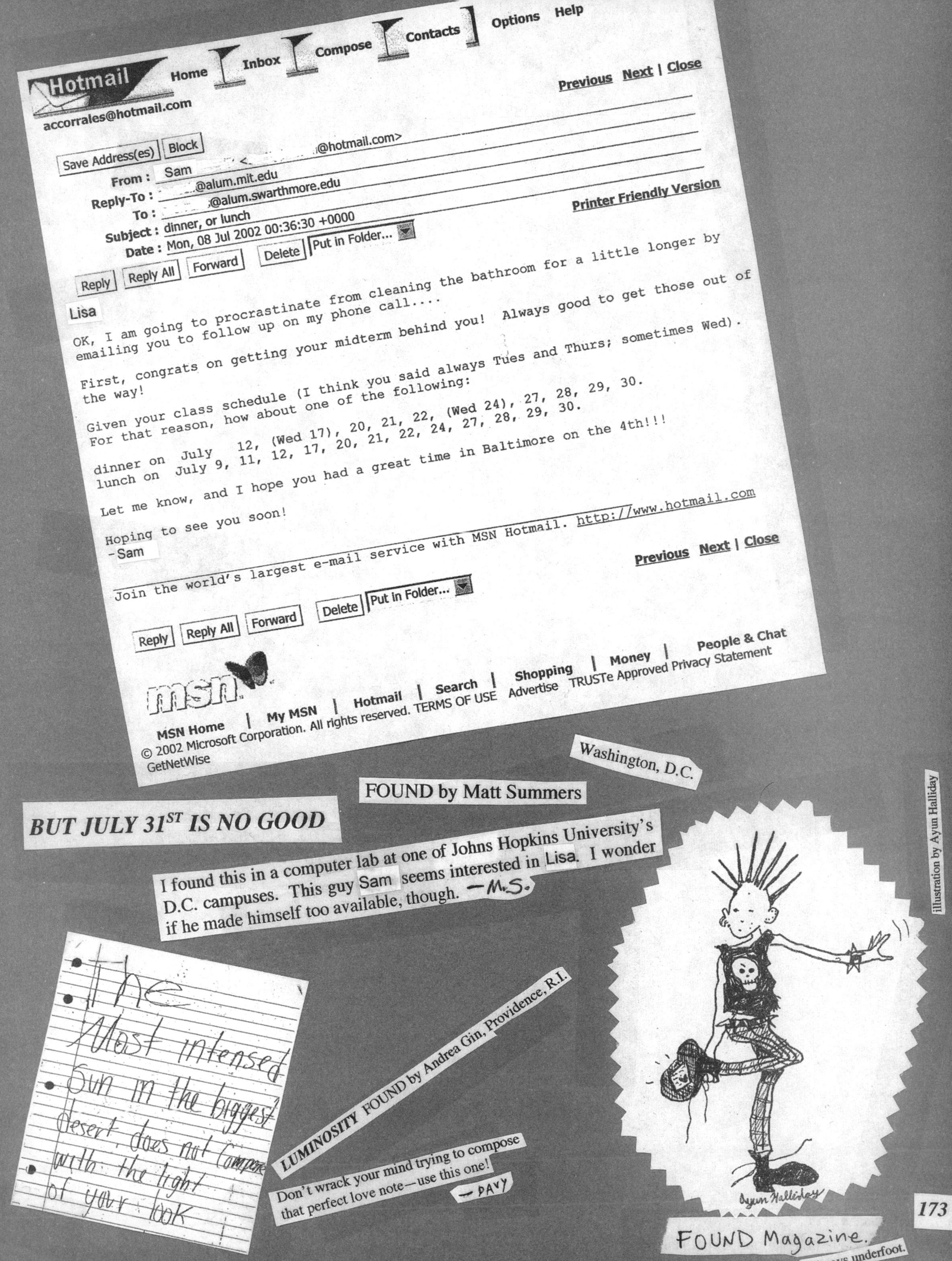
Hotmail
Home
Inbox
Compose
Contacts
Options
Help
accorrales@hotmail.com
Previous Next | Close
Save Address(es) Block
From : Sam < @hotmail.com>
Reply-To : @alum.mit.edu
To : @alum.swarthmore.edu
Subject : dinner, or lunch
Date : Mon, 08 Jul 2002 00:36:30 +0000
Printer Friendly Version
Reply Reply All Forward Delete Put in Folder...
Lisa
OK, I am going to procrastinate from cleaning the bathroom for a little longer by emailing you to follow up on my phone call....
First, congrats on getting your midterm behind you! Always good to get those out of the way!
Given your class schedule (I think you said always Tues and Thurs; sometimes Wed). For that reason, how about one of the following:
dinner on July 12, (Wed 17), 20, 21, 22, (Wed 24), 27, 28, 29, 30.
lunch on July 9, 11, 12, 17, 20, 21, 22, 24, 27, 28, 29, 30.
Let me know, and I hope you had a great time in Baltimore on the 4th!!!
Hoping to see you soon!
- Sam
Join the world's largest e-mail service with MSN Hotmail. http://www.hotmail.com
Previous Next | Close
Reply Reply All Forward Delete Put in Folder...
msn
MSN Home | My MSN | Hotmail | Search | Shopping | Money | People & Chat
© 2002 Microsoft Corporation. All rights reserved. TERMS OF USE Advertise TRUSTe Approved Privacy Statement
GetNetWise
Washington, D.C.
FOUND by Matt Summers
BUT JULY 31ST IS NO GOOD
I found this in a computer lab at one of Johns Hopkins University's D.C. campuses. This guy Sam seems interested in Lisa. I wonder if he made himself too available, though. —M.S.
The Most intensed Sun in the biggest desert does not Compare with the light of your look
LUMINOSITY FOUND by Andrea Gin, Providence, R.I.
Don't wrack your mind trying to compose that perfect love note—use this one!
—DAVY
illustration by Ayun Halliday
Ayun Halliday
FOUND Magazine.
Always underfoot.

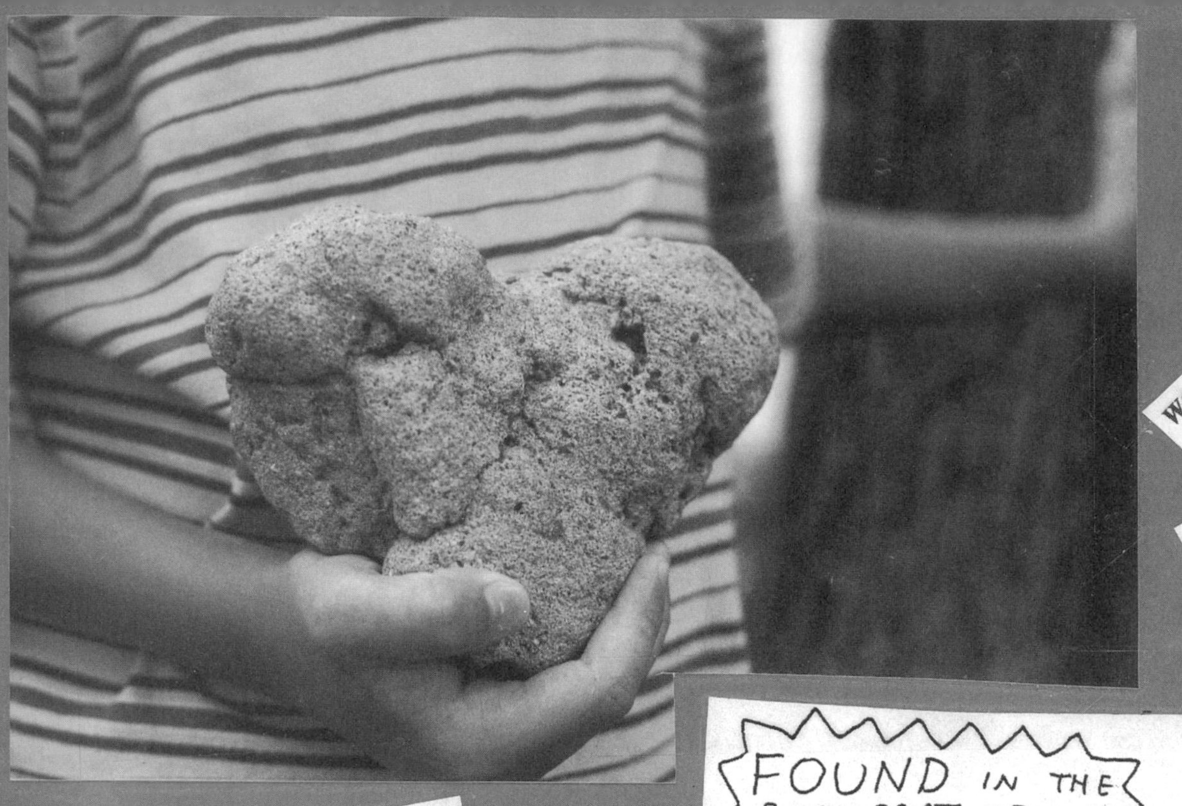

WOW! I WAS SO FULL OF EMOTION WHEN I SAW THAT GIRL DIE ON T.V. WHEN WE WERE IN BED TOGETHER!

FOUND by Charles Negendank

Knoxville, TN

**MY STONE HEART**

FOUND by Robert Hall

Clarksville, IN

The elements have sculpted this piece of concrete into the shape of a valentine heart. A friend and I found this twelve years ago in a waterfall; it now resides in my house in a display case. —R.H.

FOUND
3455 CHARING CROSS ROAD
ANN ARBOR, MI
48108

FOUND IN THE BACK SEAT OF MY BEST FRIEND'S CAR

BY JEFFREY BROWN

"DEAR TEDDY"... HEE HEE.. "I JUST WANT TO KNOW HOW SPECIAL YOU ARE AND HOW MUCH I'VE MISSED YOU THE LAST TWO DAYS..." HEE HEE HEE

"... AND THANK YOU FOR THE NOTE YOU LEFT ME IT WAS SOOO SWEET AND MEANS SOOOO MUCH TO ME.." HEE HEE "... AND I KNOW WE'LL ALWAYS HAVE A SPECIAL CONNECTION" HEE HEE

~APOLOGIES TO TED~

Hugs & more hugs & kisses
and more Kisses for V

Vanessa, oh what music to my ears!
You are what "they" are talking about-
pure beauty, oh what a feeling.

I know I love you
I know you love me
Gosh this is so cool, isn't it?
We are like perfect together. You make me feel a way I was sad to think I'd never feel, before. I'm smelling your smell in my sheets and on your jacket. I'm hugging your bear and snoopy. I call your bear "the sweetest thing." You are the sweetest thing. Wow! I was so full of emotion when I saw that girl die on t.v. when we were in bed together. It made me ill. I don't know what I'd do without you - you fullfill me in such a way. Thinking about being with you is like what helps me - w/ grades, life, myself, etc etc The list is endless. You are the blood that pumps my heart and the air that my lungs breathe in. How refreshing. I could explode with my feelings for you, my sweet Vanessa.

P.S. You're so fucking cool
the coolest ~~the~~ girl in the world

TEST OVER CHAPTER 7 (Alg. II-2) Good Luck

NAME Aaron H.

0

Determine if the example models exponential growth or exponential decay. Then find the percent increase or decrease.

① $y = 620(.94)^x$

② $y = 54(1.07)^x$

Graph each function.

③ $y = 5.3(.4)^x$

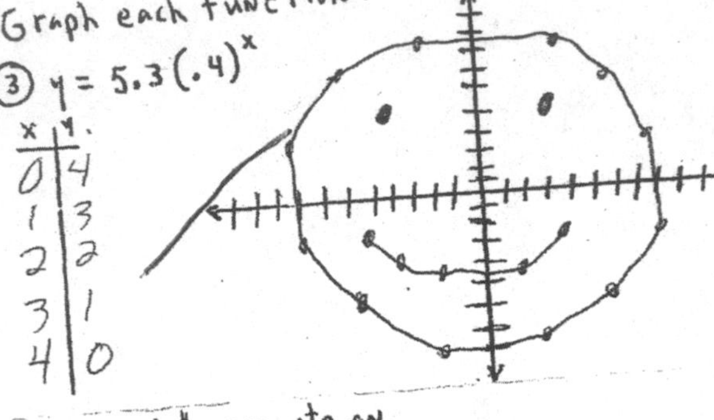

④ $y = 3(2)^x$

| x | y |
|---|---|
| 81 | 48 |
| 64 | 10 |
| 420 | 56 |
| 69 | 75 |

⑤ You put $2,000 into an account earning 4% interest compounded continuously. Find the amount at the end of 8 years.

Not enough

⑥ Write an equation to describe each exponential function $y = ab^x$. The base is 8 and the graph passes through the point (1,3).

X−Q = ABCDEFGHIJKLMNOPQR TUVWXYZ

Evaluate each expression by first rewriting it as an exponential equation.

⑦ $\text{Log}_2 16$

Loggggg 8

⑧ $\text{Log}_5 125$

Logggggg 25

⑨ $\text{Log}_4 \frac{1}{64}$

Logggggg 16

Expand the following.

⑩ $\text{Log } 3x^2$

$\text{Log } 6^{x^{12}}$

⑪ $\text{Log } \frac{4y}{x^3}$

Condense the following.

⑫ $\text{Log } 7 + 2 \text{ Log } A - 5 \text{ Log } B$

It's Small enough

⑬ Expand $\text{Log}_3 14$ into an expression with two logarithmic terms.

150 ÷ 2 = 75 × 2 = 150 ÷ 2 = 75 × 2 = 150 ÷ 2 = 75 × 2 = 150 ÷ 2 = Correct answer

⑭ Use the properties of logarithms to evaluate $\text{Log } 5 + \text{Log } 10 + \text{Log } 2$.

Get off my Property !!!!

(fron

## AARON'S ALGEBRA TEST

FOUND by David Meiklejohn

Portland, ME

This algebra test has become one of my very favorite finds of all-time. It's clear that Aaron is having his struggles with Algebra II, but I love what he's done here: He's decided, "you know what, I'm here for an hour, I might as well have fun with this." I think his answers are positively delightful! If he's my student, he's getting an A+, best grade in the class. But check out the ruthless humorlessness with which this test has been graded—the teacher gives no comment toward his creative spirit, no encouragement, just a simple red slash through every single problem. Aaron's total score for this test—which includes a series of rhymed couplets on the back? A zero.

—DAVY

Solve the Following Equations.

(15) $\sqrt{x^4} = 81$

Yahoo
Yahoo
Yahoo
Yahoo

(16) Log 5x = 3

Yahoo
Yahoo
Yahoo
Yahoo

(17) $10^{2x} = 40$

Yahoo
Yahoo
Yahoo
Yahoo

(back)

(18) $x^{\frac{3}{2}} - 5 = 59$

(19) $4e^{2x} = 14$

(20) $\ln(2x+5) = 10$

My name is Aaron
Im in Algebra Two
I sit in class for an hour
And nothing I do

What Killian is talking about
I guess I'll never know
But its stuff I should've learned
A long time ago

But I just sat in his room
watching the time pass
And all I would do
Is sit on my as—

My hopes of passing
Is no hope at all
I just stare at the board
And watch my grade fall

Maybe Someday
My grade will go higher
But who am I kidding
Im only a lyer.

This Algebra year
In June will soon stop
And that means my grade
Can no longer drop

YAY!!!

Me

You

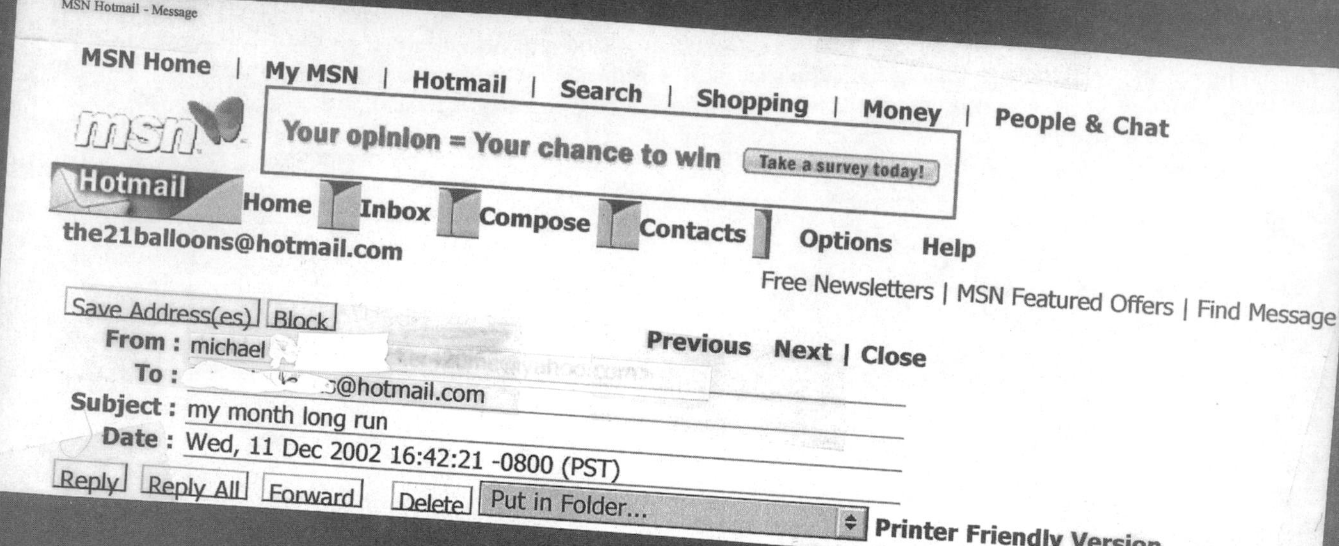
MSN Hotmail - Message

MSN Home | My MSN | Hotmail | Search | Shopping | Money | People & Chat

msn

Your opinion = Your chance to win [Take a survey today!]

Hotmail Home | Inbox | Compose | Contacts | Options | Help

the21balloons@hotmail.com

Free Newsletters | MSN Featured Offers | Find Message

[Save Address(es)] [Block]

Previous Next | Close

From : michael

To : @hotmail.com

Subject : my month long run

Date : Wed, 11 Dec 2002 16:42:21 -0800 (PST)

[Reply] [Reply All] [Forward] [Delete] [Put in Folder...] Printer Friendly Version

Hi, I just wanted to tell you about my month and a half run :-)

Lets just say that is was very enjoyable until the end. But lets not get ahead of my self here first some background I'm 19 I've been doing crystal for about 3 years now off and on (pretty hard-core the last year or so) anyway.... I was hit by a van when I was a little kid (2 yrs old)...so my mom sued the hell out of them and now I get

Settlements every year...7500$ a year pretty nice huh? Lets just say

That that whole check went into my pipe...and up my nose...anyway to the story

This started in about May. My mom kick me out once again (I said some very hurtful words to here and I regret it everyday that I live) I never new my dad but I ended up meeting him one day and I was homeless so he offered for me to live on our boat. So I move in and I ask him if does crystal. And he said "hell yea" so we party every now and then. (We mostly drank) Just enjoyin' our self's. (It was nice to get to know him) The months tick away and July comes around. So I got to my lawyer's office and pick up my big old check (yea!!) First thing I do is go to the bank and cash it. Then I went about looking for an 8 ball (3&1/2 grams) so my dad call up his friend who sells and he comes on by. We get the ball and do it that day (and night). This is how I met my friend John (he really is a good dude even if he narcked me out) so me and John go out and get a quarter oz the next day and the next day and the next day (you get the point) but anyway I must say that we had a blast we used to go pick up hookers just to party with them (no sex) we were all over the place(the whole month and a half was kind of a blur) but anyway...

We had it on lock down. We programmed it hard. 6:am strait to jack in the box...go smoke some more...12 noon. Go to taco bell go right next store to pick up food for Bill . ( John's Big ol' dog) then we would go to a friends house and smoke some more...go back to the boat and smoke some more.... and smoke some more next morning comes around and guess where we go? That's right... jack in the box...then we would smoke some more go call our dealer up and see if he wanted to play darts. We would play darts for days on end...

But sure enough back to the boat ...to smoke some more...we got kicked off the dock and went to some derelict dock. But it was all-good because we had a generator.(you really don't carte about to much when your tweeking) So we continued to party all night (nothin' like being wide awake drunk all night)

Our job was to smoke and find more crystal...that's it...what a job huh? So to wrap it up toward the end of the time when my money stared to run low I got arrested. All because I was coming down and so was bob. he ran out of gas. And so this is what he told me (I don't remember much I was passed out) he tried to get me to push the van to the curb but I just could not. I was just too dead. (There was no

this drawing FOUND by Katie and Nina, St. Louis, MO

amount of crystal in the world that would wake me up at this point.) Anyway...so the next morning comes and I wake up to a clink clink clink sure enough it was the cops. Both me and bob passed out and we ended up parking about 4 ft. away from the curb "can you step out of the car please" asked the officer and as soon as I opened the back door to get out a beer bottle fell out ::gasp:: I got caught with a gram of crystal. (But thankfully I had safety-pinned 4 sacks to the inside of my sweater and they never found it. There was a gram in each sack.)The cops would have got me with intent to sale and then I would have gone away for a very long time. But anyway... They propped 36'd(for those of you who don't know that is a drug diversion program) me out so it was nothin' to me...this is where it started to suck...

Me and Rob where getting really paranoid

Things that we would do at the begging of the trip where out of the question...I remember one time I would refuse to go down to my boat

Because I swore that I heard my dad saying that the police where they're which they weren't...constantly looking in the mirrors of the van because I thought that someone was following me. (Lol)

Anyway.... about a week later a got arrested again...this time I got to go visit good ol' hotel Sana-Rita (county jail) for a month... I had something like 8 pipes, 1 crystal

Bong, 3/8 of good ol' Mary Jane and can you believe this?? .1 grams of crystal!

That was all! But because of my priors I went in. but somehow bob only stayed for 3 days...what's up with that??? (me and him got arrested for the same charge)

# MY MONTH LONG RUN

FOUND by Davy Rothbart

Redding, CA

I was using the computers at the public library. The kid at the next computer, maybe twenty years old, was typing furiously and singing softly to himself. Every few minutes he sat up straight, laced his fingers together above his head and stretched, then went back to battering the keyboard. I wondered what he was writing about. At one point, he started freaking out all of a sudden and asking everyone if they had a disk he could borrow. I guess the computers shut off after you've been there for an hour, and he was afraid he'd lose the long piece of writing he was working on. No one had a disk, and his computer wouldn't let him save to the hard drive, so I suggested he copy and paste his essay into an e-mail and e-mail it to me. He got the e-mail off seconds before his computer shut down.

A few minutes later he'd signed on to a new computer, and also found a disk he could save his file to, so I e-mailed it back to him. He was grateful and for a few minutes we had a pleasant conversation; then I left. The next day I finally got a chance to read what he'd written. I e-mailed him again, asking how the story ended. For a couple months I didn't hear anything. Then at last he responded. He said he was still out of jail and off of drugs, though living drug-free was a struggle. Best of all, he said, he'd reconciled with his mom. Now, a year later, he's just been hired at the same library where we met.

—DAVY

***RICE*** FOUND by Karen Cutter, Belmont, CA
Found this list left behind by a 19 year-old girl who housesat for us in 1989.

NEEDS
RUG SPOT REMOVER
NAIL CLIPERS
Q-TIPS
SEX AND UNDERSTANDING
OIL, VEG.
RICE
WART STUFF + BANDAIDS

"The Clear Choice in performance"
Fully integrated/modular system


***THE NEW, NEW THING***
FOUND by Katherine Allred, Salt Lake City, UT
Found this business card on the ground at the Utah State Fair. *I have no clue what this is advertising.*

DON'T ASK
DON'T KNOW
MORE INFO. IN HAT

***MORE INFO IN HAT*** FOUND by Arnie Rutkis, Birmingham, AL

SHUT UP
I'M WATCHING
THE GAME

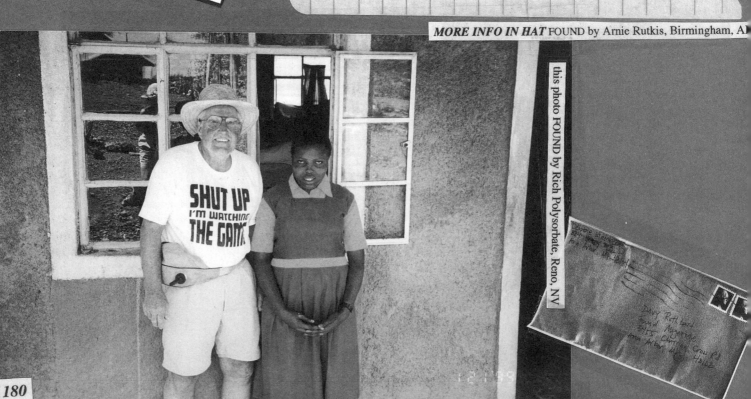

this photo FOUND by Rich Polysorbate, Reno, NV

USIC LOVERS BE WARNED FOUND by Dan Miller, Philadelphia, PA

PLEASE DO NOT
BOUNCE HEAD!
THANK YOU

No:
J's lover
D.U.I.
Temessee

NO FOUND by Elizabeth Crane, Chicago, IL

mett me down by the big
bush from the kid whith
the green Backpack

RENDEZ-VOUS FOUND by Trevor Harris, Columbia, MO

this drawing FOUND by Debbie Steinberg, Ann Arbor, MI

2085
1455

I WANT TO GO SOMEWHERE WHERE I DON'T ALWAYS HAVE TO CLENCH MY TEETH AND I'M NOT AFRAID OF SCORPIONS IN MY WATER. I LEFT A LITTLE LIGHT FOR YOU, EVEN THOUGH I KNOW I SHOULDN'T EXTEND YOU THAT COURTESY. I KNOW SOMEONE WHO WOULD GIVE ME ADVICE. BUT I LOST TOUCH. IT'S HARD WHEN NO ONE WANTS TO HELP. A FLOWER SHOP AND A STUDIO APPARTMENT. A DARK GREY CAR AND A BOY NAMED CHRIS. I DON'T ASK FOR MUCH.

*A BOY NAMED CHRIS*
FOUND by Lori Sartin, Billings, MT
I found this deep in a couch at the community college where I take night classes.

# Erika Rioja

Erika we the boys want to know why are you going out with Nathan and you like all of us in a way. Tell us why and list how much you like the person with there name for example, Fred/not at all I think. Sorry for asking you all of these questions but we the boys want to know and get to the bottom of this. I'm always having to write the letters because they are some punks. You don't have to tell us right away but do tell us. Me, Fred, and Ricky thought of it, well it was really just Fred. All of the boys in the 6th grade likes you expect for some. That means that you are the finest girl in the whole 6th grade. A few them like you because of you know what but I don't. I like you because you have a pretty face/smile and your the only girl that has a little piece of hair going down your face. I think that makes you even prettier. You said that was your own style and I think that it's cool or whatever. That's all for now so i'll see you on the flip side, peace out.

P.S. Call me if you want to tell me about myself or just to talk about something. You know my number and if you don't then i'll tell you in your ear or something because I don't want any other girl but you to know my number. Not even Aisha

WE THE BOYS

FOUND by Amy Price & Brian Farmer

Austin, TX

# I'M IN HERE THINKING

FOUND by George Prince

San Francisco, CA

Dear Husband,
I'm in here thinking
about you. About how much
I love you. I'm proud of
you for finding a job you'll
like and be happy in.
You're so smart & thoughtful. I've never known a
person as sweet as you —
you truly think of other
people before you think
of yourself. That's a rare
quality. You're much nicer &
beautiful then the average
person and I don't deserve
you.
I know I fuss at you
too much but I swear I'm
never (hardly) really mad
at you. I'm too impatient.
I hope I don't hurt your

feelings too often. I never
want to make you feel
bad although I know I
do sometimes because I'm
so mean. I love you &
I'm sorry I make you
unhappy sometimes.
Please don't ever
leave me or your gentle
ways behind.
Thank you for being
my best friend.

photo by Dorothy Gotlib

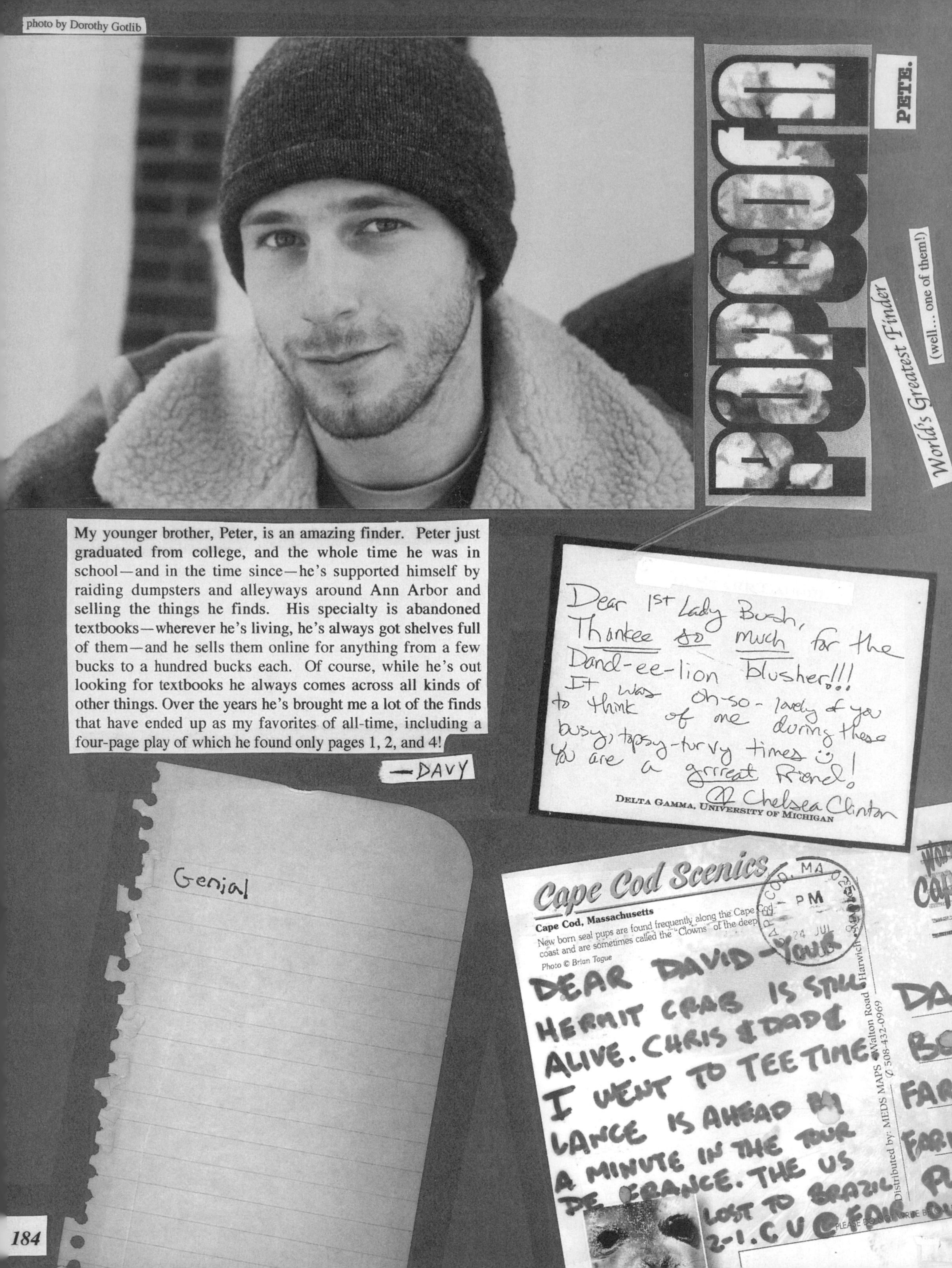


My younger brother, Peter, is an amazing finder. Peter just graduated from college, and the whole time he was in school—and in the time since—he's supported himself by raiding dumpsters and alleyways around Ann Arbor and selling the things he finds. His specialty is abandoned textbooks—wherever he's living, he's always got shelves full of them—and he sells them online for anything from a few bucks to a hundred bucks each. Of course, while he's out looking for textbooks he always comes across all kinds of other things. Over the years he's brought me a lot of the finds that have ended up as my favorites of all-time, including a four-page play of which he found only pages 1, 2, and 4!

—DAVY

Dear 1st Lady Bush,
Thankee so much for the
Dand-ee-lion blusher!!!
It was oh-so-lovely of you
to think of me during these
busy, topsy-turvy times ☺
You are a grrreat friend!
♡ Chelsea Clinton

DELTA GAMMA, UNIVERSITY OF MICHIGAN

Genial

Cape Cod Scenics

Cape Cod, Massachusetts

New born seal pups are found frequently along the Cape Cod coast and are sometimes called the "Clowns" of the deep.

Photo © Brian Tague

CAPE COD, MA 026
PM
24 JUL

DEAR DAVID— YOUR
HERMIT CRAB IS STILL
ALIVE. CHRIS & DAD &
I WENT TO TEE TIME.
LANCE IS AHEAD BY
A MINUTE IN THE TOUR
DE FRANCE. THE US
LOST TO BRAZIL
2-1. C U @ FAIR

Distributed by: MEDS MAPS • Walton Road • Harwich • MA
☎ 508-432-0969

*After leaving the building, please...*

# LOCK THIS DOOR

*It will prevent unauthorized people from entering the building and* **defecating** *in the washing machine. Many thanks!*

**POPCORN PETE SAYS:** Note that those who are authorized to defecate in the washing machine will be given a key for entry!

October 15, 1997

Professor W
College of Engineering
University of Michigan
Ann Arbor, MI 48105

Dear Sir:

If this letter reached you with this address some good fortune has already smiled on my effort. I saw you quoted in a newspaper article reporting the planned inspection of commercial aircraft after the TWA 800 disaster.

While inspections may prevent some future mishap, no inspection could have prevented the TWA 800 explosion.

I am the helo pilot who saw the plane struck and saw the series of explosions leading up to the fuel burn. The first two explosions appeared to me to be military ordnance. They were high velocity explosions; one multi-colored similar to HPX and the second brilliant white light. The third event in the chain was a low velocity explosion; the fuel burn which occurred 3-5 seconds after the initial explosion.

I believe that TWA 800 was struck by one or two missiles. Whatever brought it down was not initiated by a fuel explosion.

I graduated from U of M in 1962. The quality of the Engineering Department has been internationally recognized for generations. Therefore I know that you and your colleagues have the skills to find the truth. Please inquire.

Cordially,

Milton H. White II

all Found by Peter Rothbart

WHOLE FOODS
Customer Communication
Please take a moment to give us your comments, suggestions or questions. If you need a personal or confidential reply please include your phone number.

Date:

The bunny or rabbit are stupiel get rid of them.

Response: I am not sure what bunny or rabbit you refer to here. Please be more specific. Thanks.

Team Member Name: David Lott, Store Team Leader
Date: 2/13/01

NAILED!

FOUND by dan zatkovich, janice smith, & dan smith

*DAN ZATKOVICH EXPLAINS....* So janice's brother dan comes into town (san diego) for a couple days before leaving for china for a year. we take him to a pizza place in ocean beach and we're just sitting there eating. there's this door near our table that separates the kitchen from the dining area and dan points out the sign on it—CAUTION!! DOOR WILL SWING OPEN AND NAIL YOU! It's pretty funny to all of us. i mean, usually you see a sign like that and it says, "Careful, door opens quickly" or "watch for swinging door." something about the "and nail you" part just seems hilarious. it provides such a concrete image; its so full of malice. janice says, "hey, that would be great for davy's magazine." we have a lengthy debate, the 3 of us, about what exactly constitutes "FOUND." i mean, does it have to be blowing down the street? or can it just be a sign you see hanging somewhere?

eventually we decide that one of us is gonna have to grab the sign. actually, janice and her brother decide that *I* have to grab the sign. so when we're done eating, we're kind of hanging out, waiting for a quiet moment by the kitchen door. for some reason i get real nervous about getting caught. i mean, realistically, they're not gonna have me arrested or anything. but there is a real potential for a big scene and some serious embarassment. finally there's no employees around. i go over to the door and take out the bottom two tacks. janice and her brother are watching from the front door, ready to book out of there if any of the employees swoop in on me.

AUTION!!
DOOR WILL SWING
OPEN AND NAIL
YOU!

from up close i can see how much time someone put into making the sign—there's pencil underneath, like they did a rough draft, putting it down, erasing, putting it down, and then once they got it right they retraced their letters with a thick pen or thin marker. i've got no idea why I'm so goddamn nervous, but i keep looking all around, making sure the coast is still clear, then i turn back to pull out the top two thumb-tacks and WHAM!!! the door flies open and fuckin *NAILS* me!! a dude comes out of the kitchen with a platter full of food and drinks, and he's like, "oh, sorry," and he walks off toward a table in the next room. my head and my face are throbbing from the blow. i yank the sign down and walk woozily outside—janice and dan are squealing and collapsing with laughter, practically peeing themselves. looking back on things, now that the bruise has healed up a bit, i can imagine how funny it must have been to them. i got so caught up in how COOL and FUNNY the sign was, i forgot about the practical nature of its message. davy, tell people to be careful collecting FOUND stuff—it could get them killed.

SEPT, 16, 95

PETER! AKA "CHICO PUNK SPONGE" "THIEF" "TEAR DROP" "SHIT STAIN"

THANK'S SO MUCH. FOR STOPPING BY FOR FIVE MONTH'S AND SPONGING. LEAVING SPUNK TRACKS ON MY CLEAN BLANKET'S. LEAVING EVERYTHING NAMELY BILL'S UNPAID. TAKING MY STEREO WATCH CASSETTE TAPE.

I KNOW ITS A HORRIBLE THING HAVING PEOPLE GIVE YOU FOOD WHEN YOUR HUNGRY, SHELTER, TABBACO, MONEY. HOW COULD I HAVE BEEN SO CRUEL.

HEY I KNOW THE CLOTHES I GAVE YOU JUST WERNT COOL ENOUGH. I KNOW CLEANING UP AFTER YOU WASNT GOOD ENOUGH I SHOULD HAVE CLEANED YOUR ROOM WASHED YOUR CLOTHES AND WIPED YOUR STINKING ASS. AT LEAST THAT WAY MAYBE YOUR SPONGE FREINT'S COULD STAND YOUR STINK!

LET'S NOT FORGET BRINGING A WONDERFUL 15 YEAR OLD FAT CHICK RUNAWAY TO OUR PLACE. OF COURSE HIDING HER HERE HAS BROUGHT THE COP'S. THE NEIGHBORS ESPECIALY APPRECIATED THE COP'S BUSTING IN TO THEIR PLACE. THEY THINK SO MUCH OF YOU NOW! GOSH GOLLY WE ALL DO!

HUGS AND KISSES, Chad YOUR FREIND FOR LIFE!

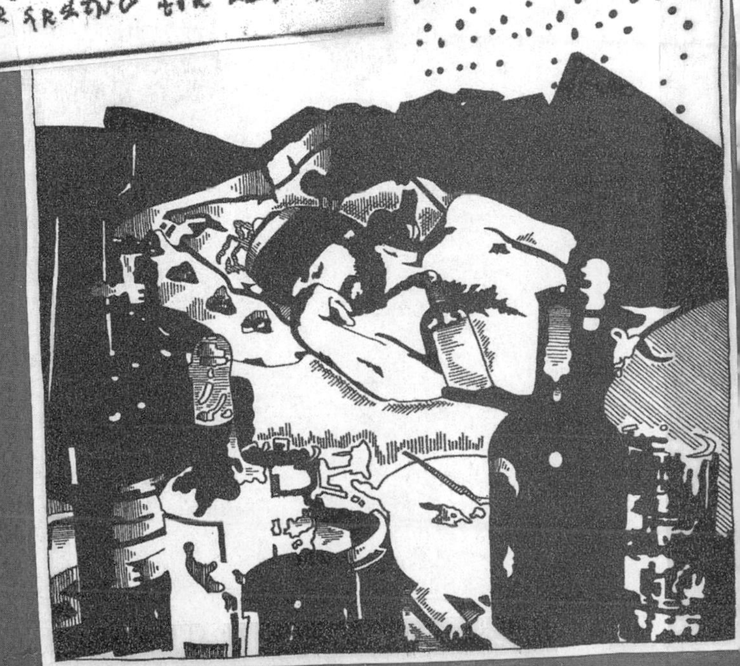

CHICO PUNK SPONGE

FOUND by Tae Won Yu

Olympia, WA

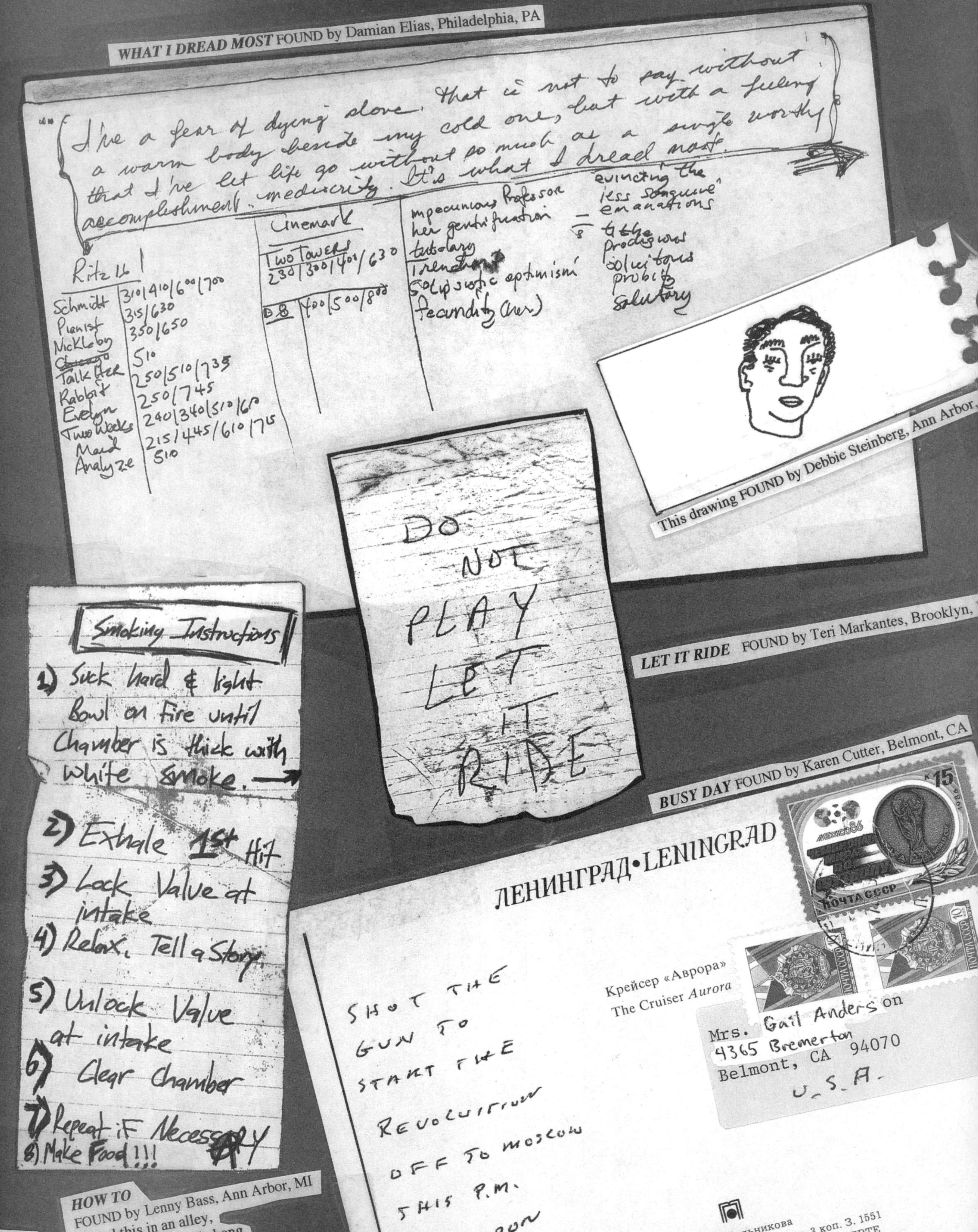
WHAT I DREAD MOST FOUND by Damian Elias, Philadelphia, PA
I've a fear of dying alone. That is not to say without a warm body beside my cold one, but with a feeling that I've let life go without so much as a single worthy accomplishment. mediocrity. It's what I dread most.
Cinemark
Two Towers
230/300/400/630
DB 400/500/800
Ritz 16
Schmidt 310/410/600/700
Pianist 315/630
Nickleby 350/650
510
Talk Her 250/510/735
Rabbit 250/745
Evelyn 240/340/510/650
Two Weeks 215/445/610/715
Maid
Analyze 510
impecunious Professor
her gentrification
tutelary
trenchant
solipsistic optimism
fecundity (ness)
evincing the
less sanguine
emanations
the
prodigious
solicitous
probity
salutary
This drawing FOUND by Debbie Steinberg, Ann Arbor,
DO NOT PLAY LET IT RIDE
LET IT RIDE FOUND by Teri Markantes, Brooklyn,
Smoking Instructions
1) Suck hard & light Bowl on Fire until Chamber is thick with white smoke.
2) Exhale 1st Hit
3) Lock Value at intake
4) Relax. Tell a Story
5) Unlock Value at intake
6) Clear Chamber
7) Repeat iF Necessary
8) Make Food!!!
BUSY DAY FOUND by Karen Cutter, Belmont, CA
ЛЕНИНГРАД•LENINGRAD
ПОЧТА СССР
Крейсер «Аврора»
The Cruiser Aurora
SHOT THE GUN TO START THE REVOLUTION
OFF TO MOSCOW THIS P.M.
GORDON
Mrs. Gail Anderson
4365 Bremerton
Belmont, CA 94070
U.S.A.
Фото В. Мельникова
© «Планета», 1985. 7/8в-6456. 400 тыс. 3 коп. З. 1551
ОТПРАВЛЯТЬ ПО ПОЧТЕ ТОЛЬКО В КОНВЕРТЕ
HOW TO
FOUND by Lenny Bass, Ann Arbor, MI
Found this in an alley, taped to a homemade bong.

this picture FOUND by Morgan C. Zernich, Oberlin, OH

"We love, because He first loved us." 1 John 4:19

*I CARE...*

About My square head

Who lives at Circleville

Because I have a Big Square head

....and I want my church to help me put concern into action.

+++++++++++++++++++++++++

*I WISH...*

We would sing give me a circle head

The Pastor would preach a sermon

on different people with different heads

Someone would visit the Square headed dude

Name □ head

Date Who cares

I/We communed X

I would like to.......

get a normal head

**THE SQUARE-HEADED DUDE** FOUND by Susanna Peck, Caldeonia, MI

ANY 2 OF THE 3

FOUND by Tyrone White

Wilmington, DE

HEY GROUCHY!

Don't call me til you have good news about my lines, the Goonies, and Rhode Island, well — any 2 of the 3.

Later Dude!

this drawing FOUND by Amy Carter, Bloomington, IN

# A MESSAGE FROM ROGER

Standing on a Clearwater pier, a little boy put a note in a bottle: "To whoever finds this, please write me a letter and let me know." Nineteen years went by. Roger, we got your note.

reprinted with permission from the St.Petersburg Times

STORY BY LANE DEGREGORY

At first, he thought it was trash.

The bottle was bobbing in a canal behind Don Smith's house in Venetian Isles, drifting toward his dock. He saw it on the Fourth of July, while he was playing with his grandchildren. He grabbed a fishing net and scooped the bottle out of the murky water. One side was fuzzy with algae. The other was clear. Black electrical tape was wound tightly around the top. The rusty cap said "Pepsi" in an obsolete logo.

Inside, there was a note.

The paper was folded, scorched sepia by the sun. It had been ripped from a school writing tablet, the kind with dotted blue lines. Smith pulled it out and smoothed it on a table. "To whoever finds this letter please write me a letter and let me know," the note said in shaky pencil. "Roger J. Clay, 890 Linwood Ave., Fairfield Ohio, 45014." Don and his wife, Carol, know the place. They are from Cincinnati, about 25 miles from Fairfield. Their son Sean works in Fairfield. "What are the odds?" Don asked.

Then he saw the date. On the bottom right corner, the paper said: 12/27/84. That bottle had been in the water for almost 19 years.

Don's daughter-in-law is a teacher. By the handwriting, she said, whoever wrote the note was probably 7 or 8 years old. Roger J. Clay would be 26 or 27 now. "Wouldn't it be great if we could find him and let him know we found his bottle?" Carol said. "I'll try," said Don. "But 19 years is a long, long time."

That night, after the fireworks, Don got on the Internet. He didn't find Roger J. Clay. He found this: "Roger K. Clay, 890 Linwood Ave., Fairfield, Ohio."A few more clicks and Don found public records showing Roger K. was 49. "Must be the kid's father," Don told his wife. "And it looks like he still lives at the same house. What are the odds?' Don tried to find a phone number, but had no luck.

So he wrote a letter: "I found your son's message in a bottle behind my house in St. Petersburg, Florida," he wrote. "I just thought you would want to know." He mailed the letter the next morning, Saturday. On Monday, he called the St. Petersburg Times.

Don and Carol Smith are 56 and retired. Don owned a Cincinnati business that manufactured trailers to haul mobile television studios. Carol was a Realtor. "I couldn't believe it. Could a bottle really last that long out there? In Tampa Bay?" Don asked. "Geez, 19 years!"

Back at work, we tried to find out more about the boy who wrote the message. Caryn Baird, a Times researcher, tapped into electronic databases, tracked all sorts of records. But she couldn't come up with a Roger J. Clay. Then she scanned Social Security files. There he was.

"He's dead," she said.

There had been an article in the paper. Nine days after his 21st birthday, Roger J. Clay was driving home on his new Suzuki. "His motorcycle went left of center and collided head-on with a pickup," the Columbus Dispatch reported. "Police are still trying to determine why Clay's motorcycle went left of center." It happened on July 10, 1998. Five years ago today.

Courtesy of Clay family

I called Don Smith and read him the news. He coughed. Or choked. Or something. "Oh my God. Oh my God. I knew it," he said. "That's terrible. I can't explain it. Oh my God. I just had this feeling something had happened to that kid." Now Don was even more determined to find Roger's parents. "Imagine what that message would mean to them," he said.

So Caryn found a new address and a phone number for Roger's dad. Then she found a number for someone she thought might be his mom, at a different address. I gave the numbers to Don. A half-hour later, he called me back. "You're not going to believe this," he said.

Roger's dad wasn't home. So Don had called the other number, the one for Lisa M. Ferguson, who used to be married to Roger K. Clay. A woman had answered. No, Lisa wasn't home. "I'm Lisa's sister," the woman said. "Can I help?" Don explained why he was calling. "Oh my God!" the woman gasped. "Lisa is away," she said. Every year this time, she goes away. "She can't stand to be in Ohio around the anniversary of the accident." She gave Don a cell phone number. "Lisa is down in Florida," her sister said. "In Seminole."

Lisa had just come back from the pool when her cell phone rang. She and her husband, Al, were cooling off in their hotel room. When Don told Lisa he had found a bottle, she started screaming. She knew the rest. She remembers that note. She remembers the day her son wrote it. They were in Clearwater, celebrating Christmas with her sister. Roger was 7. His dad took him fishing on Pier 60. Roger wrote the note and took tape from the tackle box and sealed the note in the bottle and tossed it off the pier. Lisa remembers telling him he was littering.

Roger was a happy, active kid. He liked to pretend to climb the walls like Spider-Man. He liked shooting squirrels with his dad. He raced dirt bikes. He fished. And he dropped a Pepsi bottle in the water even though his mother disapproved. Now, 19 years later, a stranger had called and given her back her son. "Here I am, trying to escape Roger's death, and he reaches out and gives me this message, this gift," she said. Lisa told Don she wanted to see him. She wanted to hold that bottle. She wanted to touch that note, trace Roger's childish letters with her finger. Don wanted to see Lisa, too. He wanted to learn about Roger. They agreed to meet for dinner at 7:30 Tuesday night. How does it happen? Can a message really float around in a bottle for 19 years and surface so close to where it started?

"I'm not at all surprised," said Robert Weisberg. He is a professor in the College of Marine Science at the University of South Florida, St. Petersburg. He makes models of currents, tracks tides and studies how objects travel in water. "There would be no problem at all getting a bottle from Clearwater's Pier 60 to Tampa Bay. Water does move," he said. "There are currents out there that are driven by wind. There are tides. It certainly is reasonable for something like that to stay in circulation around this area."

The bottle could have gotten hung up in a mangrove somewhere and stayed there for 15 years, Weisberg said. It could have moved around a bit, floated down to Sanibel Island and come back up into the bay again. It could have circulated up the gulf toward the Panhandle, then gone to Texas and come back under the Sunshine Skyway bridge. "Once something drifts offshore, there's no telling," he said.

Vembu Subramanian, who works in USF's office of Coastal Ocean Monitoring and Prediction Systems, said the bottle could have traveled thousands of paths from Clearwater to Venetian Isles. "There could have been boats moving it. It could have bounced through all those little islands. Who knows what kinds of influences could have impacted its path all those years?"

All day Tuesday, Roger J. Clay's mother couldn't stop smiling. And crying. And smiling. She called her daughter in Ohio. She called her brothers and sisters. She called Roger's dad, who cried so hard he had to hang up. "I had forgotten all about that bottle. It's kind of hard to put into words, all the emotions that brings back," Roger K. Clay told me from Ohio. "I told Lisa, it was like he was trying to remind us he was still with us."

Lisa told Roger's dad she would get to see the bottle that night. She and Al got to the restaurant early. At 7:40 p.m., a man with blue eyes and salt-and-pepper hair walked up, holding a bubble- wrapped bottle. Lisa smothered him, weeping, without even introducing herself. Don hugged her back. Hard. Then they stood there, in the lobby of the restaurant, holding on and sobbing into each other's shoulders. Their spouses stood by, dabbing at their eyes. "Isn't this unreal?" Carol Smith asked. "He's still touching lives," Al Ferguson said. "He was an amazing kid."

Over Diet Cokes and iced teas, salads and flaky rolls, the two couples talked about Roger. How he loved to play practical jokes, rig buckets of water above his sister's bedroom door, string fishing line across the hallway. How he lettered in football three years in high school. How he played varsity baseball. How the girls all loved him. He loved country music, they said, and fishing and deer hunting.
"He was buried in his blue jeans."

Ever since he was a kid, Roger had wanted a motorcycle. He begged his mom, then - after his parents got divorced - he started in on his stepdad. They kept saying no. Too dangerous. So the day he turned 21, Roger bought a brand new Suzuki GSX- R750W. He drove it to his mom's house, where he still lived. She turned white. He grinned. But his bike kept breaking down. The fuel hose kept popping off, killing the engine. Roger took the bike back to the dealership four times the first week. Five years ago today, he picked it up after it was supposed to be fixed again. He and two friends headed down the highway. Roger's fuel hose dropped off a few miles from home. The engine cut out and he crossed the center line. "It's not natural," Lisa said. Under the table, she cradled Roger's Pepsi bottle in her lap. "You're not supposed to have to bury your baby."

Lisa slipped her wallet from her purse and pulled out a photo. Roger's high school graduation portrait. He was wearing a blue oxford and jeans. "What a nice-looking kid," Don said. "What a shame." "He was studying to be an FBI agent," Lisa said. "He was going to school during the day and working third shift. Everyone loved him. More than 400 people came to his funeral." A few weeks after the funeral, she said, a notice came in the mail. Suzuki was recalling its GSX-R750W line because of a fault in the fuel system. Lisa called a lawyer. She spent five years suing Suzuki. Finally, in February, she settled out of court for an undisclosed amount. "The money will never bring back Roger," she told her dinner companions. "But you all have."

"I dread this time of year every year. It's the worst. But now I have something wonderful to think about," Lisa said. She reached across the table, grabbed Don and Carol's hands. "You all have given me so much to be happy about. You have given me this message from Roger. He's still playing tricks on me." When dinner was over, the two couples walked out into the dark.

"Why don't you all come visit us in Ohio?" Lisa asked the Smiths. She plans to put the bottle on her mantel, and wants them to see it.

# NONE OF US ARE GAY

FOUND by Paul McCarthy

Aaron

~~Tonights Tonites~~
Tonight's event was just a
tradition of the house. It was
not gay even though you had to
pull down your pants. At least
you didn't have to show it to all
the actives! Just your pledge
master.. No meaning: To
prove your manhood and
that you are not a boy.
You swear we want to see
your dick! Everyone has done it
but none of us are gay.
Aside from all this, I want
you to know that I've
seen some improve-
ment out of you

+265

since
you 1st
pledged. Keep up
the effort and have a positive
attitude of things. I tell ya,
its all worth it once you crossed!
Take my word for it! Just hang
in there ok? I want you
to have dinner w/ me
when you are free someday.
It's a great chance for you to
get to know me better and
for me to answer questions
you may have, alright?
Good shit lil' bro.

A.J. Wilson

+265

ET

This is one page from some kind of pledge journal found outside a fraternity house at the University of California in Berkeley.

—P.M.

May your life
be filled with all the
special magic of this
wonderful time of year.

Merry Christmas

✝ THE SLAPPY FAMILY ✝

DeWayne, Angela, Angelina,
DeWayne, II & DeAngelo

## SLAPPY TIME

FOUND by Debbie Steinberg

Ann Arbor, MI

It seems that the parents here, DeWayne and Angela, weren't very creative coming up with names for their children. —D.S.

## DECAPITATED HOLIDAY GREETINGS

FOUND by Bonnie Schulkin

Oakland, CA

I can't decide which is sadder: that someone felt compelled to rip the heads off of this photo, or that one of the four people pictured is not acknowledged as a sender. —B.S.

12-29-87

To All,

Could you please send me ~~a~~ a complete catalog of Zippy
~~med~~ merchandise. Bill Griffith - if you read this - here's some idea
you should use for the ~~pro~~ perovial pinhead - Zippy joins a heavy
metal band, Zippy meets David Letterman, Zippy meets ~~[illegible]~~
Donald Trump, Zippy meets Charles Manson, Zippy goes to Carmel & meets
mayor Clint, Zippy meets Jim & Tammy Faye, Zippy meets Gary Hart,
Zippy meets Donna Rice, Jessica Hahn, Fawn Hall & has affairs with all
of them in one night, ~~Ste~~ Zippy meets Gumby & Pokey, Zippy meets
Rocky, Bullwinkle, Fearless Leader, Boris Bentiof, & Natashia, Zippy meets
the Noid, Zippy meets Teddy Ruxpin, Zippy meets Sean Penn & doesn't
get hit!, Zippy meets the Pope & takes his place, Zippy meets
Hulk Hogan & becomes the new World Wrestling Federation world champion
Zippy meets his sonn's heir apparent - Zee-pee, Zippy meets Jerry
Faldwell & Oral Roberts, Zippy meets Ozzy Osbourne, Zippy & Claude
go back to Haight-Ashbury & People's Park in the summer of 1967,
Zippy meets the Freak brothers & gets his stomach pumped
after too much partying with the Fat Freddy, Phenias, & Freewheelin'
Franklin. Zippy meets Slegehammer!, Zippy meets Morris the Cat,
Zippy meet Steven King, ~~&~~ Zippy meets Bugs Bunny, Zippy meets &
goes bowling with Fred Flintstone, Zippy meets ALF, Zippy meets Joe
Bob Briggs, Zippy meets Siskel & Ebert & Rex Reed. Zippy meets Pee-Wee
Hermann. Zippy meet Elvis, Zippy meets Joe Montana, Zippy meets
Howard Cosell, Zippy meets pit bulls & freeway gun shooters,
Zippy meets ~~Mikeal Gor~~ the Gorbechev's in the U.S.S.R., Zippy
meets Richard Simmons, Zippy meets Judy & Audrey Landers ~~[illegible]~~
(lucky Pinhead!) & Yow!, The best of all Zippy meets
the 3 Stooges! We don't get ~~[illegible] the [illegible]~~ Zippy in any of
the local papers except the Bay Area Spectator which
is supposedly illegal for me to buy. When is the Zippy movie
due out, I heard Randy ~~[illegible]~~ Quaid was going play the
Pinhead. I heard that a few years ago they gave out free
Zippy t-shirts for eating Ding-Dongs ~~[illegible]~~ & Taco sauce, are
there going to be any more events like that in the →

Bay Area, I have had the ~~delacy~~ delicacy before & it's ~~so~~ quite good. Next year ~~I~~ I get to vote-I'm not voting for Gary Hart - he can't keep his pants on & I'm not about to vote for Albert Gore because his wife is head of the Parents Music Resource Center & they're not my favorite people in the world. I definatly want a real Pinhead in the office!! Who is going to be vice ~~presi~~ president-Tuesday Weld, Griffey, Claude, Tuxedo Sam, Mr. Bushmiller? I want to have a ~~pi~~ Zippy picture painted on my guitar some day.

Oh yeah I almost forgot, Zippy meets Robin Leach, Garfield, Spudds Mackenzie, the Peanuts gang, Richard Nixon, G. Gordon Liddy, Dr. Demento, Cheech & Chong, Marget Thacher, Sammanth Fox, Queen of England, Mormar Kadaffi, the Iyathola, Rambo, ~~Ch~~ ~~Chase~~ George Zimmer of the men's where hase, Vanna White, Cal Worthington Jr., Gary Hart, Malcam Forbes, Liz Taylor, Joan Rivers, Eddie Murphy, & a pack of weasels, & the California Raisins.

Thanks A Lot,

Jason Daniels - The only person in town that knows anything about - Zippy the Pinhead

Jason Daniels

Pleasanton, CA 94109

P.S. - How ~~how~~ 'bout Zippy meets - Godzilla, King Kong, Robocob, Alfred E. Neuman, the Fat Boys, Ollie North, William Deaver, Cherry Pop-Tart (~~or~~ the cartoon character), Alice Cooper & Frank Zappa.

Yow!!

Zippy in 1988
Put A Real Pinhead in the White House

**YOW INDEED!**

FOUND by Genevieve Balleveau

San Francisco, CA

I adore this kid's letter to Bill Griffith, author of the subversive comic strip *Zippy*. Pit bulls, Alf, the California Raisins, Spuds McKenzie, Robocop, and Teddy Ruxpin, what an amazing time capsule of '80's culture!

—G.B.

*FOUND Magazine* meets Donna Rice, Jessica Hahn, and Fawn Hall and has affairs with all of them in one night.

Dear Josef & Thalia,

Given what happenned last night, I don't feel safe the two of you driving long distances together. Anger and driving or riding in sports cars don't go together. What if you had a fight & one of you Would one of you

Step on the gas and the other jump out of the car?

It's too much responsibility for Josef and Thalia you need to show more self control & better judgement to go on long trips like that! Sorry, Mom

ANGER AND SPORTS CARS

FOUND by Jared Rodocker

Davis, CA

illustration by Dylan St

Bell's Pizza

#734-995-0232

OPEN 7 DAYS TIL 4 AM

## DAVY'S CHICKEN SCRATCH

FOUND by Niels Damrauer & Kim Hamad-Schifferli

Davy explains:

*A* lot of folks have asked me how I'd react if someone found something that *I* had lost and sent it in to FOUND Magazine. Well, a few months ago, I was digging through a bunch of mail, tearing envelopes open and checking out the finds inside, and suddenly my heart jumped—it was a note in my own handwriting!

Let me back up. A couple months before, I'd gone on tour with my friends from the radio show *This American Life*. At each stop I read some FOUND notes, same way I'd read 'em at FOUND parties, but because these were way bigger venues than I'd ever read at before, I thought I might get nervous and forget all the stupid shit I say between each note. So right before the first show of the tour, at the Berklee Performance Center in Boston, I quickly scribbled down some little reminders to myself on a few Bell's Pizza napkins. I must have dropped this one into the first row of seats, where Niels and Kim found it.

I'm pretty sure Niels and Kim knew that the napkin came from me but they played it straight-faced when they sent in their find. This was their take on it: "Looks like notes to oneself though we don't know how they could decipher this chicken-scratch. Self-mutilation reference sounds particularly ominous." Ha! Y'all two want to see somebody get skewered, keep talking junk about my handwriting, dang! —DAVY

This napkin is made from recycled fiber. Please do not litter.

don't always paint themselves
in best light

skewer themselves

## FINDS ABOUT FINDING

Hey Chuck!!

Look what I found! I still need to get a new form to fill out, as the info on this one is no longer valid,

Jojo

FOUND by Pete Cropley, Jamaica Plains, MA

Colleen,

I found this letter in my papers that Nora Sanchez returned to me.

You sure abandoned me doing a life sentence as a result of a wrongful conviction - you + Marks. Thanks a lot.

$ was not our barrier as you wrote - I had plenty of $ to hire you. after Marks, I was just being cautious.

Why are lawyers all alike?

B. Watson

FOUND by Becky Hutchinson, Oakland, CA

GUESS WHAT CINDY FOUND THE CANCER THE SKIN CANCER THIS MORNING.

FOUND by Chris ...

That was when I stopped caring about the gaping hole in my side and stooped to look for her missing pinky in the corrigated steel culvert.

I never found it...

but I did find a really Nifty swatch and two old silver notes in a half rotten pencil box.

Score!

FOUND by Kovar Lee, Lincoln, NE

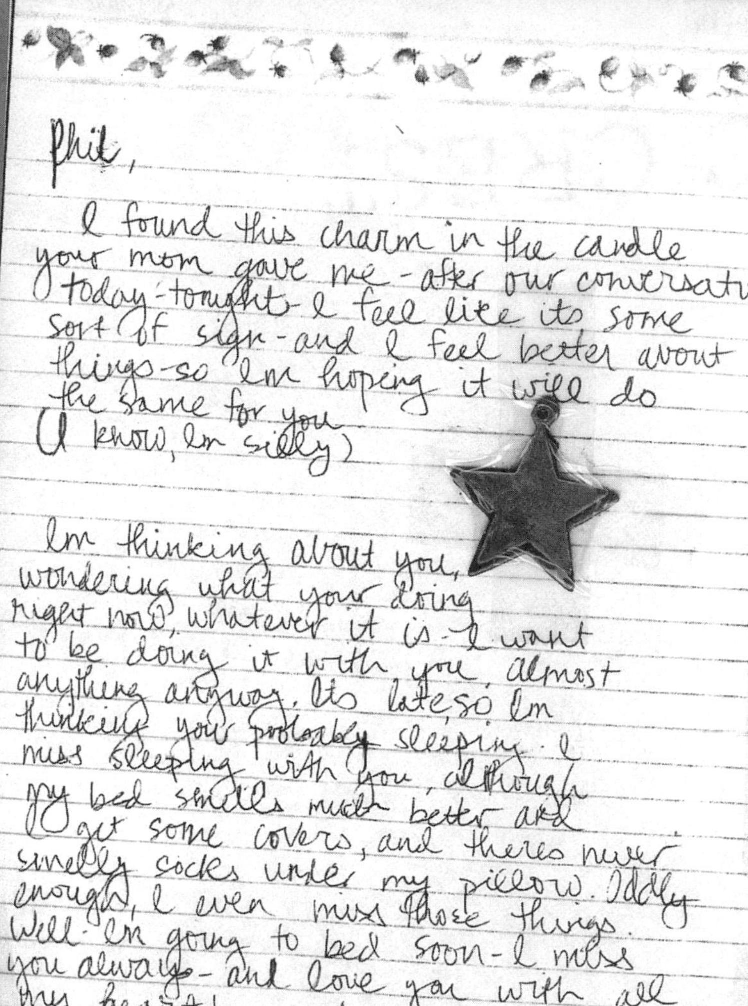

Phil,

I found this charm in the candle your mom gave me - after our conversation today-tonight - I feel like its some sort of sign - and I feel better about things - so Im hoping it will do the same for you (I know, Im silly)

Im thinking about you, wondering what your doing right now, whatever it is - I want to be doing it with you. Almost anything anyway. Its late, so Im thinking your probably sleeping. I miss sleeping with you, although my bed smells much better and I get some covers, and theres never smelly socks under my pillow. Oddly enough, I even miss those things. Well - Im going to bed soon - I miss you always - and love you with all my heart!

Kristy

FOUND by Elizabeth Crane, Chicago, IL

We might be able to find

FOUND by Ruth Wielgosz, Washington, D.C.

CASE OF THE PERFECTLY PURPOSELY-PLACED PEEL

FOUND by Jacqueline Wood

Boston, MA

This morning I found a banana skin in the middle of the front doorway, which appears to have been purposely placed there. This could have been a hazard for anyone walking through the doorway and could have caused someone to fall and hurt him - or herself.

If it is found out who did this, we will take action against the person responsible for endangering the lives of others (whether intentional or not). Be considerate of your neighbors and clean up after yourself. Don't leave your trash in areas where it can pose a hazard to other people.

Please contact me if you have any information regarding who may have done this.

Lillian Hew 5/5/03

Lillian Hew

JUST FRIENDS

FOUND by Jen Devoe

Brooklyn, NY

I wonder if Delane ever got the subtle hint that she just wanted to be friends. —J.D.

Dear Delane, October 21, 2003

You and I are just friends. Thats the way I wish to remain. I like you but only as a friend. I would be happy If this doesn't effect our bond - as friends.

Please understand it is not because your black. It's not because your not handsome enough it's because you and I are just friends. And that's it.

The reason you can't be my boyfriend is because I am not attract to you as you are to me. To be honest I just want us to be friends that's all. It's your choice whether you want to be my friend or not.

Julia

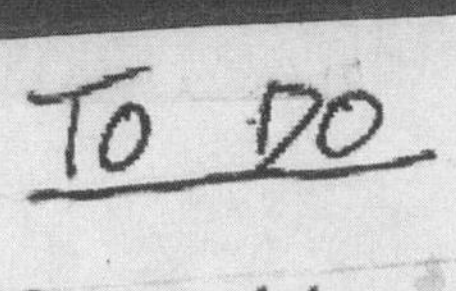

TO DO

Turn in Library Books
Find out about college
Mail Dads shit
Pay bills in advance
Write Crystal
Hide Guns
Pack
Get medication
Do Taxes
Sew Pc up
Change adresses
Pay Columbia bill

FOUND by Holly Henderson, Bellevue, WA

Barrel Chamber Firing mechanism Breech Grip

# TO-DO LISTS

*I* love FOUND to-do lists—and we've received a ton of remarkable ones here at FOUND headquarters. I especially like the way items like "Turn in Library Books" and "Hide Guns" end up next to each other. Or the way folks will follow a bunch of mundane, specific things like "Water plants" and "Return movies" with something grand like "Learn to live free!" But to me, most remarkable of all is the entirely crossed-out FOUND to-do list where every last thing that needed doing has been done.

—DAVY

Go get "The Paper
from Buttcheeks

FOUND by Kevin McGuire, Mt. Pleasant, MI

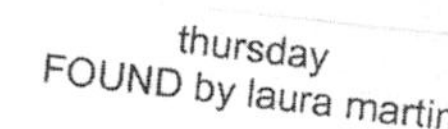

thursday
FOUND by laura martin

Thursday

- Lizards
- Infuse relationship
- Gym
- Transcrip #1 (night)
- After Cart
- Crewing up
- Sailing off.

i found this rather cryptic to-do list in the alley behind my apartment building in santa monica, california; there are always little whirlwinds of interesting debris out there. the back of the list has part of a computer print-out of this person's bank account, which had $50,860.92 and then shows a withdrawal of $49,753.42 - perhaps because he or she was "sailing off?"

i like to imagine it as a to-do-before-leaving-town-for-good list: give away pet lizards, give that relationship a final "infusion" before long distance sets in, that one last workout, then setting sail...

A Note from Jesse

~~Stampede~~
Oakleys car
laundry (again!)
Sharpen knives
Call E.
Zims project

FOUND by S. Dorothy, Middlebury, VT

CORPORATION

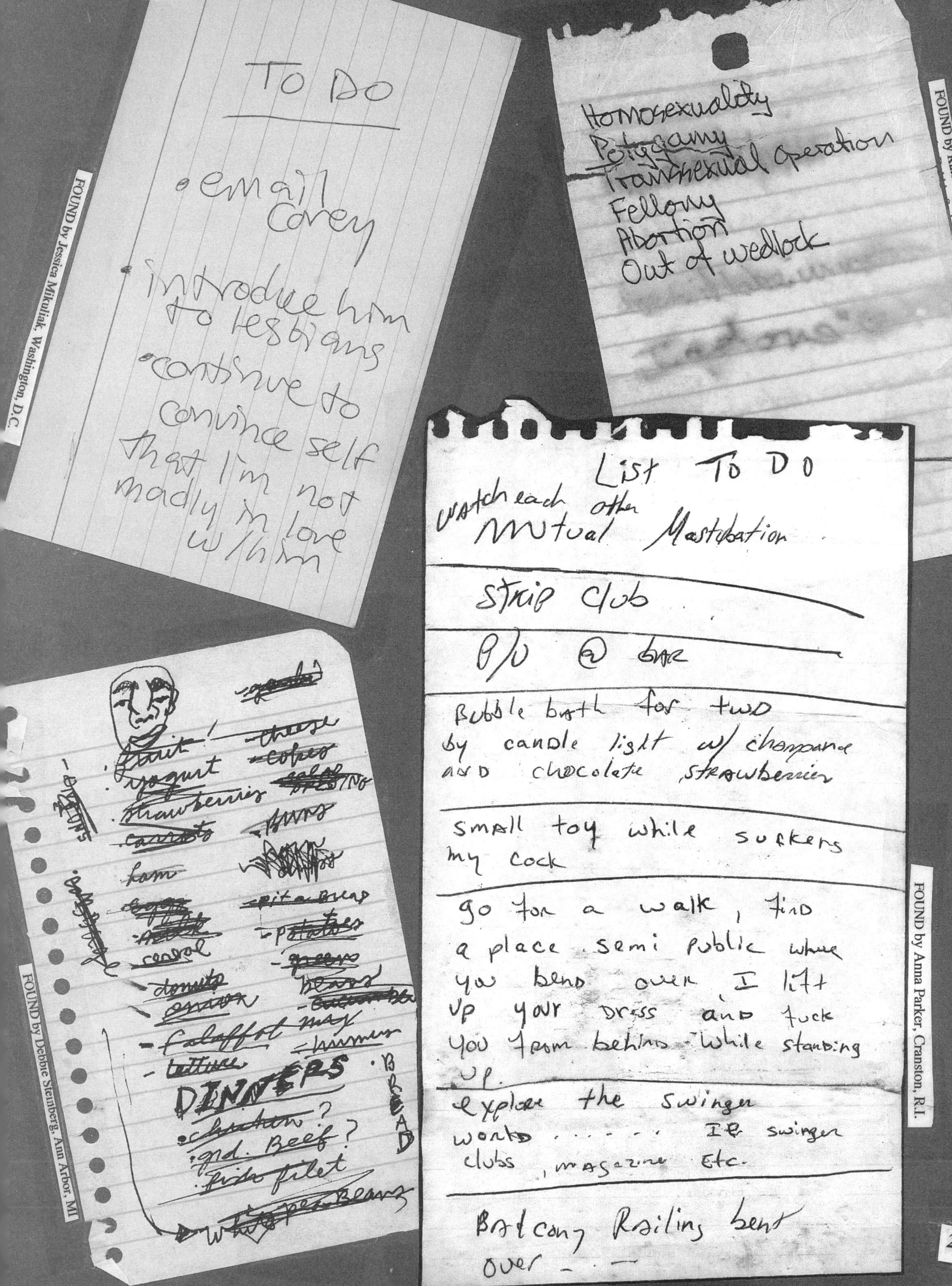

TO DO
• email Corey
• introduce him to lesbians
• continue to convince self that I'm not madly in love w/him
Homosexuality
Polygamy
Transsexual operation
Fellony
Abortion
Out of wedlock
LIST TO DO
watch each other
Mutual Mastrbation
STRIP CLUB
B/J @ bar
Bubble bath for two by candle light w/ champane AND chocolate strawberries
small toy while suckers my cock
go for a walk, find a place semi public where you bend over, I lift up your dress and fuck you from behind while standing up.
explore the swinger world ..... IE swinger clubs, magazine etc.
Balcony Railing bent over . . .
yogurt
strawberries
ham
DINNERS
gnd. Beef?
BREAD

FOUND by Jessica Mikuliak, Washington, D.C.

FOUND by Kate Taylor, Salt Lake City, UT

FOUND by Debbie Steinberg, Ann Arbor, MI

FOUND by Anna Parker, Cranston, R.I.

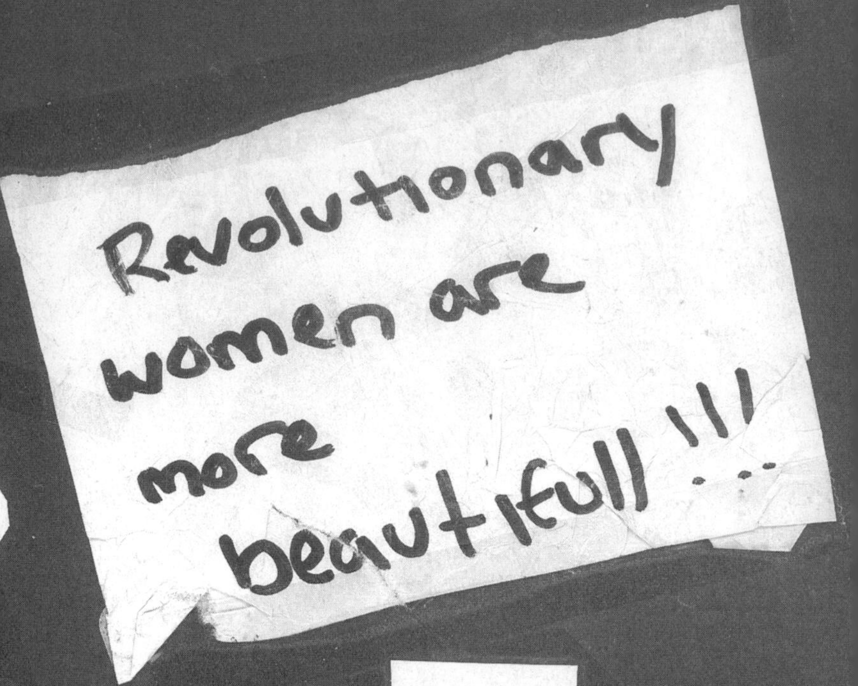

Revolutionary
women are
more
beautifull !!! ...

**REBEL**

FOUND by Miriam

Madison, WI

KAGAN

www.kaganmcleod.com

illustration by Kagan McLeod

# A QUIET, SOOTHING WARMTH

FOUND by Miriam

I found this next to a dumpster.

Tucson, AZ

do I still love him? I honestly don't know anymore. if you question love, doesn't that mean it's gone? I never question my love for my brother, even though he can be a huge pain, but maybe that's because *he's been* in my life forever…or maybe it's because I truly and deeply love him. I know I care immensely for **stan**; *I'm anxious* to talk to him after a hard day of work, and I like it when he comes over…at first. he gets here and sudden*ly I'm* very tired or angry or other emotions that I haven't felt all day. I go about my day thinking of him often, *but* sometimes those thoughts turn to frustration or disgust if I think about him with **Dave**. I really don't have anything against **Dave**, except that I think that he's attractive to my boyfriend. it would be different if I were ignorant to their past together; knowing they are together all the time and touching and flirting just makes it hurt more. what if **stan** is subconsciously trying to replace me because I've grown tiresome and uninteresting? if he's is getting sick of me, that could almost be a relief because it would mean less heartbreak for both of us. listen to me, talking as if this is the end! I just don't want to give up, because it was so recently that I felt that this was IT, the real thing; it was only weeks ago, and that feeling urges me to keep trying to make it work..

he doesn't fit into my family; my relatives disgust him. knowing this changes what I say and how I behave because all I want is for him to be pleased with me.

I resent that he doesn't have a job, that a huge majority of his time is free time, that his life is largely problem free. I hate myself for even considering this, but sometimes I wonder if **stan** will end up getting what he wants in life largely because of who his father is.

my mom doubts he's "the one," and my dad seems to tolerate him, no more, because they don't have enough in common to become close. **stan** despises my mother, I think, though he'd never admit that to me. I think he finds my family's lifestyle somewhat "lower" than that of his family, and I know he doesn't mean to, but I feel he'll always be a rung higher on the sophistication ladder than me. which I shouldn't care about, I know, but **stan** makes dressing well and manners and politeness such a priority that somehow I get the feeling that I was brought up poorly or raised with no social graces. I know my parents did a great job with us. they love us to no end, have given us what we need, and have supported us in helping ourselves attain and achieve the rest. I should not be ashamed of the way I am, but, I can't help it—sometimes I am.

the lip piercing is another story, but I'm over it. some situations just require compromise. I'm willing to give in on some things. other things I am not.

case in point: I will not stay with a person who shows and vocalizes affection infrequently. I will not be in a relationship where sex is not often and pleasurable. physical affection is as important to me as personality compatibility. I need touches, kisses, smiles, caresses and "I love you"s, and, most of all, I need to be able to reciprocate all those and feel loved as well.

**stan** must know he's mostly my everything, and that sometimes his selflessness and generosity astonish me. he's very likely the smartest, most curious person I've ever been close to, and I've gained a lifetime's worth of knowledge in the nine months we've spent as a couple. he's integral in my life, and as much as I want to think I don't, I'm certain I need him, for better or worse. rage and frustration such as this rambling memo need an outlet, and perhaps when I find it, the boiling waters will calm and I'll be left with only a quiet, soothing warmth, enveloped in the arms of a man I'll never be able to forget.

# GIVE ME ONE TOO

FOUND by Deb Schimmel

Chicago, IL

Jacob,

Hi what's up boy? me? just Chill'n. I know you ain't know who I am but I see you around alot. Every time I see you you be look'n fine like always.

I always see your cousin IN-Law or whatever she is to you always with my Girl Samantha. So I decided to tell you I Like you alot and give this letter to my Girl Samantha to Give to you.

I found out you have a baby well that's good now maybe you can give me one, too.

ALWAYS,

TASHA

Don't tell your Lady I wrote to you!

Dear Baby Jacob,

I fell in love with your father the absolute second I saw him. He was the most beautiful man I had ever seen. That was around Feb. of 1998. He helped me get through so many insecurities. That only made me love him more. I'm telling you this first because I want you to know that we loved eachother. (or rather, I loved him.) It didn't matter to me that he already had 2 kids - your 1/2 Bro and Sis. or that he was married to someone else because I loved him so much. And if I had it to do all over again the only thing I'd change would be the abortion. I wanted to have you the second I found out I was pregnant. It was your father that made me change my mind. He didn't want to leave his wife for anything. He kept claiming that he didn't love her and that he really loved us. He could never tell me what I should do with you. When I saw how much pain he was in because he had to tell his wife about you, I felt like I was dying inside. I knew that I had to give you up through abortion because I couldn't hurt the one I loved so much. I regret it because he's the one who so thoughtlessly hurts me now. See your grandma, my mom, Told Daddy's wife about all of us. She produced an out for your father and he didn't take it. He apparently didn't love me like he did before you came to be. He now avoids seeing me, Tells me that if his wife wants to work on the marriage he would transfer away from our jobs to stay with her - Remember he said he didn't love her. I'm seeing a Therapist now, Baby Jacob, to learn to forgive myself for what I so needlessly did to you. I had the abortion so Daddy to tell his wife and leave her with some dignity instead of just saying he had an affair. I wish that you were still in me - you'd be 5 1/2 months old by now. I'd be getting ready to have you. I love you, Baby Jacob, and I'll never forget you for as long as I live. Sorry to say that I don't think your Daddy cares about us anymore, But I hope someday you and God forgive me enough for what I've done and maybe I'll see you in heaven.

I love you

Jacob.

Mom

Daddy wasn't there, he couldn't think of something to tell his wife.

Abortion date July 19th 1999 - 11 1/2 weeks along

**JULY 19TH**

**FOUND by Heather Boyer**

**Glen Ellyn, IL**

I found this inside a bottle in Churchill Woods.

—H.B.

These two notes (facing page and this one) were found by two different people and were apparently written by two different girls living about twenty miles apart. It's eerie how the two notes seem to speak to each other—a Before and After.

—DAVY

after all the years of relentless heartbreak, one might feel like giving up on the "game." If only it ~~those~~ were as easy as the silver screen portrays it - so that's when ~~people~~ you feel that urge to live on the wild side, in the fast lane in the party scene. Companionship is instinctual to all of us - ~~but then why are there so many~~

~~rules~~ you get lost in your own pool of thoughts without it.

# UP FOR ANYTHING

**Perfect ways to play in Vegas, if you don't need to sleep.**

**By Elaine Glusac • Illustration by Douglas Fraser**

These might be random thoughts - but the pt is on the inside I know that life is pointless & repetitive this thought makes me incredibly sad. On the inside I'm so sad, ~~I guess that's~~ why I put up this shield of the "always smiling, never a dull moment - ~~diva~~" but the truth is it's all a play - i'm an actor - just like everyone else in the "game" this might be a cry for help - self pity or plain craziness - but it's how I feel.

EMERGENCY SIGNALS CASINO ROUGE

| | |
|---|---|
| FIRE: | Continuous ringing of the general alarm Bells for not less than 10 second. |
| MAN OVERBOARD: | Hail and pass the word "OSCAR BRAVO" to the Pilothouse. |
| DOCKSIDE EVACUATION: | 7 short blasts & 1 long blast on whistle & same signal on general alarm bells. |
| ABANDON SHIP: | 7 short blasts & 1 long blast on the whistle & same signal on general alarm. |

***ABANDON HOPE***

FOUND by Josh Noel

Baton Rouge, LA

## UP FOR ANYTHING

FOUND by Kristin McCaman

I found this on a Southwest Airlines flight from Las Vegas to San Jose, California.

MUST WIN
$

4321 WEST FLAMINGO ROAD / LAS VEGAS, NEVADA 89103
TOLL FREE 866.725.6773 / WWW.PALMS.COM
TEL 702.942.7777 FAX 702.942.6999

## NOTE TO SELF

FOUND by Chris Connolly

This was in the elevator at the Palms Casino in Las Vegas.

Addictions 616.860092 Recoveries

Bankruptcy 332.75

## *ONE THING LEADS TO ANOTHER*

FOUND by Bill van Sickle

I plucked this up as it tumbled across the parking lot of the Natrona County Public Library in Casper, Wyoming.

*FOUND Magazine*. OSCAR BRAVO!

FOUND INTERVIEW BY BROTHER MIKE

# Tom Every / doctor Evermor

**Down a winding dirt driveway in the cornfields of central Wisconsin,** visitors are unexpectedly greeted by columns of knee-high metal bugs and a platoon of *Happys* – squat, smiling sculptures that look like a cross between a dwarf and an anchor. Artist Tom Every - who also calls himself Doctor Evermor - has created an outdoor gallery of giant metal sculptures from an assortment of industrial machinery parts and other scraps of metal he has found or salvaged over the decades.

To call Evermor's site a sculpture park is misleading. The chaotic place more resembles a junkyard that has somehow come fantastically to life, or perhaps a Mardi Gras parade, frozen and cast in metal. A 20-foot tall spider with menacing pincers lurks beside the Bird Band, a full orchestra of human-sized birdlike creatures constructed from banged-up brass and percussion instruments rescued from a local high school. The musicians appear to play themselves while facing the head Bird Conductor and his companion, the Bird Music Stand.

Towering above all these creatures is the *Forevertron* - Evermor's masterpiece - a 40-foot tall Victorian-style rocket launch, which the Doctor claims he will someday use to blast off into the heavens. It is hard to tell whether or not he is serious. Until 1999, the *Forevertron* held the *Guinness Book of World Records*' title as the world's largest scrap metal sculpture; Evermor estimates that it weighs 400 tons.

An antique fire engine rusts away in another corner of the clearing next to oversized rows of shelves stuffed with detritus dating back to the Industrial Revolution. There are crates full of old propellers, Bunsen burners, bicycle handlebars, birdcages, gears, railroad spikes, and faucets – a cacophony of raw materials, that Doc has collected over time for his artwork. In his pieces giant springs transform into the neck or legs of a creature; rusty shears become bird beaks and fish scales. Currently a stack of propane tanks is slated to be cut into sections; Doctor Evermor imagines spikes jutting from the Kimodo Dragon sculpture underway beside the *Forevertron*.

**brother mike:** To start, could you tell us how you became an artist? How did you get started making these gigantic sculptures?

**doc:** All my education is in the scrap industry. I was a salvage wrecker tearing down factories and breweries and stuff. Old Navy ships. Then I got tired of tearing things down all the time. We were done on a job, and there wasn't any sign that we had ever been there. We didn't leave anything behind, we didn't contribute, and there were all these historic parts, hand-cast machinery, and I felt this should be saved.

So I started making stuff out of it, in my shop, welding it back together. I decided I wanted to create something, not be a destroyer of history. I think we evolve from whatever we do. It certainly wasn't any preplanned thing to be an artisan; I just build the stuff. It's a passion. Everything's a passion.

**rother mike:** You have a huge amount of materials lying around here. Where did it all come from?

**doc:** I'm of the World War II era, and we saved everything: toothpaste tubes, newspapers, rags. Eventually I went into scrap iron and marketed it, but I always saved all the unusual things that came. I must have enough here for 10 men for 100 years working on it full time. I've probably got 3,000 tons of stuff around here.

**brother mike:** Tell us about some specific found objects you have used in sculptures.

Visitors are welcome to drop in any time. Doctor Evermor can be found at the park most weekends. Visit the doc's web page

www.drevermor.org

**doc:** Well, what you're looking at is the shop where I do the building of stuff. See on the *Forevertron*, under the gazebo, where the generators are? That's a decontamination chamber from NASA, from an Apollo space mission. I'm afraid I can't tell you how I got that.

Everything around here has the historic integrity that comes along with it. The most important thing is it gets people to think outside the box. Anything can become anything. And so they can look at it, go home and look at what they've got in their garage, "Gosh, that looks like something here," and they can come up with whatever they want to, and get thinking outside the computer box, and look at their lives a little differently, and then the whole world will get better and a little bit more flexible towards each other too, you know. Instead of having it all being categorized for some reason or other.

**brother mike:** How do you decide what you are going to make?

**doc**: I don't know about this, I'm not making anything that's a sculpture. I'm just making stuff. Heck, these are fantasies. But before you know it, I'm building it, and it becomes reality, and whether you like it or not, that's what happens. I'm working with scrap materials, and not going out and trying to buy new stuff, so the cost is entirely realistic to put things together.

I don't take any measurements on anything. I just go and do it. If I find a spot that's not exactly right, I'll put a blender in to make it right. I just keep adding until it's right.

I'm really pushed by a driving force which in normal terms would be considered kind of insane. I locate all these pieces and go zip-a-dee-doo-dah, blending them together, and I don't have any previous idea of what the heck might even come out.

So you can have some very ornate piece of material, dating back to the 1800s and maybe use that as central catalyst. You go zip-a-dee-doo-dah and you build it up. I like to see things finished immediately, and not come back to it. Only the big things do I come back to. The little ones I build in their entirety, from start to finish.

**brother mike:** Tell us about the *Forevertron*. It's your largest and most complex sculpture. What does it mean to you?

**doc:** Well, the *Forevertron* is designed to perpetuate myself back into the heavens on a magnetic lightning force beam inside a glass ball inside a copper egg. And the mechanics of the unit is, we got Edison bipolar dynamos on it, and you go up the spiral staircase, crank the crank, the ball goes up, signaling to everybody on the ground that you're ready to highball it to heaven. You go across the little bridge and get inside the little glass ball inside the copper egg, and on the *Forevertron*, the stop-and-go lights will signal everybody on the ground, the red, green and amber, and when it's green, that means power on, and it fires you back to the heavens on this magnetic lightning force beam.

**brother mike:** So this is the fantasy, the legend behind the *Forevertron?*

**doc:** Well, of course, we have lots of doubting Thomases-type people, who think this is just going to go into a cornfield over the Thames river, or something like this. On one side of the *Forevertron* is a giant telescope for the non-believers, to see if I make it. There's all this wonderment about "Is this going to work? Will the dear doctor be fried?"

**brother mike:** Before, you've made a differentiation between the fantasy ascension into heaven and the reality. If that was the fantasy, could you explain the reality of how you built the *Forevertron* and why?

**doc:** They're both the same, the fantasy and the reality.

**brother mike**: Then do you have a plan for when the final takeoff will happen?

**doc:** Yeah, I would say that the final liftoff would be about '05. Mmhmm. I take that totally under the advisement of an intergalactic specialist. I thought he'd be here today, and he could tell you the date that this was all going to happen, but he hasn't arrived yet.

**brother mike:** We heard that a museum in Baltimore wanted to buy your two Double Bass birds for a hundred grand, maybe more, but you refused to sell them. You wanted the whole bird band to stay together. Is this true?

**doc:** The answer to that is yes. But this is something of a lucky project. This was never built with the intentions of buying and selling. Some things are for looking at, and not buying and selling. And that's why we never entertain the thought of selling any of it.



**brother mike:** But you sell some of your smaller sculptures to support yourself?

**doc:** These people come along and they wanted to buy something, and I said, well, let's go back, let's put it on the scale, and weigh it. And we put the little Happy on there; it weighed seven pounds. I said, "Well, let's try three dollars per pound." So we put $20 on it, and they sold like popcorn.

Putting a monetary value on sculptures, well I don't think much of it. Some of this stuff is irreplaceable. These are kind of national treasures, and I'm just a steward watching over that. The happiness that it brings other people by seeing the whole thing intact is much more of a positive thing for culture than it is for me to be able to lay down in a castle or ride around in a Rolls Royce, or something like that. I'd just as soon pass on that kind of good stuff.

**brother mike:** Aside from blasting into space in 3 years, what other plans do you have for the future?

**doc:** The challenge is what I like. I did eleven breweries. I'm not interested in going to wreck another brewery just because I'm an expert on breweries. I have no interest in building another *World's Largest Merry-Go-Round* or going to buy any more carousel horses, even though I may be one of the foremost authorities of the world on carousel horses. It's more of a challenge to me to do this crazy Kimodo Dragon, and work the sound aspect out. Have it so you can ring it, like Tibetan bells. Essentially, I'm not interested in making functional things.

**brother mike:** I have to admit I'm confused by the way you use two different names. Could you explain to us why sometimes you talk as Tom Every, and sometimes you talk as Doctor Evermor? How do you manage to be both? Or are you both?

**doc:** Well, those are names. I represent a spirit force, so you could have as many names as you want to add to that without getting some psychiatrist thinking you're crazy. But in this particular timeframe I inhabit the body of Tom Every, which I date back to 1066, the time of my grandfathers. So I'm a purebred Englishman, and that may be the body that I'm walking around here on this planet with. Other than that I do know Dr. Evermor very well.

In the land of Evermor, the doors are always open. You'll have to come that special day. I'll take your reservations now, if you'd like to.

gail lamberty a.k.a. princess of power

**brother mike:** So the part of you that is Tom Every, is that just the past, what you know in your memory, but Doctor Evermor is your future?

**doc**: No, it's not. It's...I don't know. Do you have to get things into some kind of logical perspective? Because I don't know how to answer that. Dr. Evermor is an idea and a thought and a spirit guide. To attach a body to him is not really necessary because he may be gone but he isn't, he's already gone up in the egg. Time and space are relative.

**If you want to visit,** Evermor's Art Park is on US Highway 12, one hour northwest of Madison, Wisconsin. From Madison, take University Avenue west through Middleton to US 12. Take 12 northwest 19 miles, across the Wisconsin River at Sauk City. Stay on 12 North for 9 miles; Evermor's is on the left, 100 meters before the entrance to the Badger Army Ammunition Plant. Look for the giant red heart at the side of the road.

*some of the material in this interview originally appeared in the documentary film "evermor, forevermore," directed by alyssa bailey.*

*photos, interviews, and introduction* **by michael forster rothbart.**

PAY MY FUCKIN BILL FUCKIN BITCH!

***BILLS*** FOUND by Ashley Rogers, Asheville, NC

I'm sorry, a car push me off the road on my bike and I hit your Mirror, sorry

***CRACKED REAR VIEW*** FOUND by Sosi Malta, Santa Rosa, CA

Aug 20 2003 pt Reye
I found a pretty Rock and got to keep a nice boy.
Aug 21, 22 2003 Butano State park - where are we going to sleep? excitement, Blair witches Camping and breakfast at Duante's olallie-berry syrup - did you throw away the map Pat?

***BERRY SYRUP*** FOUND by Bruce Gerstman, Berkeley, CA

Thank you for helping me ~~rember.~~ remember.

***REMBER***
FOUND by Miriam DeSharnais
Baltimore, MD

"Are you sure?"
"Yes I'm absolutely positive."

---

"Sure thing!"
Absolutely. Definitly

---

"Do you love me?"
"Sure I do!" (Of course!)

***DRESS REHEARSAL***
FOUND by Alyssa Banta
Manhattan, NY

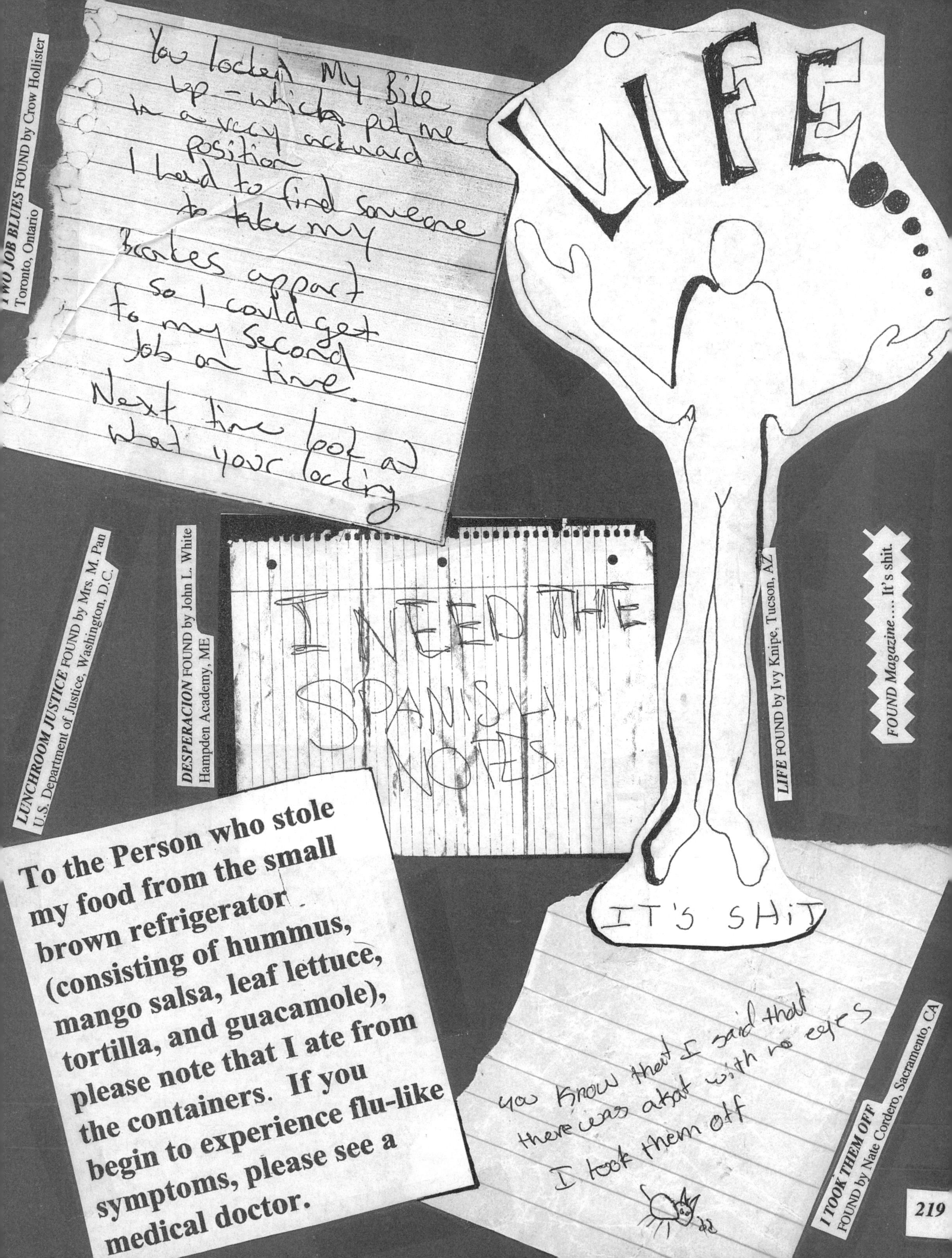

You locked My Bike
up - which put me
in a very ackward
position
I had to find someone
to take my
Brakes appart
so I could get
to my second
Job on time!
Next time look at
what your locking

**TWO JOB BLUES** FOUND by Crow Hollister
Toronto, Ontario

LIFE...
IT'S SHIT

***LIFE*** FOUND by Ivy Knipe, Tucson, AZ

I NEED THE
SPANISH
NOTES

***DESPERACION*** FOUND by John L. White
Hampden Academy, ME

**To the Person who stole my food from the small brown refrigerator (consisting of hummus, mango salsa, leaf lettuce, tortilla, and guacamole), please note that I ate from the containers. If you begin to experience flu-like symptoms, please see a medical doctor.**

***LUNCHROOM JUSTICE*** FOUND by Mrs. M. Pan
U.S. Department of Justice, Washington, D.C.

you know that I said that
there was a bat with no eyes
I took them off

***I TOOK THEM OFF***
FOUND by Nate Cordero, Sacramento, CA

***FOUND Magazine....*** It's shit.

# ROOM FOR RENT

FOUND by Geoff Greene

Portland, OR

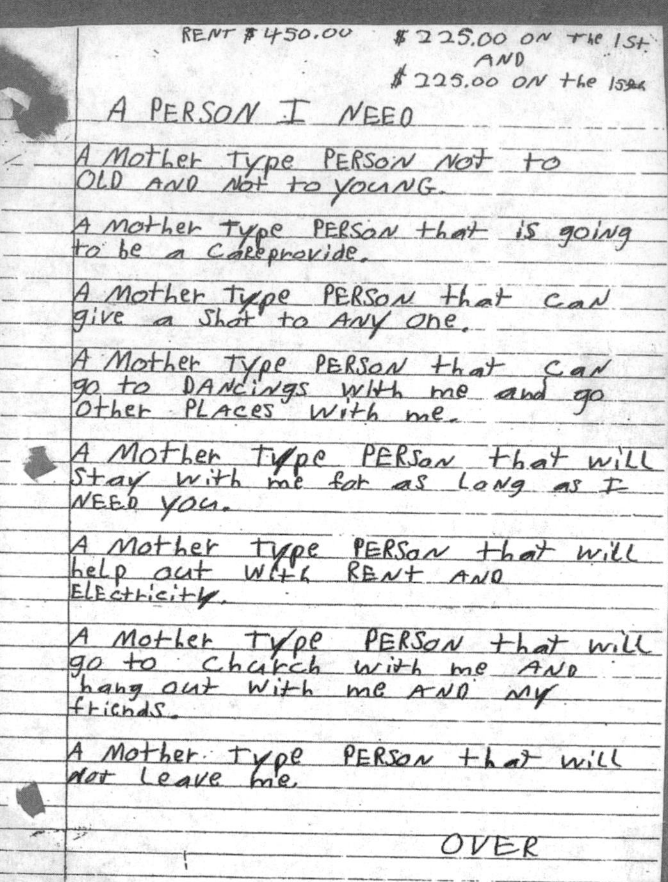

RENT $450.00 $225.00 ON the 1st AND $225.00 ON the 15th

A PERSON I NEED

A Mother Type PERSON Not to OLD AND Not to YOUNG.

A Mother type PERSON that is going to be a Careprovide.

A Mother type PERSON that can give a Shot to ANY ONE.

A Mother Type PERSON that can go to DANCings with me and go Other PLACES with me.

A Mother Type PERSON that will Stay with me for as Long as I NEED you.

A Mother type PERSON that will help out with RENT AND ELECtricity.

A Mother Type PERSON that will go to Church with me AND hang out with me AND my friends.

A Mother Type PERSON that will not Leave me.

OVER

A Mother Type PERSON that Love's Any type of ANIMALS.

A Mother Type PERSON that is Single AND is going to STAY Single.

A Mother Type PERSON Here with me Just in case of a fire or ACCIDent.

A Mother Type PERSON Here with me Just in case Someone BREAKS in.

SOMEONE Who is Not too LOAD AND Not have too MANY friends over.

SomEone who DOES Not SMOKE OR DRINK (OR Who will Smoke outSIDE).

SomEone who will go GRocley Shopping ~~with~~ with me.

A Mother Type PERSON that I CAN tALK to ANY time in the DAY OR Night.

A Mother Type PERSON that has a GOOD AND fuNNY Sense of Humor.

A Mother Type PERSON that has a CAR.

A Mother Type PERSON that will be A very, very good friend to me.

OVER

A Mother Type PERSON that will Not get upset at me for Any thing.

A mother Type PERSON that is Not going to be to fussy about things.

A mother Type PERSON that I CAN trust.

A Mother Type PERSON That will be understanding about every thing.

A Mother Type PERSON that can teach me things I don't know.

A Mother Type PERSON Who is clean AND not messing.

If this is You CALL ME At 503-4...

Ryan, this was something
I made for you out of a promise from a long
time ago, I bet you did not know I
was doing this in my spare time in the
academy. Well now you do. I am very
Sorry about your truck. I was just very
hurt and thought you would have told me
about this relationship you kept from me.
Sorry I interrupted your life and I
will miss you very much. You've been
fun!

Daria

## CRIME OF PASSION

FOUND by R.J. Sidwell

Champaign, IL

illustration by Rama Hughes

# MY HANDS ARE BAD TODAY

FOUND by Lily Engle

Alexandria, VA

I found this letter in a mystery novel I got out of the public library.

6/29/03

Dear Joyce,

It was good to hear from you. I don't have much to write the days are mostly the same everyday.

I was moved down the hill from the Range to Cottage 24. Instead of Range I put Cottage 24 on my mail now. The rest of the address is still the same.

Instead of a large room with over a hundred women I am now in a room with only 3. It is a lot nicer + a lot quiter.

I hope you can read this my hands are bad today.

Bobby came from Louisianna to visit me today. We had a good visit. He has to fly home from O'Hare tomorrow.

Love Them

this photo FOUND by Lisa Bee, Milwaukee, WI

# WHAT YOU MUST D

FOUND by Mandrake Sumners

Washington, D.C.

Worth noting that the notepad is from a pharmaceutic company advertising an HIV drug. —M.S.

TRIZIVIR®
abacavir sulfate 300 mg + lamivudine 150 mg + zidov
ONE TABLET TWICE A DA

You have No legal right of your disposition...
Embrace a Living Will!
Preparing your plans of disposition w/ Legal Power of Attny.
"You must release yourself!"

# SWALLOW WHOLE

FOUND by Laura Seals

Brownsville, TX

I found these pages under a Coke machine in the lobby of the hospital where I work. Looks like someone was taking somebody else's blood pressure and they didn't make it.

—L.S.

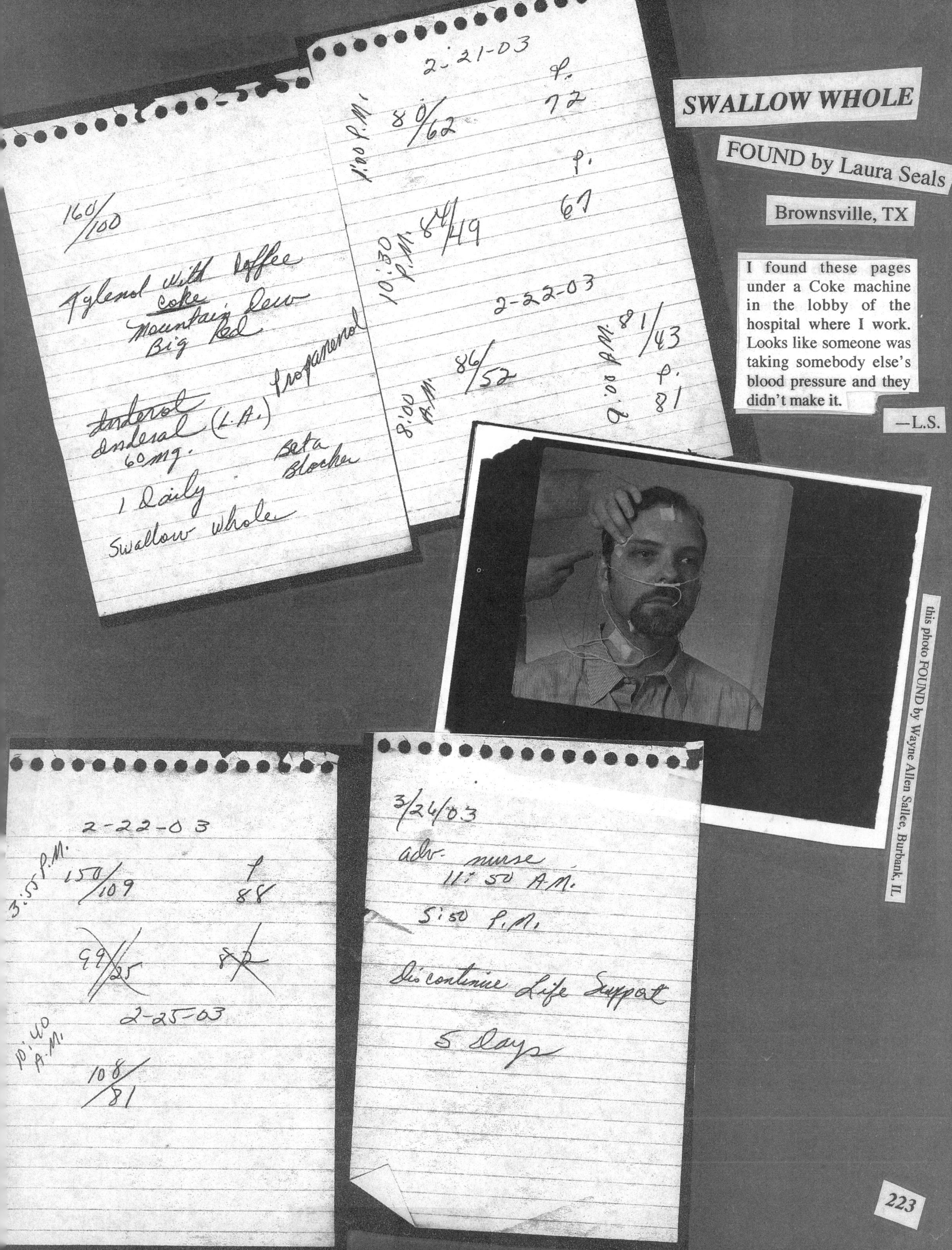


this photo FOUND by Wayne Allen Sallee, Burbank, IL

# THE RINGS

FOUND by Tina Marie Davis and Willie

Berea, KY and Clarksville, IN

TINA explains ↘

Dear Found Magazine:

I graduated from high school in 1990 and moved to Berea Kentucky to attend Berea College. During my freshman year, I met an art major and fell completely in love with him. Being immature and young, our relationship was very tumultuous and we dated off and on –breaking up and getting back together at odd intervals. During one date, in November of 1993, I saw something shiny near a tree and picked it up. It was a woman's ring and it was encased in mud. The ring cleaned up very well and was exceptionally pretty. Willie and I discussed whether or not I should report finding the ring – and fearing that someone may be heartbroken over losing it, I put up a notice in the college post office.

By January of 1994, no one had come forward to claim it so I decided to keep the ring. To tell the truth, I had become rather fond of the ring and was wearing it all the time. Willie and I broke up and got back together about 10 times that year, but we always remained good friends. Often we would sit and talk about the ring we found and thrill at our special found object story. The memory remained special to the both of us, but we had no idea that this was only the 1st part of the ring story

Several years after our college graduation, Willie and I decided to try dating again. He moved to Indiana, where I live, and we moved in together. After being in Indiana only a ~~few months, the 2nd part of the ring story took place. Willie came to pick me up at work~~ and I realized I had left my jacket in the employee's break room. Being deep in discussion, we walked there together to retrieve my jacket. On the shelf directly above where my jacket was hanging was something shiny and Willie saw it first and picked it up- it was a ring. A man's ring. *And it matched the ring I had found 4 years earliar*!!! Once again I posted a notice for finding a ring and once again no one came forward to claim it; we took the ring home. Now we had a matching set!

It would be lovely to say that we worked out and got married using those rings that we found, and maybe that was what was supposed to happen, but sadly that is not how our story ended. Willie and I are no longer romantically linked but we have remained very close and we are best friends to this day. I keep the rings in my jewelry box and every once in a while we take them out and put them on and reminisce about how we each found one and how they match and how this probably meant something…and then we smile and wink at one another because these 2 found objects have made us – and our odd relationship – special. No matter what happens in our life, and no matter where life takes us, Willie and I shall remain best friends until we die and we will always have this special bond that transcends our college days and our past romantic escapades. Just because of 2 found objects that were 200 miles and 4 years apart – we are forever linked.

Thank you for hearing my long and rather mushy found object story! Enclosed is a picture of the rings.

Tina Marie Davis

# YOU WILL SHOCK OF POWER

FOUND by Seth Combs & Chris Connolly

San Diego, CA

*M*y friend Seth found not only this note but also its author in the back of his car.

Seth was waiting for his food at a drive-thru when suddenly the back door of his car opened and an old woman got in. The woman was agitated and started shouting at Seth. In order to calm her down—and because he couldn't understand what she was trying to say—he gave her a pen and paper and asked her to write down what she wanted. She gave him this note, then climbed out of the car and disappeared.

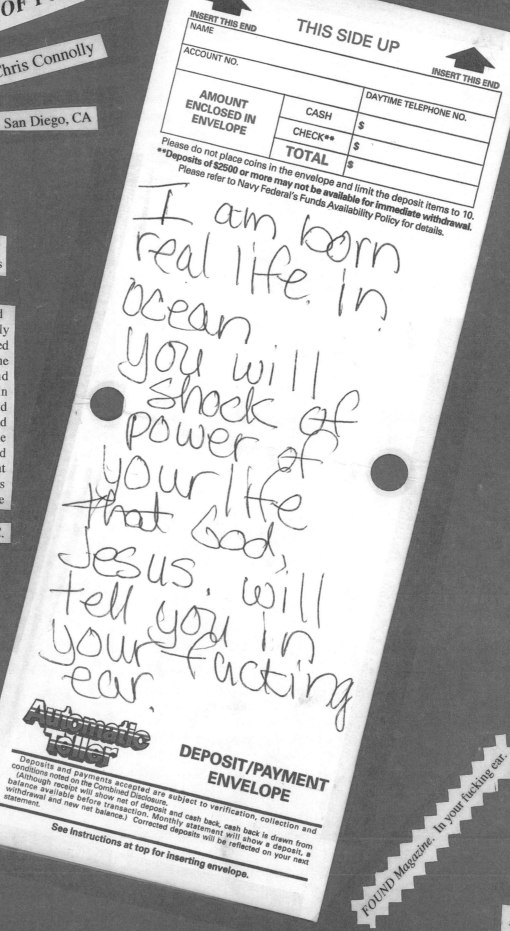

—C.C.

INSERT THIS END

THIS SIDE UP

INSERT THIS END

| NAME | | |
|---|---|---|
| ACCOUNT NO. | | |
| | | DAYTIME TELEPHONE NO. |
| AMOUNT ENCLOSED IN ENVELOPE | CASH | $ |
| | CHECK** | $ |
| | TOTAL | $ |

Please do not place coins in the envelope and limit the deposit items to 10.
****Deposits of $2500 or more may not be available for immediate withdrawal.**
Please refer to Navy Federal's Funds Availability Policy for details.

I am born
real life, in
ocean
you will
shock of
power of
your life
~~that~~ God,
Jesus, will
tell you in
your fucting
ear.

Automatic Teller

**DEPOSIT/PAYMENT ENVELOPE**

Deposits and payments accepted are subject to verification, collection and conditions noted on the Combined Disclosure.
(Although receipt will show net of deposit and cash back, cash back is drawn from balance available before transaction. Monthly statement will show a deposit, a withdrawal and new net balance.) Corrected deposits will be reflected on your next statement.

**See instructions at top for inserting envelope.**

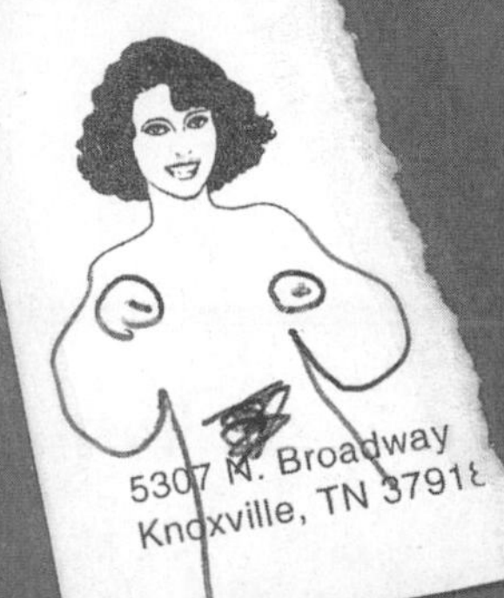

# DEAR LYLE

FOUND by Sam Costello

Ithaca, NY

Dear Lyle

Listen to me I just came back from planned pa
because I wanted to make sure that your nasty
god that I was good and I didn't have nothing
mandatory that they give female pregnany test
positive and they gave me a sonagram and I'm
have a baby on the way and look if it was up
you 'r not gonna have anything to do with
and all I feel you have the right to know bu
to get around in this little ass town that I'm p
feel it can't happen because you pulled out,
happened,and it is is very possible for a fem
what you call precum and it can get a fema
and you took that chance and now look w
can do this and be mature about it and d
that me and you hate eachother and we c
will be the best mistake of my life so list
and you and not the whole god dam Itha
reguardless and I feel that the best thing
parential rights to the baby and nobody w
sorry I never thought that this would've b
getting past this and so these 9 mounths th
know that this is your baby I'll make sure
touch with you and all you gotta do is go
before you know it and
We can go on with our lives. So please d
tell non of your little friends and just ke
Don't say anything to anyone because I
when the time comes when I have the b
johnson ave in Riverdale N.Y. so I'll ho
Fed into all the bullshit but you know w
best for you and not what other people th

P.S.

Listen you know what when we was in yo
sweet you went to the store for me and b
nice person and deep down inside you're
the wrong people that's all and I'm not m
got a baby on the way and you need to ge

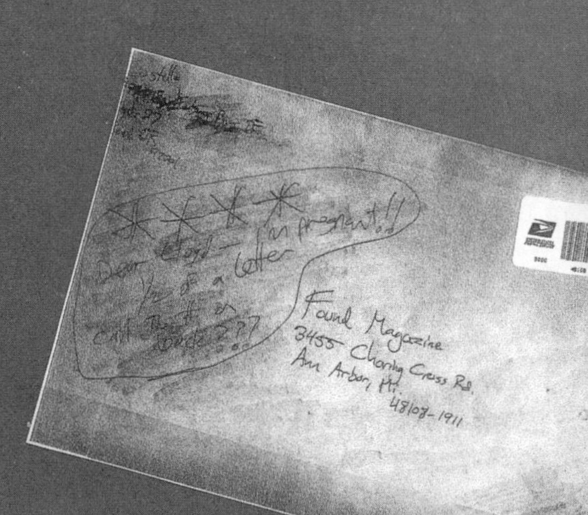

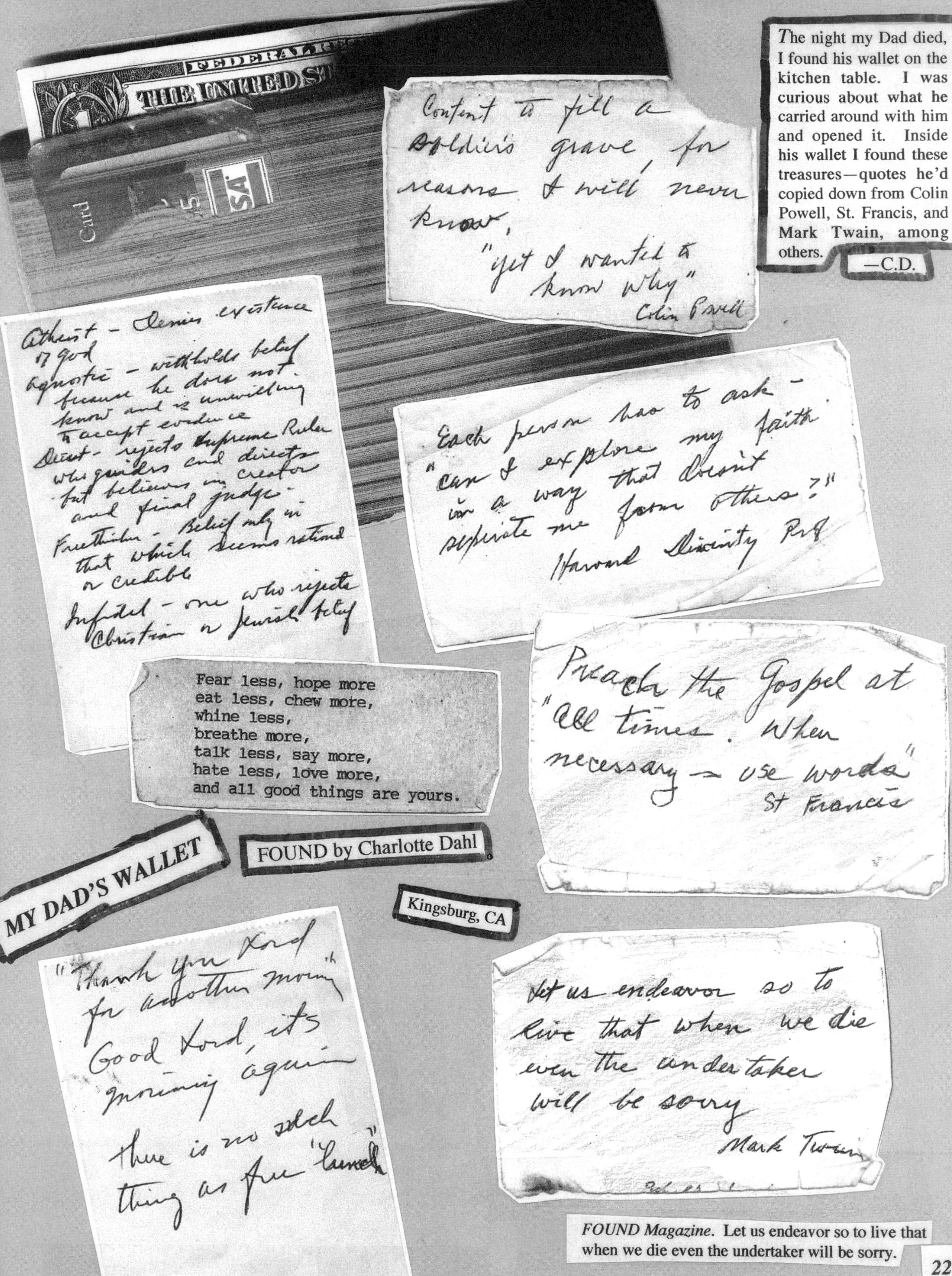

The night my Dad died, I found his wallet on the kitchen table. I was curious about what he carried around with him and opened it. Inside his wallet I found these treasures—quotes he'd copied down from Colin Powell, St. Francis, and Mark Twain, among others.
—C.D.
Content to fill a soldier's grave, for reasons I will never know, "yet I wanted to know why" Colin Powell
Atheist – denies existence of God
Agnostic – withholds belief because he does not know and is unwilling to accept evidence
Deist – rejects Supreme Ruler who guides and directs but believes in creator and final judge
Freethinker – Belief only in that which seems rational or credible
Infidel – one who rejects Christian or Jewish belief
Each person has to ask – "Can I explore my faith in a way that doesn't separate me from others?" Harvard Divinity Prof
Fear less, hope more
eat less, chew more,
whine less,
breathe more,
talk less, say more,
hate less, love more,
and all good things are yours.
Preach the Gospel at all times. When necessary – use words" St Francis
MY DAD'S WALLET
FOUND by Charlotte Dahl
Kingsburg, CA
"Thank you Lord for another morning" Good Lord, it's morning again
there is no such thing as free "lunch"
Let us endeavor so to live that when we die even the undertaker will be sorry Mark Twain


FOUND Magazine. Let us endeavor so to live that when we die even the undertaker will be sorry.

Grandpa smell like poopy

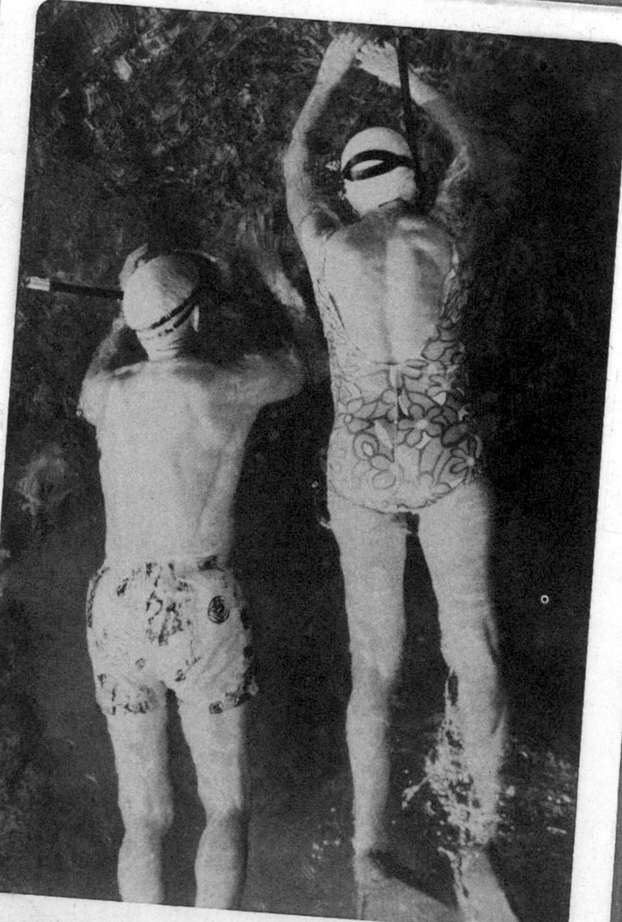

this photo FOUND by Christopher Peterson, Berkeley, CA

## POINT OF INFORMATION

FOUND by Damon Smith

Cleveland, OH

Back before X-mas, my girlfriend let someone use her e-Bay account to buy some gay porn. After the porn had come and gone, I was asked to ship a package to some friends in Boston. I decided that the porn box was about the right size. As I removed the shipping label that the porn-seller had provided, I found this (above)—perfectly intact—as though they had been cut from the same pad. It caused me to wonder several things:

1) Who was Matthew's message of "love" given to?
2) What is the content of the detached drawing?
3) How does this drawing intersect with porn sales?

—D.S.

JUNE 21, 2002

STAN

I am sorry things have turned out so badly.
I will write you a long letter once settled since
At the moment I have no home.
Give me two weeks.
It would never have been my intention to hurt you.
"Maureen" is nice and would have been an excellent
partner for us. She is helping me now in crisis.
I will always love you despite what you may believe.

( Jill )

♡ Jill,

Our last present:
Hearts to match the ring we shared.
Burn inscent on glass above candle.

My counselor said you are being cruel in your methods. Getting dumped I can eventually handle, but it is the WHY? that I need to know. I need this to heal and move on.
Something strictly between your ears?
OR something I could possibly have done?

At all points, I was open to listen, to talk, to compromise, to improve → to worship you.

Now, I go home to burn the photos and cry one last time. The pictures show such intense love for three months.

What on earth went WRONG?

Stan
7-18-02

Stan

This relationship and friendship is completely over.

Stop ... Harassing ME!

or I will get a restraining order.

Jill

August 14, 2002

Basically I am here to refute the Petitioner's statement. However: Whatever the outcome of this court appearance—I will NOT be contacting or communicating with **Jill** . I would have just let this court date go by, but for the inaccuracies written in her complaint form.

After all is known, I feel I have done fairly well for someone alone and sick in an empty house . Was it realistic for me to just disappear without the comfort of knowing why this whole nightmare was necessary? After two months, I have discovered that I really don't care anymore. The answer is obvious, my heart just had some trouble catching up to my brain. My final thoughts of **Jill** are "thank you for the best three months of my life".

I FEEL A RESTRAINING ORDER IS NOT NECESSARY OR JUSTIFIED
Based on some minor lapses which I freely admit.

At no time was I controlling, violent, verbally abusive, stalking or dangerous To **Jill** in any way.

Jill,

Why?

yes no Because I fell for someone else

yes no I just fell out of love

yes no I just wanted to delay, or date

other short reason

I did nothing so mean to you that you left so coldly. Any man in America would have tossed you out with that hair-brain story. You are a Lost Bottle on the waves.

LOST BOTTLE ON THE WAVES

FOUND by Marlin Florida

Valdez, NM

(turn the page for the last note)

from previous page

1) THREW ALL MY BELONGINGS OUTSIDE

I placed her boxes on carefully spread out plywood against my house and under the roof. Jill received all she wanted plus was given access to my home without my Presence. The alternative would be to let her moving group scatter all over my house Not knowing what items belonged to who. Very stressful time that would have been! By the way, she brought her new boy friend right to my home. I was not controlling, Verbal or violent in any way.

2) VOICE MAIL

No messages were ever threatening, controlling, or violent in any way. I was sinking into depression and told Jill my counselor and I would be greatly helped if we were given a reason for her to so abruptly tear my heart in half. She wrote that she would Do this but never did. My notes left on her car refer to this promise.I needed to understand in order to heal. I wanted to avoid future mistakes. I needed closure To move on with my life.

As for the pornographic message—Jill often requested me to leave sexy fake messages from fictitious companies. She loved it!

Another call explained that I was going to drive to California and meet some mutual friends and would she like to come along?

With Jill not responding it was hard for me to adiust. My heart led me to wishful Thinking, and thoughts of her last note of love to me. If Jill had been honest and direct, I would not have bothered her.

My counselor referred to Jill as "unnecessarily cruel". Also stating that Jill is as water seeking its own level. I perhaps was too normal for her. I was "Bonafied" with a job, benefits and yuppy desires. Of course, the counselor stated that She is free to do as she pleases, but that her behavior has been bazaar, callous and cold. I now know that I could never depend on her, but will always feel that I was the best man For her. Jill and I have never really argued or ever really raised our voices to each other. She has no reason to be afraid of me.

3) THE NOTE ON EMPLOYER'S DOOR

This was her personal calendar that SHE highlighted our special days together. I simply circled my birthday, vacation times etc. and encouraged a romantic response.

this drawing FOUND by Debbie Steinberg, Ann Arbor, MI

4) BAG WITH PRESENT LEFT ON CAR
About July 18, I left a romantic present on her car at work. I had completed my vacation without her and happened to see something that matched a ring I had purchased for her previously. Remember, I was experiencing the effects of deep depression until I could find The right medicine that works for my body during July and was experimenting with Prosac (which did not work). My heart held onto 1% hope of reuniting. Her response in a letter was that I had harrassed her. She did mention a Restraining Order. This runs opposite of her speech and letter of June 21—my only two notes from her during all this period of turmoil. I needed answers for my peace of mind, and hopefully to get her to look into the mirror and think better. My notes were asking for common sense, respect and compassion. They were NOT threatening.

5) MAIL TO WORK PLACE
I simply forwarded a letter from Sears to **Jill** at her office. **Jill** 's boss led me to believe that possibly **Jill** had quit that job. I wrote, "If not here-send to circus". This was an inside Joke meant only for **Jill** . Her boss "involved" herself and proceeded to write copious sour messages all over two personal letters from me To **Jill** —returning them unopened. The letters contained requests to peacefully Meet and finalize, clarify what is going on. I offered to chat with the new man In her life also.

6) NOTE ON CAR AT **Jill** 'S APARTMENT
I did NOT follow **Jill** anytime or anywhere. It is also perfectly legal for anybody To print ADDRESS CORRECTION REQUESTED on a letter, and the new address will Be sent back to the sender for a small fee. However, I knew approximately where **Jill** Resided and simply looked for her car.
I left my final note asking, "Why did you leave?) This was about 7PM July 29. I never would have driven that far from my home (Woodinville is about 65 miles South) But just happened to be going by on my way to Bellingham. As I pulled back onto the Freeway I noticed that I did not feel good about what I had just done. After more thinking I realized that I no longer cared for her answer—it did not/would not matter to me anymore. I was happy to know that I was finally healing. I made a mental note to pull the Note off her car on my way back home. When that time came, I chose to be a BRAT and Kept driving.
I AM TRULY SORRY FOR THIS, AND SINCERELY APPOLOGIZE TO **Jill** , AND TO THE COURT.

Due to modern medicine and counseling, I am just pulling out of a deep and momentous depression as of August 6. The color is coming back into my life again.
The key basic facts that I feel are vital are:

1) **Jill** has not seen me since her move out day of June 18.
2) I was broken hearted and clinically depressed
3) My heart and mind were pulling in opposite directions
4) I failed to act maturely by writing that last note.
5) I will not be going near **Jill** , her car, her job, her apartment for the next millennium. No phone, No letters, No nothing.

*FOUND Magazine*. I failed to act maturely by writing that last note.

*I* THINK THE THING I've owned the longest is this little girl's lost shoe. It's tiny and navy blue, with little white stitching. It's for the left foot. My best friend, Felicia, has the one for the right. Six years ago I was visiting Felicia in Chicago, where she used to live (I was living in New York) and we had just left a bar and were feeling all drunk and giddy. We were both about 20 and very much in that time of our lives when everything had a higher meaning and was in some way magical and important. We were somewhere in uptown, on a residential street near Felicia's apartment, and the shoes were lying in the middle of the street. I don't know who saw them first, but we both immediately loved them and wanted them and understood them to be intended for us to find.

THERE COULDN'T BE any other explanation for why they would be there, a perfectly fine pair of shoes just waiting to be buckled onto some spastic little foot. Basically they had been placed there for us to crack up about, which we did for like twenty minutes in the middle of the street. And then the shoes just became permanent fixtures, crazily important to us. Like bizarre, moderately gross Best-Friend charms, I guess. We've always displayed them prominently in our rooms, always made sure they went with us in all our moves -- I've been living in Chicago since last November and still haven't managed to retrieve any of my furniture from New York or even my blankets and pillows and stuff but when I came out here that creepy little shoe was the first thing I packed.

– S.K.

***CHILD'S SHOE WITH BUCKLE***

FOUND by Starlee Kine and Felicia Ballos

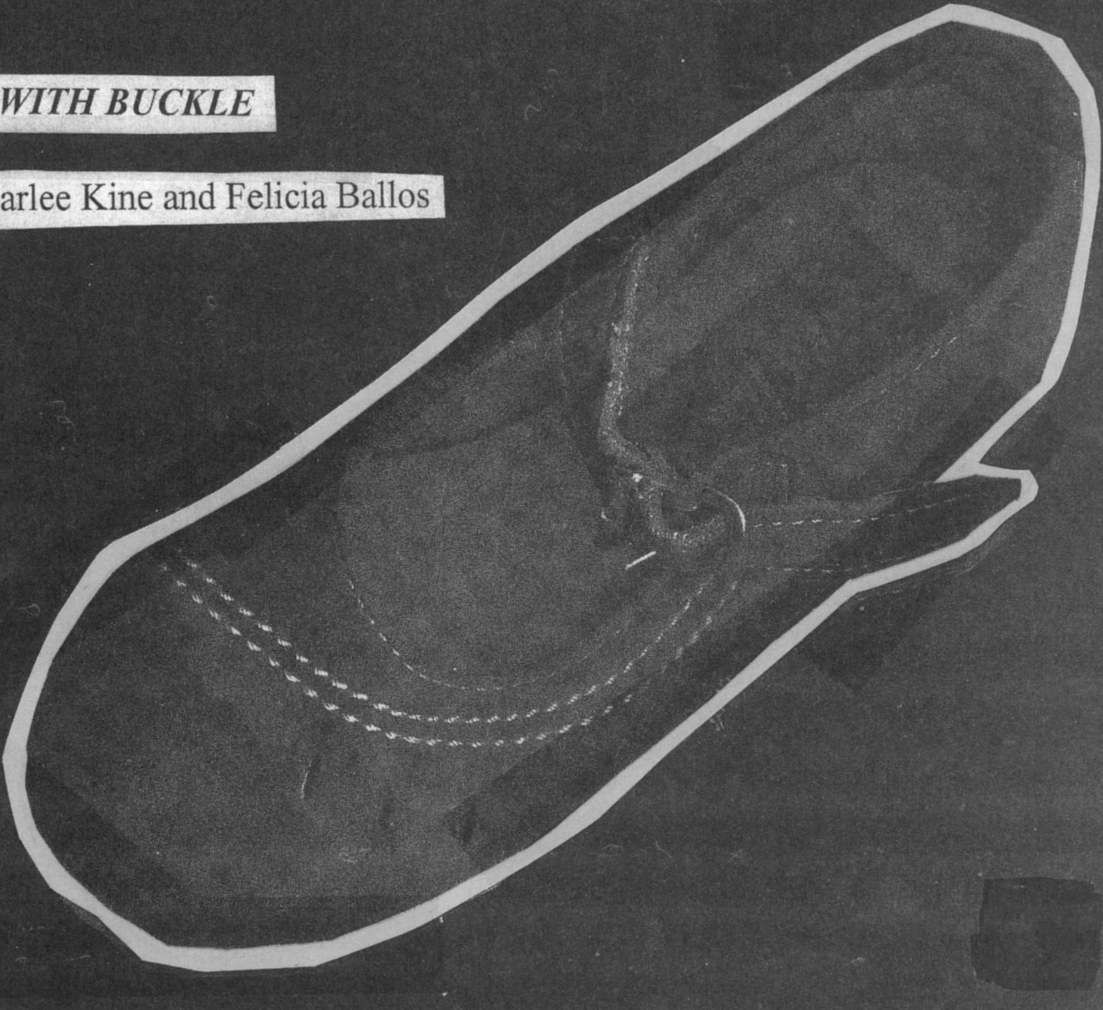

***GREETINGS #1*** FOUND by Alice Freda, Los Gatos, CA

Have a nice day!

HI, FUCK OFF!

***GREETINGS #2*** FOUND by Matt Stilt, Houston, TX

***WANTED: GOOD WOMAN*** FOUND by Karen Haan, Chicago, IL

# NOT MOVED YET

FOUND by Rory Carroll

Portland, OR

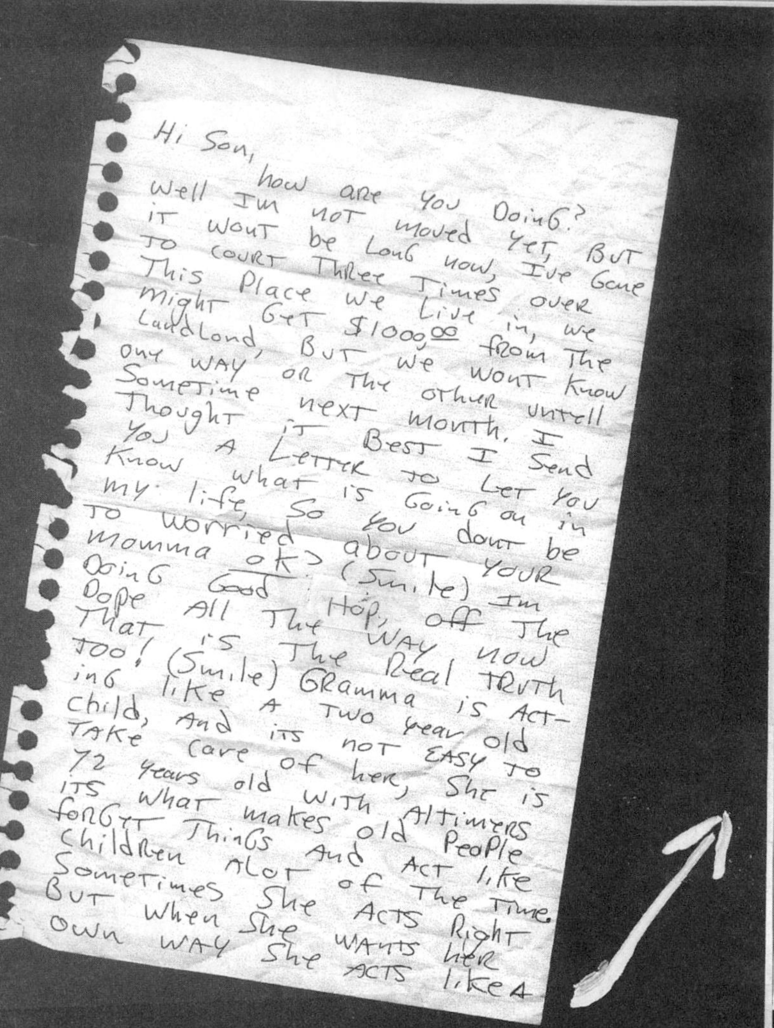

Hi Son,
how are you Doing?
Well Im not moved yet, But it wont be long now, Ive Gone to court Three Times over This Place we live in, we might Get $1000.00 from The Landlord, But we wont know one way or The other untell Sometime next month. I Thought it Best I send you A Letter to Let you know what is Going on in my life, So you dont be to worried about your momma ok> (Smile) Im Doing Good Hop, off The Dope All The way now That is The Real Truth too! (Smile) Gramma is Acting like A two year old child, And its not easy to Take care of her, She is 72 years old with Altimers its what makes old People forgtt Things And Act like Children Alot of The Time. Sometimes She Acts Right But when She wants her own way She Acts like A

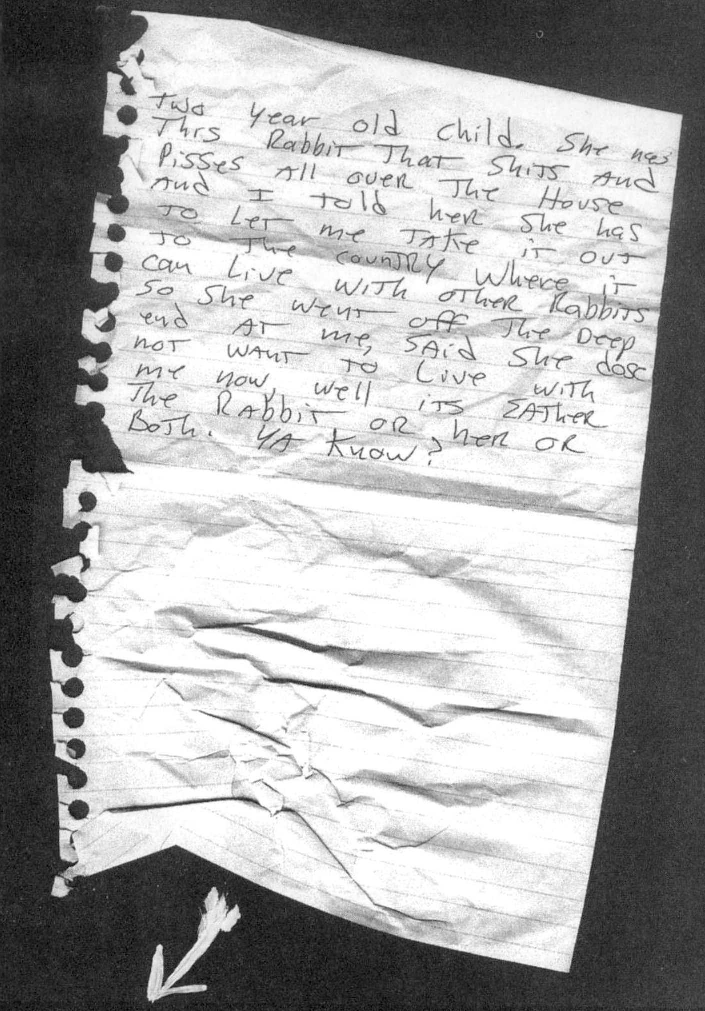

Two year old child. She has This Rabbit That Shits And Pisses All over The House And I told her She has to let me Take it out to The country where it can live with other Rabbits so She went off The Deep end At me, Said She dose not want to live with me now, well its Eather The Rabbit or her or Both. YA Know?

Hello Hop,
So you injoyed Those Picture's Did You? (Smile) Im Sending you some more, I Do Hope you like Them, Ive Got Some Picture's of when we was out in The country in GoldenDale WA. I Do Hope You injoy Them Alot? I cant find The one of winkie The cow, Do you like The Horse? I Hope So, because Im Gonna Try to Buy one when you come Home. Anyway I Am Sending you These Picture's of your uncle Ken And your momma And Little Dimray TinGerson KeeGo's son. God Bless Jerry And you And All The People in our lives who we Love very Deeply. Well Son Im not Gonna Keep writing Right now because I have to fix Dinner And clean up After, Hey Hey how YA Doing there? Well Dinner Sucked The Big one, Guess I need to Learn how to cook, YA Know?

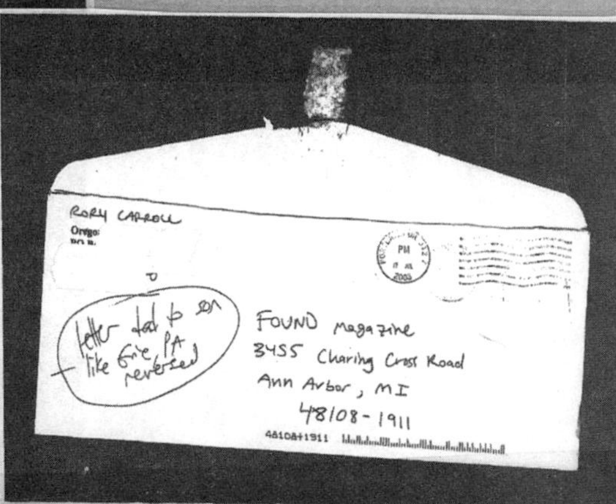


I especially like 3 things about this letter:

1) "(smile)" — seems like she's saying that she's smiling, but it also seems like a request. I get the feeling that no one is smiling.
2) "I'm doing good Hop, off the dope all the way now that is the real truth too!" — this sentence has kind of a natural acceleration to it. It also rings with hopefulness—not accomplishment—and suggests past lies and failures.
3) Reminds me of the letter Davy read on *This American Life* from the son in Erie, PA to his father in Arizona—only reversed. (see pg.42)

—R.C.

**COMFY**
FOUND by Dave Narter, Palatine, IL

I got new
bras & they're so
comfy. I'll show
you in
gym.

Everything
is
going to be
all right

**REMINDER**
FOUND by Gretchen Ames
Cambridge, MA

This note was taped outside the turnstiles of the Central Square T stop in Cambridge Mass this morning (7/1/03)… it made me, and all the people getting off the train behind me, smile and comment ("Finally", "I needed that", and "it's about time" were uttered). Coincidentally, I had been reading FOUND on the Train, and felt compelled to share the good vibe that the note was promoting—but didn't want to end the good will with you, so I took it down, copied it, and went back and replaced the note with the copy and am sending the original to you. Hope the good will continues….

~G Ames

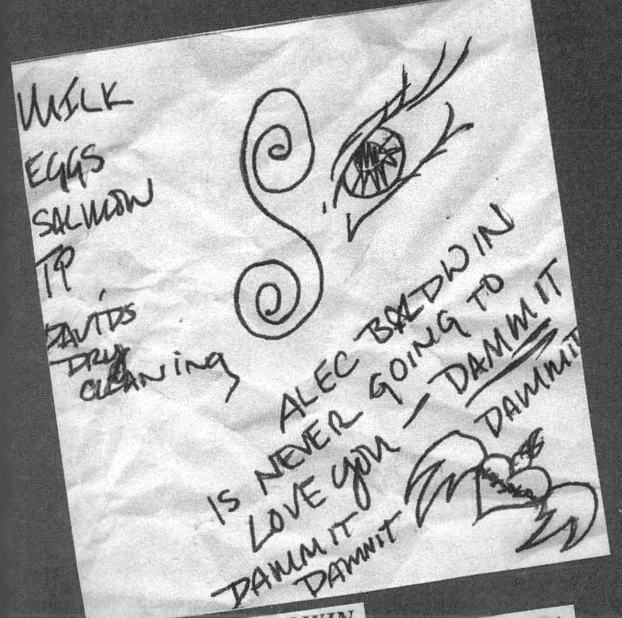
MILK
EGGS
SALMON
TP
DAVID'S
DRY
CLEANING

ALEC BALDWIN
IS NEVER GOING TO
LOVE you — DAMMIT
DAMMIT DAMMIT
DAMMIT DAMMIT

**ALEC BALDWIN**
FOUND by Jhone Daniels, Bel Air, CA

Grant-
I hope ~~ate and enjoyed~~ the cookies brought your stomach joy,
as was promised, here is your toy.
Baseball fan, you are tis true.
Although your A's lost, your
spirit ~~shoved~~ shined through.
~~Try your arm and see~~ win ~~you do!~~
~~Stress relief I hope~~ this ~~should~~ bring
~~When the financials bring troubles~~
When the bank, card the creditors, ~~our crea-~~
~~bring stress and bad news.~~ make you want to shout
Take Aim and have fun, ~~don't blow~~
~~as focused~~ and strike them out!
~~What surprises will one tomorrow bring you ask?~~

**FINANCIAL TROUBLES IN OAKLAND**
FOUND by Stefan Salinas, S.F., CA

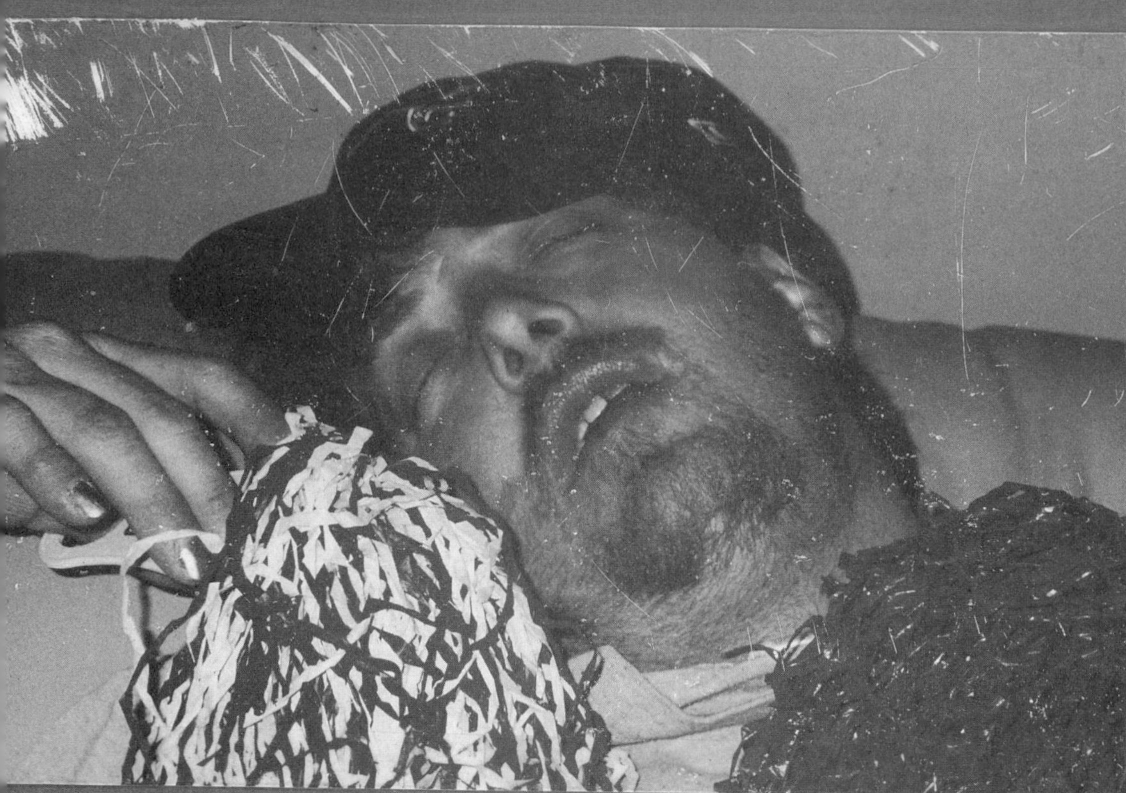

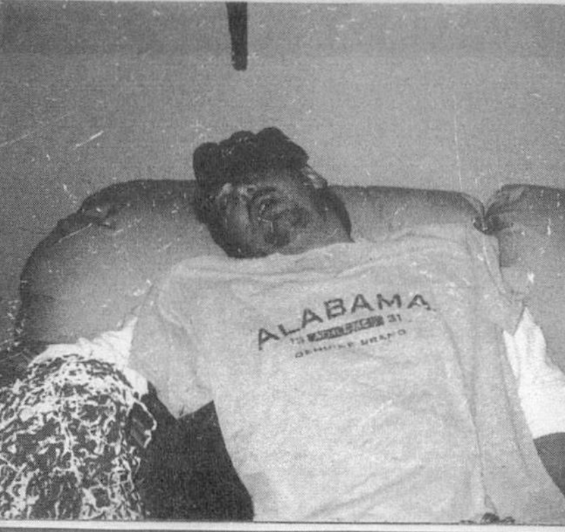


# ROLL TIDE

FOUND by Doug Aycock

Montgomery, AL

*O*ne of the fiercest rivalries in sports is the one between Auburn University and the University of Alabama. These four photos, which I found in the rainy parking lot of Home Depot, seem to document an Auburn fan's transformation to Alabama fan—while sleeping. Looks like his friends have painted him with rouge and lipstick, too, but it's the Alabama shirt he's "wearing" which is sure to have given these pictures such unlimited value as blackmail material. Roll tide!

—D.A.

February 28, 2003

Dear Parents,

The fifth grade students have been invited to attend a performance by the Houston Symphony on Wed., April 2, 2003 at 9:30. Due to the behavior of some of the students at the play "Johnny Tremain" in January, we have decided that only those students who have an E or S in conduct from now until March 13th will be invited to go. We will send home the permission slips with those students on March 13th.

Thank you for your help and support.

The fifth grade teachers

# JOHNNY TREMAIN

FOUND by Michael Powell and Janelle Gunther

Houston, TX

illustration by Ayun Halliday

***SCARY***
**FOUND by Kim Finale, Rohnert Park, CA**

Kayla,

Hey wuz up? OMG, yesterday I went to the ranch with Ashley and I have second thoughts about going to highschool in like 9 months. Im not ready. Im so scared. Are you ready? Are you scared? yea I wanna get out of MSMS but, wutz gonna happen when we get there? we might not all be together! Are we all still gonna be friends? Are we gonna have classes together? who are we gonna be friends with? what gonna happen? Is it the same as MSMS? We've never thought about this! Just promise me we'll always be friends!~ Well im hella tired so w/b/ASAP!

Valwayz,

Donna

AKA: Devil-Child or Bad Girl

this photo FOUND by Pavlina Fonville, Berlin, NH

I'M going to 2nd grade. I hope I pass.

***MOVING ON UP***
FOUND by David Kanthor, McCune, KS

***BOMB THREAT***
FOUND by Chris Rush, Tucson, AZ

Dear MoM and DaD
I hate school I don't want
to go aney more
I jest want to go to
your school and stay
home! Thanks.
Chanel

MB

Marjolein Bastin

***YOUR SCHOOL***
FOUND by Colleen Kennedy, Mahwah, NJ

**SCHOOL**

**SCHOOL** is one of our most important institutions.

Allo françois!

Si tu demandes pourquoi ça sent le thinner à plein
nez c'est parce que le thinner en question a passé à
travers mon verre de plastique (yé dans la poubelle si tu
veux le voir...) et s'est répandu sur le dessus du poêle,
dont les 2 ronds de gauche. Je suis vraiment désolée!!!
Donc, si j'étais toi, je ne me servirais pas de ces 2 ronds
avant de savoir si le feu va pogner quand ça va
devenir chaud. J'ai ramassé tout ce que j'ai pu et j'ai
gratté les ronds, mais on sait jamais... J'appellerai à un
magasin de peinture en arrivant pour leur demander
quoi faire, mais je ne sais pas à quelle heure exactement
je vais revenir... Si tu veux pas attendre au
cas que ça fuckerait le poêle, tu peux toujours le faire.
Encore une fois, je suis désolée! Et essaie de ne pas me
crier après quand je vais revenir ok?! J'ai pas fait exprès
pour faire ça! :) Bonne Journée!

Sandra

**Translation:**

Hi Français!

If you are wondering why it stinks of thinner, it's because the thinner in question leaked through my plastic cup (it's in the garbage if you want to see) and spread to the top of the stove, the two left-hand side burners especially. I'm really sorry!!! So, if I were you, I wouldn't use these 2 burners before finding out if they will catch fire when they heat up. I wiped up as much as I could, but you never know… I will call a paint store when I get back to ask what to do, but I do not know what time, exactly, I will be home… If you don't want to wait in case it fucks up the stove, you can always do it. Again, I'm sorry. And try not to yell at me when I get home, OK? I didn't do it on purpose! :) Have a good day!

Sara

**THINNER**

FOUND by Renae Mécha

Montréal, Quebec

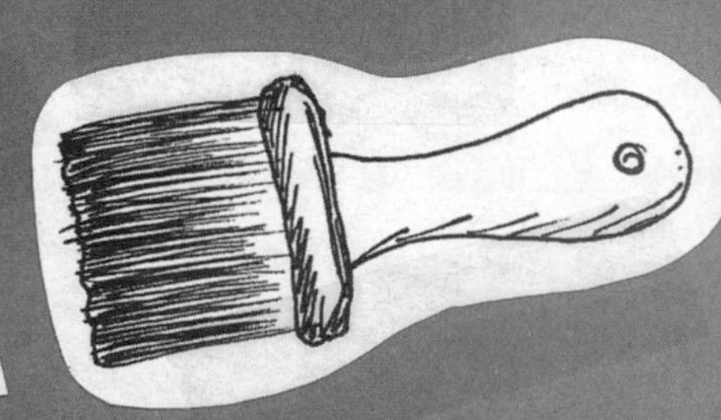

this photo FOUND by Gia Palmer, NYC

## NEW YEAR'S EVE

Though they were discovered in three different parts of the country, this note and both photos all share the same date: December 31, 1997.

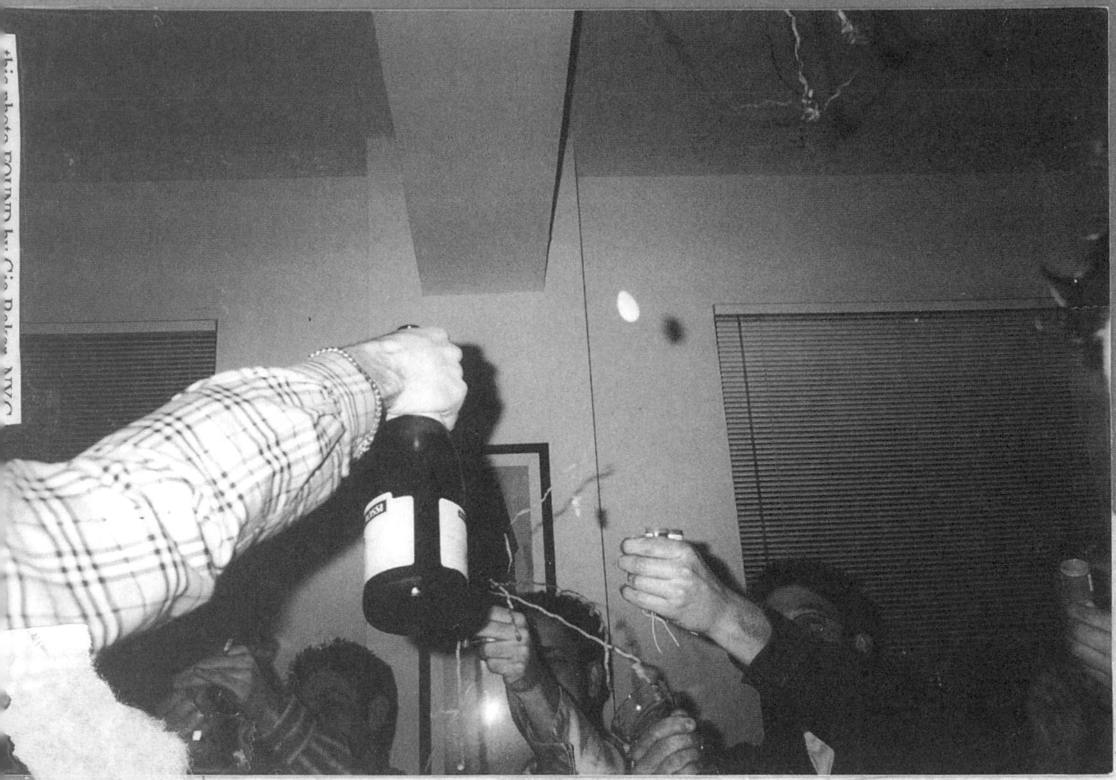

12/31/97

MoM,
Don't, panick, I'm safe and sound,
I'm spending the night at Gimpy's,
I'll be back tomorrow sometime, Don't
call + yell, yell at me when I get
home please, I want to have a good
New year's.

Love,
Kevin

this note FOUND by Peter Martin, Fond du Lac, WI

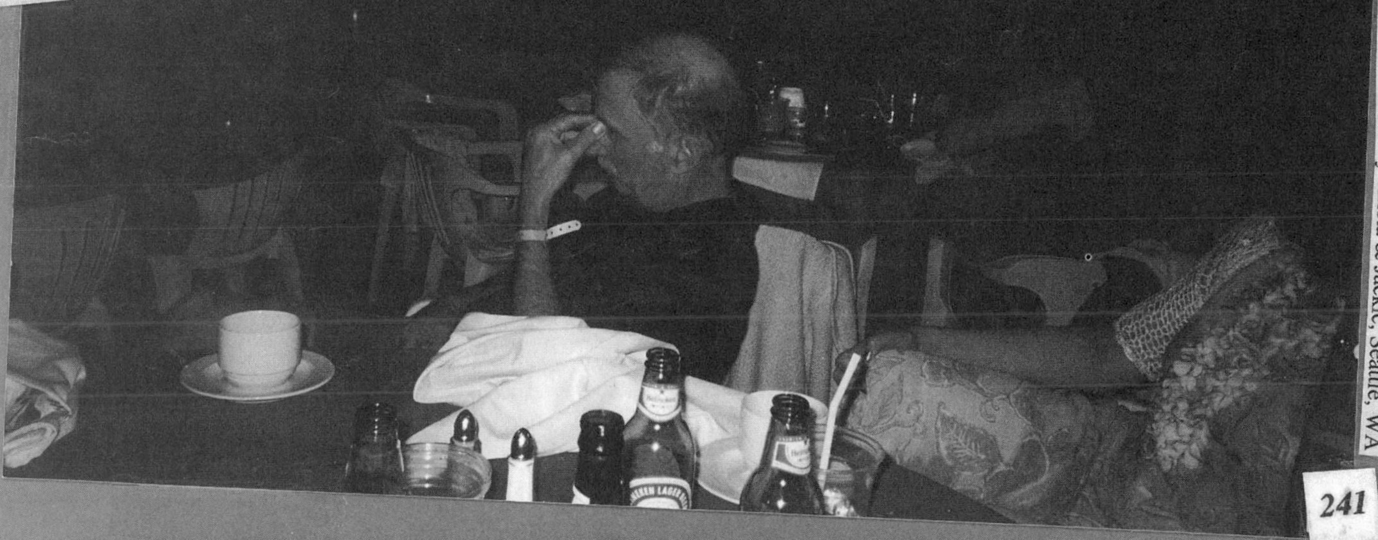

this photo FOUND by Krista & Jackie, Seattle, WA

(1)

problem
- exemplified by sex. - ~~I want~~ I want once
per month - I want 3-4 times/wk. We
do not compromise at even once/wk. -
Julie gets her way. or else. - or else she
(like - tapping fingers on shoulder)
* makes sure it is no fun. (like says Mom
"I got him turned around") It's not just
a numbers game. It's the quality (just
lies there - no response, - etc) ~~go~~
- comes down to a basic of giving &
receiving - of touching - I don't comprehend
~~how we~~ we were both deprived of touching
when young yet I need it & need to give
it & J. doesn't seem to need either.
- J. talks about how I must be gentle
w/ her during sex (or any other time) yet
when was last time you touched me
that way? (claim to be like animals
ie - once a month - yet what animal
is gentle during sex)
- J. ~~refuses to~~ says it's normal & be like
the animals (once/month).. refuses to
to get hormone, etc. check (has her
way again) biggest thing shes done is
admit she has PMS & sometimes
takes vitamins & now depression medicine
* J. gets her way - sex once a month, little or
no touching etc. then she thinks every
thing is going great - when I tell her it isn't
it busts her bubble & she thinks I
"always ruin (not right word) everything"

Sex doesn't always have to end in intercourse
can enjoy the foreplay

1 or 2 or both things J. must do -
#1 have hormone, endocrine balance
checked - & do something about it,
#2 finish therapy - must deal w/
sexuality - get emotionally ~~past adolescence - or will continue to~~
have problem w/ me & w/ raising
kids, especially R.

this drawing FOUND by Alisha McKinney, Rochester, NY

**FRIGID**

FOUND by Brett Grossman

Chicago, IL

Scott

Kinsey started the sex revolution
"I think we should finish it!!"

Endorphins help relieve headaches.
↑ released by the brain

Endorphins can be stimulated
by guess what? SEX!!!

Lets Do It!

Julie

**NOT FRIGID**

FOUND by R.J. Sidwell

Charleston, IL

Question: Can Scott take a hint?

—R.J.S.

this photo FOUND by Marcus Kenney, Jackson, MS

Rick ,

I used to do this thing when I was a sophomore up the suites called a 'slapdance'. Basically I have a big long numb dick. So I would get out of the shower and go out into the common room where all the guys in the suite would hang out, and I would have only a towel on and I would pull it out in front of me, like I was about to fight a bull, and then slap my penis up against my stomach with a violent rocking motion. It would make a loud slapping noise on my belly behind the towel. I also would shake my hips a lot. Hence, a slapdance.

I did this in other dorms around campus but I was most famous for it in the suites. In fact, people would call upon me to do it and I can't remember turning down a request.

There is also a picture circulating somewhere of me in that same suite wearing nothing but a tutu. Also one with just pink women's underwear.

There was also the time I wore nothing but waiters and danced on two chairs in Tawny.

I love dryhumping my friends.

There was also the time, in Tawny that I locked the door with only a latch and pulled my penis through the crack in the door and wiggled it for everyone to see out in the hall.

When I was young, I used to intentionally open up all the windows in my room and turn on the lights and masturbate, hoping someone would walk by and see me.

All of my family members have seen me nude on many occasions.

Everyone except my dad has caught me masturbating or having sex. My dad suspects that I was masturbating at some point during my time in the household.

Nice to talk with you, Rick .

"TALKING WITH RICK"

I FOUND THIS ON THE STEPS OF THE BROADWAY-LAFAYETTE STOP OF THE F TRAIN IN NYC. IT WAS IN A STACK OF ABOUT 20 COPIES

-ANTON
BROOKLYN, NY



this drawing FOUND by Michael Svoboda
Portland, OR

Mark Herber and BRE,

Two years ago in San Jose I was able to orchestrate a procedure
with corpses as marionettes in a hospital morgue I want no strings attached.
I own a preserved human head and upper torso which was used for medical study
(photo enclosed). Would like to mechanically animate it. Have an idea of what it
could look like, though this can be changed. I haven't any experience in the
mechanical or robotic fields, nor do I know how to technically accomplish this.
Am hoping you will want to undertake such a project. Maybe you'd like to integrate
it with something you're doing. My concern is not to make a political nor moral
demand, but only to animate the dead. I am not concerned with the power to do so
as like an orlock but am interested in the differences within the isolated
comparison between the mechanically animated dead and the mechanically animated
living. This is done in creating an oasis for the animated so called inanimate.
My interests are adaptable within your plans. Would like to do this whenever possible.
I would travel to aid in its completion and its destruction.

# NO STRINGS ATTACHED

FOUND by Ken Lieck

Austin, TX

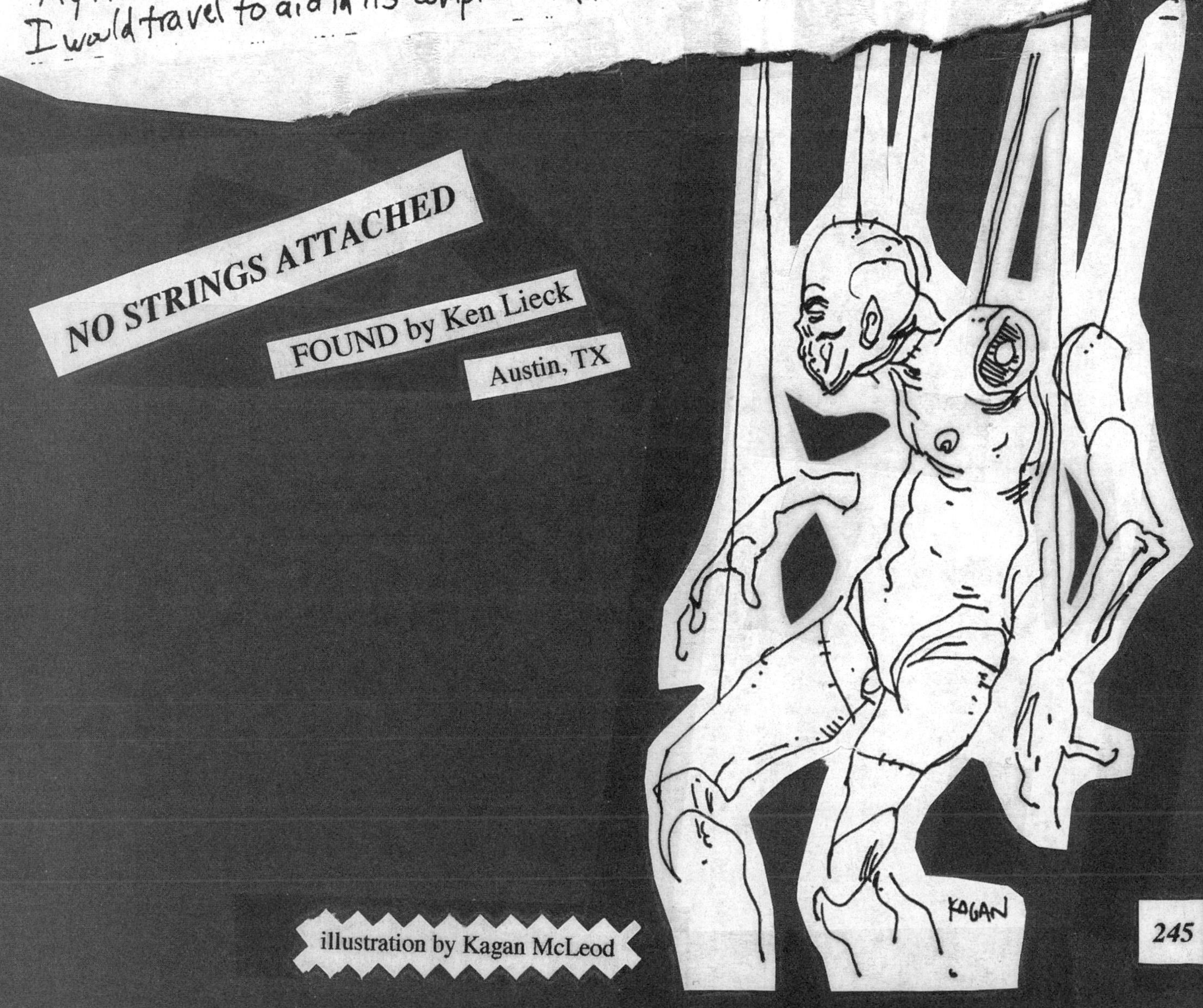


illustration by Kagan McLeod

DAD,
Come get me
@ the coffee
shop when
your done
taking a
Crap. -Hill

FIRST THINGS FIRST

FOUND by Dylan Strzynski

Ann Arbor, MI

this drawing
FOUND by Jon McDonald
& Ron Strelecki, Arleta, CA

Dear Mom.
I miss you. I really wish you
were here. Theres been alot of bad stuff in
my life but I'm sure you already know that.
but theres also been some really good things
like Justin hes my best friend and so is
bethany. Hey mom guess what is the best part
of all. theres a girl her name is Jenna were
been dating for about a month and a half
now. I love her so much. I know if you
were here you would like her alot. She
makes me soo happy. Theres nobody I've ever
been more happier with. She has changed my
life in so many ways. Shes there for me,
and that there actually is someone who cares
about me. I pray to god everyday that I got
her. Its unbelievable, remember when I was suicidal,
well not anymore. I wouldnt even think about
it. I just love her so much for biens with
me you know. This girl is wonderfull mom she helps
me through alot. I love her more than she can
imagine i've never felt this way about anyone. I
would die for this girl mom. I love her so
much and she's scared that were not going to
see each other when I move but I promised
he we would see each other just like normal.
Well, I get my liceanse this summer and I
will be out here everyday. So yeah I g2g
I love you soo much mom. I'll ~~waig~~ write
you again. bye. your son Colin

P.S. Trevor missed you too.

**DEAR MOM**

FOUND by Alison Berent

At a cemetery near my house I saw a small balloon caught in the highest branches of a tree. Dangling from its ribbon was this letter.

—A.B.



Grayslake, IL

this photo by Dorothy Gotlib

you don't see me in the hood, it's 'cause i'm doin this man—here it is, the last night 'fore i send all these pages in. truth is, this book exists only because thousands of people all over the globe have joined forces to create it. i feel so much gratitude and love toward every single person who's been involved with FOUND these past 3 years, from the 3rd grader in homer, alaska who sent in the notes he found in the hallway of his school to the old woman in homestead, florida who i overheard on the bus telling her friends about FOUND and urging them to participate. if you've ever read the magazine, checked out the website, hosted a FOUND party and let me sleep on your floor, put a FOUND sticker on your motorcycle helmet, got a bookstore to carry the magazine, mailed a copy of FOUND to your friend locked up in warrenton county jail, wrote an article about FOUND for your school paper or helped spread word about this project in any way—I just got to say THANK YOU! and my most heartfelt, giddy, enthusiastic and profound thanks goes to EVERY SINGLE ONE OF YOU WHO HAS EVER SENT IN A FIND!!! every single find—whether it ended up inside the magazine, on a hand-decorated magazine cover, on the website, or in this book—has been appreciated, treasured, and adored.

big ups to everyone on the FOUND staff, past, present & future: Mike Kozura, Rosemary Darigo, Michelle Angus, Malkah Spivak-Birndorf, Aimee McDonald, Genevieve Belleveau, Emily Long, Aaron Wickenden, Lara Markovitz, Erica Frumin, Sarah Mann, Susan Hollar, Josh Noel, Meagan Lamberti, Aaron Chaet, Vinh Nguyen, and all the folks who have helped for even one night to mail out magazines or decorate covers or open mail.

much love to the S & S family, especially London King and Liz Bevilacqua. shouts to Marcia Burch, John Wahler, Tricia Wygal, and the ravishing Miss C. Li. thanks to peter karanjia at DWT for his cheery and thoughtful legal help. and a special whut-whut to my agent and friend Jud Laghi—the Joe Dumars of the literary world.

all the far-flung FOUND operatives have done infinite good in spreading the FOUND love near and wide, especially all-stars like alissa fleet and sarah lidgus, who've been joined by such playalistic crazies as ian ellison, jonathan kidd, richard & nanette dowdy, janelle gunther & michael powell, jordan small, jenny canipe, trevor harris, reba meisels, michael svoboda, danny fenner, aimee von bokel, and many, many others. and all those fine ladies and neighborhood hustlers on the Street Team, thank you!

Thank you......

HANDMADE THANK YOU CARD

FOUND by Julie Landry

San Francisco, CA

what up VG Kids, the Sweatpants – aaron dennis and hunter blair!

world class tapes. tom slatin. matt dogg. million year picnic.

And OK Go. And Eric Peterson.

there are so many people who have been so incredibly generous in lending their time and extraordinary talents and energies to this project that it almost feels futile to try and shout 'em all out. but fuck it, i'm a try. let me start with the four people who have given the most. JASON BITNER—this dude has been at it since Day One, my partner in this crime. i can't express the extreme gratitude i have for jason's tireless work and fine sensitivities. it's crazy cuz i didn't even really know the motherfucker before we decided to run this jo'nt, but i feel unbelievably lucky for his unceasing contributions and especially for his friendship. no one can play ball or dance quite like the triple bitner. jason, you my N for real. AMANDA PATTEN—her excitement and vision for this book is what made it get born, and her constant encouragement and gentle critical eye is what made this book grow up. amanda, remember when i rolled into your office all rugged from the road, i thought i was gonna have to sell you on something. but you were already then—and have continued to be—the biggest believer in me and this book, and for that you get outkast 'aquemini' and my endless love and respect. BETH KILLIAN—she done put the whole book together while i talked about girls and battled the bats. That little yellow car pulled up out front the house with the BETHY plate and it was time to get to work. if it wasn't for beth, i'd be sitting in the basement in a big mound of FOUND notes, tangled in scotch tape and mu[illegible]ing to myself like that crazy dude in A Beautiful Mind. ahh, no more racing to the airborne express box to get the latest pages off or 3 a.m. meals standing at the washing machine. we did it beth! and then there's BRANDE WIX, who started a pattern in june 2001 when he got off work at bell's pizza at 5 a.m. and drove straight to chicago to work security at the first-ever FOUND party. now, 3 years later, he's still getting off work and coming by to help out in every way imaginable, from unloading magazines off the truck to driving on the FOUND tour from chicago to philly thirteen hours straight without a pee break. gigantic shout and one-love to FOUND's bad-boy heart and soul, the last good man, pauper and prince, Beamer, a.k.a. Short Line, a.k.a. the Good Doctor, a.k.a. Nigel Dang, yeah, it's the one and only Brande Miles Wix.

i got to say what up and thanks to all the amazing artists and illustrators who donated their skillz to this book—Lev, Ayun Halliday, Kagan McLeod, Jeff Brown, Dylan Strzynski, Jed Lackritz, Sarah Birns, Ryan Sias, Lucas Richards, Rama Hughes, Lynda Barry, Matthew Thurber, and Paul Koob. and a pinch on the ass to a brilliant artist and dear friend, Rob Doran, who designed the FOUND logo back in the day.

i madly appreciate every person who has taken the time to find something a it in and collaborate in this gigantic art project, and i've actually developed a sort-of relationship with a lot of you who have been the mo frequent contributors. You wouldn't know it since you don't usually hear back from me, but I get excited every time I see that a find has from you. these All-Star finders include—but are in no way limited to—Tom Slatin, Pete Cropley, Ryan Hennessy, Lea McKenny, Kath Philip G. Muzzy, Tim Kelly, Kevin Dole Jr., Miriam in Madison, Mike Montedoro Jr., Robert Newsome, and D. Chris Lett, a.k.a. White Samurai, a.k.a. Ghetto Goth, a.k.a. Halloween Lad.

no one would've ever seen FOUND if it wasn't for the amazing independent bookstores that bless this country. the people who work at these stores them are america's great underappreciated gift to literature. i feel lucky to have gotten to know and become friends with some of these folks—ar forever indebted to them for all they've done on the front lines in bringing this project to people. so, much love to everyone at every one of the store carried FOUND, with special shouts to a few rock stars and heavy-hitters—Cleve Corner at Politics & Prose in DC, Kevin Awakuni, Darin Klein & at Skylight Books in L.A., the folks at Book Soup, Margarita at St.Mark's in NYC, Rachel and Benn at Atomic Books in Baltimore, Liz, Hannah, Al & Quimby's in Chicago, Chloe and Reading Frenzy, Portland OR, and Kevin Sampsell at Powell's, Rob Jacques & friends at 514 Books and Book Tr Philly, Suzanne at Mac's Backs in Cleveland, and Mark, Liz, David, and Hannah at Casco Bay Books in Portland, Maine.

i deeply appreciate the media folks who've been down with FOUND and helped get the word out so that we've got more finders and this whole thing continues to grow. anyone in radio, TV, and print who's spread the word—THANKS!! Special love to all the 'zinesters, and to susannah felts at the chicago reader, adam graham at the detroit news, amy whitesall at the ann arbor news, joan anderman at the boston globe, vic maitland at GQ, whitney matheson at USA today, peter carlson at the washington post, tad friend and nick paumgarten at the new yorker, julie shapiro at WBEZ, rob elder at the chicago tribune, heidi swillinger and jim finefrock at the SF chronicle, sam grice and ben errett at the national post, charles spano and punk planet, amy fritch at spin, mary houlihan at the chicago sun-times, roman mars at invisible ink, gro skorpen at dagbladet, drew tappon at MTV, cary rodda, fiona morgan, tenaya darlington, andrew griffin, su ciampa, maria afsharian, bill radke, grant lawrence, roman mars, julia posey, jim gates, patrick hunt, dan rowe, rose george, maria guerriero, phoebe zimmerman, sabrina roach, sarah schmidt, chris borrelli, jonathan menjivar, caitlin cleary, marcus lindeen, colin ryono, steve edwards, jesse hardman, nancy, ember, and drew at flower films, and also the utne reader, KFOG, all things considered, on the media, TTBOOK, well whaddya know, rewind, the L.A.Times, and of course the man who broke it all off—Michael F. DiBella at the Philadelphia City Paper.

kate leshock, dr.kirk donaldson and dr.raymond rion, thanks!

for me, the greatest joy of this project has been discovering that there are so many other folks out there who share my wonder and love and excitement at FOUND stuff. going on tour, holding these FOUND parties in so many cities, has been absolutely incredible. i am so inspired by the FOUND communities in every town. so enormous thanks go to all the new friends i've made around the U.S. (& canada) who have helped organize events and put up fliers and given me a couch for the night, you know who you be! a few quick holla hollas—daisy and jen in louisville, krista north in MPLS, carly and twig and julie anderson in baltimore, laura D in D.C., josh hadas and josen kalra, mark higgins in toronto, joel and hayley in montreal, mark shepherd in G.R., cathy resmer in burlington, evangeline and jeff resch in chapel hill, abram and shana and Jamie in NOLA, olivia allison in houston, ben snakepit and diana and jesse in austin, elaine liner, vy, madamic in dallas, gordon, jill, ian, kim, and christa donner in cleveland, carolyn reid and sam chammas in san diego, mia schaikewitz and justin bass in LA, nick and kymmb brierly and janelle parsons in SLO, sam england in oak-town, aimee von bokel in santa cruz, andrea gin, ida nilsen, sonya ahlers, jason mclean, and fiona garden in vancouver, monica j., anna ridder and jessica in SF, doron & juju in seattle, ian mccluskey in portland, J Provine, kevin & allyson seconds in sacramento, julie G in philly, cherry and brian in san jose, kevin hamilton and conrad in champaign, dan and mrs. trommater in eugene, juliette in ABQ, the kanthor family, the lidgus', the burton's, the tominack family, and wild shouts to tracy, ron, andrea and everyone at Mad Art in St.Louis.

thank you so much to my family at This American Life—julie, jeff, alex, starlee, jonathan, wendy, adam, diane, jorge, todd, elizabeth, sarah vowell, and my motherfuckin' dogg ira G.

crucial thanks to the girls who have kept me company the last 3 years and reminded me that there's more to life than what you find on the ground—Liz Sanger, Sonny Turski, Kerry Sheldon, Hannah Gedeon, Sarah Osment, Emilie Goodhart, and Samantha Grice.

my friends keep me going and they represent hard every fuckin day. love to devin friedman, seth meisels & smeeta mahanti, eldad malamuth, tim walbridge, mike dibella, big koz, dr. wix, nicole schude, rachel frey, tim mcilrath and Rise Against, tim haldeman, dan & janice zatkovich, devon sproule, jesse P., jordan S. and all the ace deuce ballers, Bell's Pizza, my indian ultimate crew, jed lackritz, chintu kumar & dina, a.j. wilhelm, ed faktorovitch, nate wasik, dan seligmann, aaron hurst, amanda margraves, liam & marti murphy, bonnie kraybill, anne gunnison, bich & porter, claire reichstein, lu kavanagh, colleen kaman, jim thompson, josh fenton, emmanuel durant, smurf, denise, cheryl santiago, my cousins and aunts and uncles, kate leshock, kelli hicks (the 1st person ever to send in a find!), lauren hill, kevin holt, eileen pollack, judith dewoskin, charlie baxter, mike hsu, monet joe, paul redmond, nicholas depaul, shari S., jon bernstein, rodes & lindy fishburne, dan tice, meta bodewes, dean, amanda, jeremiah, natalie, ted ribbens, aimee mcD., and mr. fred rogers RIP.

finally, thanks to my dear roommates—dorothy, shawna, helen, dylan, and javan, and my neighbor todd white. and the biggest thanks of all goes to my grandma (mimi), Brother Mike, Amy, and Popcorn Pete, and to my moms and to my pops, Big Poppa we call him—this book is dedicated to him 'cuz he worked his whole life to give opportunities to his family, and shit like that don't go unnoticed.

i just wrote a bunch of names down here, but if you've contributed in any way to FOUND, or to me—like bought me a drink or tossed me some stamps for my Subway club card—and i didn't put your name in here, you better give me shit for it next time you see me. and know that even though i didn't write you a song like tupac did for his mama, you still are appreciated.

one final thanks—to the authors of the notes in this book, for sharing their humanity with all of us.

peace out for now—see you in a minute

chronic love to all the folks at WestCan in winnipeg, manitoba where FOUND Magazine is printed, especially Mr. Chris Young. yes yes y'all to all the distributors, like billy roberts at loop distro, JR Fesperman at desert moon, ed at armadillo and mary at small changes. clint johns and mike brown at Tower Records rock the fuckin house. and sick props to paul hornschemeier in chicago.

Book was
OK

very informative

If bored -
throw it
out.

Love Mom

**BOOK WAS OK**

FOUND by Adriana

Brooklyn, NY